# Microservices by Example Using .Net Core

*by*

**Biswa Pujarini Mohapatra**
**Baishakhi Banerjee**
**Gaurav Aroraa**

## Distributors:

**BPB PUBLICATIONS**
20, Ansari Road, Darya Ganj
New Delhi-110002
Ph: 23254990/23254991

**BPB BOOK CENTRE**
376 Old Lajpat Rai Market,
Delhi-110006
Ph: 23861747

**MICRO MEDIA**
Shop No. 5, Mahendra Chambers
150 DN Rd. Next to Capital Cinema,
V.T. (C.S.T.) Station,
MUMBAI-400 001
Ph: 22078296/22078297

**DECCAN AGENCIES**
4-3-329, Bank Street,
Hyderabad-500195
Ph: 24756967/24756400

Published by Manish Jain for BPB Publications, 20, Ansari Road, Darya Ganj, New Delhi-110002 and Printed by Repro India Ltd., Mumbai

# About the Author(s)

## Biswa Pujarini Mohapatra – Main/Primary Author

**Biswa** has done MCA from ICFAI university, a TOGAF certified. She has over 13 years of experience in Enterprise Software Services, Product Development & Management, evangelize and deliver new products. Drive the go-to-market strategy working closely with the sales team. Extensive experience in evolving Idealization to market reality to growth cycle with focused leadership while managing large teams through fast paced, unpredictable business environment. Deep techno-managerial skills and understanding of the Enterprise Software market. Served as an Application Architect, Project Lead and Application Developer in a wide variety of domains across Product development, BFSI and other verticals. **Specialties:** Application Design, Design Principles, Stake holder Management and Product Management. **Development experience using:** C#, ASP.NET, SQL Server, Dynamics CRM, Azure, Angular Js, RESTful API, Micro Services.

## Baishakhi Banerjee – Coauthor

**Baishakhi** has completed MCA from Techno India affiliated under WBUT and is also an MCTS. She has over 13 years of experience in working with MS Technologies but for past couple of years, while working in application design and architecture, she has started working with other technologies too. She believes that future is not about trying to find a solution within the scope of a certain technology, rather finding the technology that efficiently solves the problem. With this ideology, she is currently open to learn and explore as many technologies as possible. However, MS still holds the key to her heart.

## Gaurav Aroraa - Coauthor

**Gaurav** has done M.Phil in computer science. He is an MVP, life time member of Computer Society of India (CSI), Advisory member of IndiaMentor, certified as a scrum trainer/coach, XEN for ITIL-F and APMG for PRINCE-F and PRINCE-P. Gaurav is Open source developer, Founder of Ovatic Systems Private Limited. Recently, Gaurav awarded as 'Icon of the year – excellence in Mentoring Technology Startups' for the year 2018-19 by Radio City – A Jagran Initiative for his extraordinary work during his career of 20 years in the industry in the field of technology mentoring. You can tweet Gaurav on his twitter handle @g_arora.

# Preface

This book predominately covers Microservices architecture with real-world example which can help professionals on ease adoption of this technology. Following the trend of modularity in real world, the idea behind Microservice By Examples is to allow developers to build their applications from various independent components which can be easily changed, removed or upgraded. Also, it is relevant now because of enterprises are moving towards DevOps/ Modernization, this book will emphasize on containers and Dockers as well.

## Chapter 1: An Introduction to Microservices

This chapter starts with the basics of microservices, how and from where the buzz word came from. A brief discussion about the history of the microservices. Why one should go for microservices? When to use the microservices? Advantages of microservices etc.

## Chapter 2: Microservices Architecture

This chapter will start with the discussion of Architectural concepts. We extend the discussion of monolithic and SOA applications. We will also discuss Conway's law. We will understand microservices working as an architectural style and will explore SOLID (programing principles).

## Chapter 3: Designing the Microservice Application Layer

This chapter starts with the basics of microservices, how and from where the buzz word came from. Best Practices and Design principles to consider while designing Microservices. Why one should go for microservices? When to use the microservices? Advantages of microservices etc.

## Chapter 4: Hands on Micro Services Development of Online Hotel Booking App

This chapter delivers practical implementation of Microservices. How to design, follow best practices and Principles for Microservices. How to manage distributed transaction with a real-world example and managing DevOps?

## Chapter 5: Deployment of Microservices for App-Modernization at Scale with Docker

This chapter starts with the basics of Azure Container Service. Deployment of Microservices for app-modernization with Docker. Advantages of Docker.

## Chapter 6: Service Orchestration of Microservices using Azure Service Fabric

This chapter starts with the basics of microservices, how and from where the buzz word came from. A brief discussion about Azure Service Fabric. Why one should consider Azure Service fabric for Microservices?

## Chapter 7: Integrating Various Components

This chapter is about implementing communication between the microservices built in the previous chapter.

## Chapter 8: Hands on Integration with API Management

This chapter starts with basic of API Gateway? Why to use API gateway for Microservices. Advantages of API Management etc.

## Chapter 9: Testing Microservices

This chapter will focus on the techniques for testing an application build using Microservices architectural style.

## Chapter 10: Extending Application with Logging

This chapter is about configuring and implementing service monitoring. This chapter speaks about the monitoring strategies for micro-services.

## Chapter 11: What is Next?

Discuss future scope of microservices. Introduce reactive microservices with a programing example.

# Table of Contents

## Chapter 3: Designing the Microservice Application Layer ....... 51

## Chapter 4: Hands on Microservices Development of ................. 74
## Online Hotel Reservation App

## Chapter 6: Service Orchestration of Microservices ............... 150
## Using Azure Service Fabric

## Chapter 7 : Integrating Various Components............................. 167

# CHAPTER 1

# An Introduction to Microservices

Microservices is a new buzzword and is getting more popular day-by-day. In this chapter, we will focus to understand microservices.

To better understand what Microservices is, it is an architectural style generally used to develop large software applications loosely coupled with bounded contexts. Loosely coupled means each service are modular, small, and Independent runs on its process, each service is independently manageable and deployable.

In this chapter, you will get the understanding of all the necessary terms required to understand microservices. We will cover the following:

- Understanding microservices concepts
- Discussing monolithic and history behind it
- Explaining concepts of web services, WCF, etc.
- Discussing SOA
- Discussing important concepts
- Adopting microservices

## Understanding Microservices Concepts

To know more about microservices, we should know what it is and the history behind it. The microservice architecture is a pattern to develop an application containing a set of smaller services. Microservices are independent of each other and run in their own processes. A significant advantage of these services is that, it can be developed and deployed independently on their own process. In other terms, we can say that microservices are a way to isolate our services so they can be handled entirely independent of each other in the context of designing, development, deployment, and upgrades.

Companies like Netflix, Amazon, and Spotify have a Microservices Architecture serving their resource and requests-intensive business services that, in the average case, have to scale at the scale.

### What are Microservices

Let us understand what microservices mean; Microservices is an architecture pattern, offer a better way to build to decouple components within an application boundary. Microservice architecture is a style of designing software systems which divide significant software applications into many small services that can run independently. Each of the microservices has its own team working on it, so they are entirely separated from each other. This allows every service to run its own unique process and communicate autonomously without having to rely on other services or the application as a whole.

## History of Microservices

Term microservices came in contact in mid of 2011.

The principle behind microservices is often just good architecture principles. Microservices principles have been with us since decades; just the implementations are new. Understand the philosophy behind microservices, what microservices are, what they replaced. In the beginning of1980s with the introduction of the first significant systems distribution technology: **Remote Procedure Calls (RPC)**. RPC was the concept behind Sun Microsystems' initial ONC RPC as well as the basic idea behind DCE (1988) and CORBA (1991).

The microservices style of architecture develops complex application software from small, individual applications that communicate with each other using language-independent interfaces (APIs). Companies run into trouble if they are unable to scale monolithic architecture that has developed over time if their architecture is difficult to upgrade or maintenance becomes too complicated. Microservices can be the answer to this problem, as they break down complex tasks into smaller processes that work independently of each other.

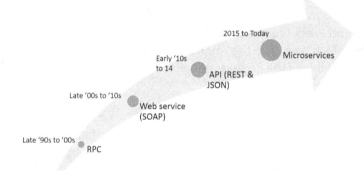

In 2014, James Lewis and Martin Fowler came together and provided a few real-world examples and presented microservices (refer to: https://www.martinfowler.com/articles/microservices.html) in their own words and further detailed it as follows:

*The term "Microservice Architecture" has been quite popular over the last few years to explain an appropriate way of designing software applications as components of autonomously deployable services. While there is no precise definition of this architectural style, there are particular common characteristics around organization around business capability, automated deployment, intelligence in the endpoints, and decentralized control of languages, and data.*

The world is moving towards the next generation of HTTP, forging strategies to create small, cross-platform containers that host independent microservices. It is very essential to know all aspect Lewis and Fowler defined above.

## Microservices are Modular and Independent

When we say, Microservices have loosely coupled; it means each service is small and designed to solve specific business function. Microservices are broken down into multiple service components by design, which can be developed by a small development team so that each of the services can be developed and deployed independently without compromising the integrity of the application. In a microservice architecture-based approach, each microservice owns its process and data so that it will be independent of a development and deployment point of view. Typically, a tiered approach is taken with a back-end store, middle-tier business logic, and a front-end user interface (UI). Microservice has evolved over the past couple of years to build distributed applications that are for the cloud. Any programming language can write it and use any framework.

## Microservices are Decentralized and Cross-functional

The ideal organization for microservices has small, engaged team where each team is in charge of a business function made out of various microservices which can be independently deployed. Teams handle all parts of development for their microservices, from development to deployment, and hence all level of team members required to deliver Microservices from developers, quality engineers, DevOps team and Product architects. This organization design is consistent with Conway's law, which says that the interface structure of a software system will reflect the social fabric of the organization that produced it. The code is organized around business capabilities.

## Microservices are Resilience

Application developed as microservices are better for fault isolation, if one service fails, others will continue to work. This is one of the benefits of building distributed systems like microservices, that is the ability of the system to resist faultsTand unexpected failures of elements, networks, computer resources, etc. These systems are resilient even within the face of errors. The concept behind this resiliency looks simple: if our Monolithic application fails, everything that it's accountable fails at the side of it; therefore let's break things into smaller modules so we can withstand individual pieces of our app failing without affecting the entire system. Dealing with fault isolation in a distribution system is not very straightforward; that is the main reason microservices needs orchestrator for high availability. It is essential to choose a better cloud computing infrastructure for microservices to orchestrate microservices because the various parts of the application are segregated. A problem could happen in one section without affecting other areas of the application.

## Microservices are Highly Scalable

In the previous section we read about several benefits of adopting Microservices, Scalability is the utmost importance of any distributed system and Microservices are designed for scaling. Scaling permits applications to react to variable load by increasing and decreasing the number of instances of roles, queues, and alternative services they use. It is easy to quantify the efficiency of a monolithic application but evaluating and quantifying the ability of a broad ecosystem of Microservices are quite tricky because Microservices are partitioned into thousands of small services. When it comes with the scalability of any system, it can be scale-in or scale out. We will learn about Scalability (both scale-in and scale-out) in Microservices with examples in the next chapter.

## Discussing Monolithic and History Behind it

In monolithic software, we mainly built as a single unit. The monolithic software is designed to be self-contained; components of the program are interconnected and interdependent rather than loosely coupled as is the case with modular software programs. In a tightly-coupled architecture, each component and its associated components must be present in order for the code to be executed or compiled.

The monolithic architectural style is a traditional architecture type and has been widely used in the IT business. The term monolithic is not new and has come from the UNIX world. In UNIX, most of the commands exist as a standalone program whose functionality is not dependent on any other program.

Enterprise applications are built in 3 layers: A data access layer, Business layer / Service layer and UI/Presentation layer. It is a single layered software application in which the presentation layer and data access layer are consolidated into a single program on a single platform.

- **Presentation layer:** Presentation (UI) layer in which user interacts with an application, all client-side logic, client-side validation related logics taken acre by this layer.
- **Business Logic layer:** Business Logic layer contains all the logic related to business context, which is a middle layer communicating between Presentation and data access layer.
- **Data access layer:** Data Access layer contains all the logic related to backend or Database.

In a traditional web application, client (a browser) posts a request. The business tier executes the business logic, the database collects/stores application-specific persistence data, and the UI shows the data to the user.

A monolithic app which is designed without modularity, each layer is tightly coupled. If the changes are required in one business function, entire application needs to be rebuilt and deployed. The major problem with this design is it's not designed for scalability and fault tolerance. If an exception occurs in one module, then the entire system will fail to function. Technical debt from a monolithic code base is a measurable reality in traditional DevOps. With monolithic code, even isolated components receive the same memory, as well as sharing access to the program itself. While that may present it a little easier to code interfaces and execute applications, it ultimately takes away the adaptability that should be a part of the agile development process.

Deploying such a monolithic application will become another hurdle. During deployment, you will have to make sure that each and every component is deployed accurately; otherwise, you may end up facing a lot of problems in your production environments.

## Demo Application – Monolithic Web App

Let's imagine that you are building an app of an online hotel booking application. The application takes request from the user, search for a room and book it. The application is deployed as a single monolithic application in IIS server.

Traditional / Monolithic Web App

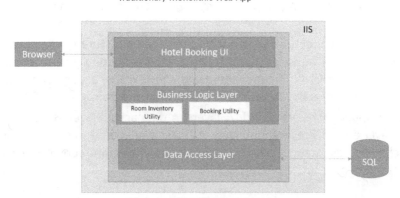

Now the requirement got changed to validate an identity of a user before booking the room, in this scenario to make the necessary changes in Booking module, we need to make the entire system down and do a proper impact analysis of dependent modules. This is not scalable as well, though we know most of our user come to our website, search for a room on a vacation season and the load on Room search module are very high still we cannot scale a particular module using monolithic architecture. We will read more on how easy to adopt this type of changes in microservices architecture in upcoming chapters.

## Use-Case of Our Demo Application

Online hotel booking application is taken as an example to make you understand Microservices architecture in this book. Using the same application we will learn the challenges of the Monolithic application, then how SOA made it better and Microservices made it most accessible.

This is an online hotel booking system where a user can search a hotel in a given city with the different category of rooms, check the hotel availability, Price, facilities and Book it.

## Requirements

- The system supports customers booking hotel rooms online and able to modify them.
- Customers can search hotels based on Room Category (ex. Radisson, Delhi (Luxury)).
- When a customer search for hotels, the search result must contain hotel information (Address, Ratings, and Price) and also its availability within choosing the check in and check out date.
- Customers are able to cancel their booking from their account.
- Customers can book online and pay with credit or debit card.
- The system must send booking confirmation email after successful payment.
- Customers can write reviews about hotels and apartment and also rate them.
- Customers are able to check their booking status from their individual account.

Main modules are as follows:

1. User
2. Room Category
3. Hotels
4. Price
5. Facilities
6. Booking
7. Review and Ratings

## Pre-requisite

To build above demo Online Hotel Booking Web Application using monolithic architecture we need Visual studio With ASP.NET, C#, and SQL.

## Overview of the Architecture of Our Demo Application

**Presentation Layer (UI):** UI layer has all client-side components, and validations, e.g., Username not blank and must be a valid email.

**Business Logic Layer:** BL layer contains all the business functionalities in a single assembly, e.g., Rom inventory, Facilities, Booking, and so on.

**Data Access Layer:** DL layer has all the backend related functionalities, e.g., all the CRUD operations, maintaining Booking transactions, and so on.

In this section, we have discussed our monolithic demo application. In the following sections, we will discuss what the challenges this application can face:

## Challenges in Monolithic Application

There are a lot of challenges to make a simple change because all the components are tightly coupled, though they are separated into 3 different layers of extensibility and maintainability point of view, it is quite tricky. Let's take a use case to see the real world challenges we can face on Monolithic.

Now we need to add a functionality to extend the requirement further to build a mobile app for our online Hotel Booking system. The pain is, we need to redevelop each and every module again because we can't offer a single business logic layer as it is tightly coupled with Data access layer and UI layer.

**Scalability:** A monolithic architecture is the one which can only scale in one dimension. It can scale with an increasing transaction volume by running more instances of the application. Some clouds can automatically create the number of instances dynamically based on load elastically . This architecture can't scale with a growing data volume. Each instance of application will access all of the data, which makes caching less effective and increases the memory consumption and I/O traffic. Also, different application components have different resource requirements - one might be time intensive while another might be memory intensive. With a monolithic architecture, we cannot scale each component independently. In order to scale the application, we just need to create more instances of that component. It is quite impossible to scale the components separately.

**Spiraling development time:** A monolithic application is also an obstruction to scaling development. Once the application gets to a specific size, it's useful to divide up the engineering unit into teams that focus on specific operative areas. For example, we might want to have the UI team, backend team, testing team, and so on. The challenge with a monolithic application is that it prevents the teams from working independently. The teams must regulate their development efforts and redeployments. It is quite difficult for a team to make any change and update application which is in the production environment.

A monolithic architecture forces you to be master to the particular technology stack (and in some cases, to a specific version of that technology) you chose at the start of development. If your application uses a platform framework that consequently becomes obsolete, then it can be stimulating to migrate the application to a newer and better framework incrementally. It's possible that, in order to adopt a newer platform framework you have to rewrite the entire application, which is definitely risky.

**Codebase complexity:** This result in a higher chance of code-breaking due to the fix requirement in other modules or services. Over time the monolith grows larger as business needs change and as new functionality is added. It becomes increasingly difficult to keep an excellent modular structure, making it harder to keep changes that ought to only affect one module within that module. Even a small change to the application requires that the entire monolith is rebuilt and deployed.

## Discussing SOA

In the previous section, we discussed the monolithic architecture and its limitations. We also addressed why it does not meet into our enterprise application requirements. To defeat these issues, we should take a modular method where we can separate the components.

**Service-Oriented Architecture (SOA)** is basically the group of services. Service-Oriented Architecture describes a set of principles and patterns for designing and developing software in the form of interoperable services. It is an architecture pattern where services are the logical representation of a repeatable business activity that has a specific business outcome. These services interact with each other. These services are generally business functionalities that are built as software components. The communication can comprise either simple data passing, or it could connect two or more services regulating some activity. SOA architecture presents a connection between the implementations and the consuming applications, creating a logical view of sets of services which are ready for the use, invoked by a standard interface and management architecture.

### Understanding Service in Service-oriented Architecture

To make SOA more effective, we need a clear understanding of the term Service.

Service, in this case, is an essential conception of SOA. It can be a part of the code, program, or software that gives functionality to other systems. This piece of code can communicate directly with the database or indirectly through different service. Moreover, it can be used by clients directly, where the client may be a website, a windows app, mobile app, or any other device app.

Services are what you connect together using Web Services. Service is the endpoint of a connection. Also, service has some type of underlying computer system that supports the connection offered. This section provides information on the specification of services. Typically, services interact with other systems via some communication channel, generally the HTTP protocol.

Service is a logical design of a repeatable business activity that has a specified outcome (e.g., Booking Service, Provide Hotel information, reports). A service is self-contained and may be composed of other services. It has three components: an interface, a contract, and implementation. The interface defines how a service provider will fulfill requests from a service consumer, the contract outlines how the service provider and the service consumer should communicate, and the implementation is the actual service code itself. Because the interface of service is separate from its implementation, a service provider can execute a request without the service consumer knowing how it does so; the service consumer only worries about consuming services.

## SOA - Architectural Principles

As a Service Oriented Architecture, it adheres to few principles, in this section; we will discuss SOA Architectural Principles.

- **Standardized service contract:** Services adhere to a standard communications agreement, as outlined collectively by one or more service-description documents in a given set of services.
- **Service longevity:** Services should be designed to be long-lived. Where possible services should avoid driving consumers to change if they do not need extra features, if you invoke a service today you should be capable of calling the same service forever.
- **Service abstraction:** The services act as black boxes, that is, their inner logic is hidden from the consumers.
- **Loose coupling:** Services maintain a relationship that minimizes dependencies and only maintain an awareness of each other. Implementations are environment-specific – they are constrained or enabled by context and must be described within that context.
- **Service contract:** Services adhere to a communications agreement as defined collectively by one or more service description documents. Services are self-contained.
- **Service abstraction:** Above what is specified in the service contract, services hide logic from the outside world.
- **Service reusability:** Logic is divided into services with the intention of promoting reuse.
- **Service discovery:** Ability to optimize performance, functionality, and cost. More natural introduction of system upgrades.

## Discussing SOA Based Demo Application

Let's take the same online Hotel booking application as a demo and see how it works in SOA architecture.

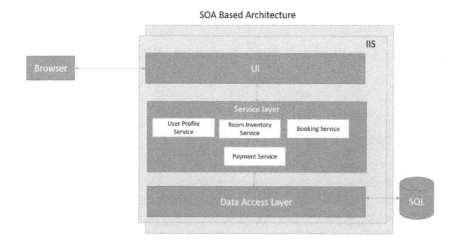

The main advantages of SOA based architecture are, it is 3 layer and 3-tier application, and each layer/tier can be deployed in the different server for better scalability.

**Presentation Layer / UI:** UI layer is same like monolithic architecture but not tightly coupled with middle layer / service layer.

**Service layer:** Middleware can be hosted as an independent layer and can be consumed by any other client. Service layer exposes proxy or WSDL to the client whereas client can consume the services by adding service proxy. Service Bus can be used to orchestrate all the services.

**Data Access Layer:** DL layer is same as the monolithic app, it is responsible for doing all data related tasks.

## Monolithic versus SOA

*In perspective, the Moore's Law states that the electronics grow at a very fast pace and with them the technology as well as the technological services.*

The development of the Internet Services has forced outlook changes in the course of the most recent decades: from the Tiered designs to SOA, and thusly from SOA to Microservices.

Rapidly, a Tiered Architecture isolates the frontend from the backend, and the backend from the Data Sources: the layers are the same number of storehouses achieving specific employment (Frontend needs to show the information and empower the collaborations, backend intercedes amongst frontend and Data Sources, and Data Sources give tireless capacity). An SOA limits into components comparative business rationale and incorporates appropriated segments with various combination designs (segments are approximately coupled yet uniquely achieving a characterized unit of work, together they can execute the general functionalities of a perplexing framework).

It is clear that a Monolith of 3-Tier Architecture is, in turn, an SOA at a higher granularity: the composed business logic spread over several components lives in the monolith, the same process, the same unit of deploy.

## Explaining Concepts of Web Services, WCF, and So On

In this chapter, we will learn about various Service-oriented Architecture implementation using Webservices, WCF, Microservices and what is the main difference between them.

### Web Services

Web services are typically middle layer reusable component of any application and use a standardized XML format. Web services are based on **Simple Object Access Protocol (SOAP)** and return data in XML form. It supports only HTTP communication protocol and can be consumed by any client that understands XML. Web services are designed to interact with other applications over the internet directly. Web services are platform- independent and language-independent, which was developed for building applications that communicate using standard web protocols and data formats such as HTTP, SOAP, and XML.

So, developers just need to understand how to send and receive SOAP messages, and no proficiency is required in the platform, object model, or programming languages to execute the service. The web services lack versatility and a lot more, which gives birth to WCF. Web service has an interface specified in a format called WSDL that machines can communicate with each other. Other systems interact with the Web service in a method directed by its description using SOAP messages, typically carried using HTTP with XML serialization in connection with other Web-related standards (W3C).

### Windows Communication Foundation

**Windows Communication Foundation (WCF)** is a framework to build service-oriented applications that enables communication over the internet using any transport protocol. WCF supports various message formats, more reliable, secure and efficient in data transmission. Using WCF, we can create a set of API which can communicate between services and clients. The same infrastructure and APIs are used to create applications that interact with other applications on the same system or on a system that remains in another company and is obtained over the Internet.

WCF Supports both SOAP and REST, Choice between WCF-SOAP and WCF-REST services will depend a great deal on the architectural objectives dictated by your application requirements.

SOAP is a protocol, whereas REST is an approach.

WCF-SOAP achieves the interoperability, but still some languages and environments don't have SOAP toolkits. WCF-REST only requires an HTTP library to be available for most of the operations.

WCF-REST relates resources to URI's and the uniform interface. You can type different URIs for accessing different resources which is much similar to typing URLs in the browser.

## WCF Jargons

We will discuss a few key WCF terminologies. Following is the description of WCF terminologies as per MSDN (https://msdn.microsoft.com/en-us/library/ms731082(v=vs.90).aspx)

1. **Messaging:** SOAP is the foundation for Web services it also defines a basic envelope that contains a header and a body section. WS-Addressing represents additions to the SOAP header for addressing SOAP messages, which releases SOAP from relying on the underlying transport protocol, such as HTTP, to carry addressing information. **Message Transmission Optimization Mechanism (MTOM)** defines an optimized transmission format for SOAP messages with large binary data contents based on the **XML-binary Optimized Packaging (XOP)** specification.

2. **Metadata:** The **Web Services Description Language (WSDL)** defines a standard language for defining services and various features of how those services can be used. WS-Policy provides specification of more dynamic characters of a service's behavior that cannot be represented in WSDL, such as a preferred security option. WS-Metadata Exchange allows a client to directly request descriptive information about a service, such as its WSDL and its policies, using SOAP.

3. **Security:** WS-Security, WS-Secure Conversation, WS-Trust, and WS-Federation all define additions to SOAP messages for implementing authentication, data integrity, data privacy, and additional security features.

4. **Reliability:** WS-Reliable Messaging defines additions to the SOAP header that allows reliable end-to-end communication, even during one or more Web services delegates must be traversed.

5. **Service:** A service is a function that is well-defined, self-contained, and does not depend on the context or state of other services.

6. **Address:** Address specifies the URL of the service where WCF service is hosted. The address provides two important elements: the location of the service and the transport protocol used to communicate with the service.

7. **Binding:** Binding specifies, "How the service and client will communicate with each other?" WCF supports various Bindings for different communication protocol.

8. **Contact:** In WCF, all services disclose contracts. The contract is a platform-

neutral and standard way of defining what the service does. WCF defines four varieties of contracts.

o   Service contracts: Describe which methods the client can perform on the service.

o   Data contracts: Determine which data types are passed to and from the service. WCF defines certain contracts for built-in types such as int and string, but you can undoubtedly define explicit opt-in data contracts for custom types.

o   Fault contracts: Define which errors are raised by the service, and the way service handles and produces errors to its clients.

o   Message contracts: It allows the service to communicate directly with the messages.

## Definitions

"Service is an important concept, Web Services or WCF are the set of protocols by which Services can be distributed, discovered and used in a technology neutral, standard form."

*"SOA is an architecture style of services adopted from a technology viewpoint, but the policies, practices, and frameworks by which we guarantee the right services are implemented and consumed. "*

*"Web services are an implementation technology; based on HTTP you don't have to use Web services to implement an SOA."*

*"WCF supports SOA, WCF Provides runtime environment for services to enable you to create and consume services, it Supports many transport protocols."*

## Discussing Important Concepts

In this section, you will learn few important concepts of .NET and .NET Core.

### C# 7.x

Visual Studio 2017 has released a lot of new features. In this section, we will discuss specifically on C#7. Following are the few main features:

### 1.   Out Variables

Before to use, we had to pass a variable as "out" parameter and it has to be declared before. You can now declare out values inline as arguments to the method where they are used.

```
if (int.TryParse(input, out int output))
    Console.WriteLine(output);
```

### 2.   Tuples

In C#7 you can create Tuples in easier, lightweight, unnamed types that contain multiple public fields. Add "System.ValueTuple" from NuGet Package.

```
(int price, int discount) GetRoomPrice(int hotelid) {
    var rooms = (5000, 500);
    return rooms;
}
```

## 3.  Pattern Matching

Pattern matching is a characteristic that allows you to implement method dispatch on properties different than the type of an object. You can create branching logic based on superficial types and values of the members of those types.

## 4.  Ref Locals and Returns

Method arguments and local variables can be sources to other storage.

## 5.  Local Functions

It is a nested function or function inside a function to limit their scope and visibility. Generally, we use private methods retain each method small and focused. However, they can obtain it harder to follow a class when reading it the first time. These methods must be known outside of the context of the single calling location.

## 6.  More Expression-bodied Members

The list of members that can be authored using expressions has grown.

## 7.  Throw Expressions

You can throw exceptions in code constructs that earlier were not allowed because throw was a statement. The extension of expression-bodied members adds more places where throw expressions would be helpful. So that you can address any of these constructs, C# 7.0 introduces throw expressions.

The syntax is related as you have regularly used for throw statements. The only difference is that now you can put them in new places, such as in a conditional expression or an initialization expression.

## 8.  Generalized Async Return Types

Methods declared with the async modifier can return other types in addition to Task and Task<T>. With C# 7.1, Main method supports additional signatures for asynchronous code:

```
public static Task Main();
public static Task<int> Main();
public static Task Main(string[] args);
public static Task<int> Main(string[] args);
```

## ASP.NET Core 2.1

ASP.NET Core which is an open source framework used to develop cross-platform, modern, cloud-based internet applications. The ASP.NET core provides benefits to build a modern, cloud-based application. ASP.NET Core 2.1 comes with a lot of new features along with GDPR. ASP.NET Core provides APIs and templates to help meet some of the EU **General Data Protection Regulation (GDPR)** requirements.

ASP.NET Core 2.1 has the following inbuilt capabilities:

1. Dependency Injection
2. App versioning
3. Ability to run and build on any OS
4. Cloud-ready environment
5. Can be deployed to cloud or on-premises
6. Client-side development
7. High performance and open source
8. It supports SignalR (for real-time web functionality)
9. Both HTTP and HTTPS
10. Identity UI library & scaffolding
11. GDPR
12. Integration Test

## To install ASP.NET Core 2.1 follow below steps

You can download and get started with .NET Core 2.1, on Windows, macOS, and Linux:

.NET Core 2.1 SDK (includes the runtime) << https://www.microsoft.com/net/download/dotnet-core/sdk-2.1.300>>

.NET Core 2.1 Runtime << https://www.microsoft.com/net/download/dotnet-core/runtime-2.1.0>>

.NET Core 2.1 is supported by Visual Studio 15.7, Visual Studio for Mac, and Visual Studio Code.

## EF Core 2.1

Entity Framework Core is the latest version of Entity Framework after EF 6.x. It is open-source, lightweight, extensible and a cross-platform version of Entity Framework data access technology. EF Core can serve as an object-relational mapper (O/RM), enabling .NET developers to work with a database using .NET objects, and eliminating the need for most of the data-access code they usually need to write. EF Core supports two development approaches 1) Code-First 2) Database-First. EF Core mainly targets the code-first approach and provides little support for the database-first approach because the visual designer or wizard for the DB model is not supported as of EF Core 2.0.

In the code-first approach, EF Core API creates the database and tables using migration based on the conventions and configuration provided in your domain classes. This approach is helpful in **Domain Driven Design (DDD)**.

In the database-first approach, EF Core API creates the domain and context classes based on your existing database using EF Core commands. This has limited support in EF Core as it does not support visual designer or wizard.

## Major New Features in EF Core 2.1

In this section, we will discuss major released new features of EF Core 2.1:

**Lazy Loading:** EF core 2.1 offers this new feature to load navigation properties on demand. The simplest way to use lazy-loading is by installing the Microsoft.EntityFrameworkCore.Proxies package and enabling it with a call to UseLazyLoadingProxies.

**Data Seeding:** With EF core 2.1 new release now you can seed your initial data, unlike EF6. Seeding data is associated to an entity type as a part of the model configuration. Then EF Core migrations can automatically compute read, insert, update, or delete operations need to be applied when upgrading the database to a new version of the model.

**Query Types:** An EF Core model now include query types. Unlike entity types, query types do not have keys established on them and cannot be inserted, deleted, or updated (i.e., they are read-only), but they can be returned instantly by queries. Some of the usage outlines for query types are as follows:

- Mapping to views without primary keys
- Mapping to tables without primary keys
- Mapping to queries defined in the model
- Serving as the return type for FromSql() queries

**Value Conversions:** It can be applied to transform the values obtained from columns before they are applied to properties, and vice versa. We have a number of conversions that can be applied by convention as necessary, as well as an explicit configuration API that allows registering custom conversions between columns and properties.

## To install EF Core 2.1 follow below steps

### *Database Provider*

EF Core also requires a database provider for the database system you wish to use. The database providers for Microsoft SQL Server and the in-memory database are included in the ASP.NET Core meta-package. For other providers and for non-ASP.NET applications, the provider should be installed from a NuGet package. For example, using dotnet on the command-line:

```
$ dotnet add package Microsoft.EntityFrameworkCore.SQLite
```

It is suggested that you also add a direct reference to the relational provider package to help guarantee that you get all the newest EF Core bits. For example:

```
$ dotnet add package Microsoft.EntityFrameworkCore.Relational
```

*When updating packages, make sure that all EF Core packages are updated to the 2.1.0 version. Mixing EF Core or infrastructure packages from older .NET Core versions (including previous 2.1 previews/RC bits) will likely cause errors.*

## Azure Environment

Microsoft Azure is an open, flexible, enterprise-grade cloud computing service by Microsoft for building, testing, deploying, and managing Applications and services.

There are broadly three types of cloud computing:

1. **Public cloud:** The cloud resources (like servers and storage) are owned and operated by a third-party cloud service provider and delivered over the Internet.

2. **Private cloud:** A private cloud consists of computing resources used exclusively by one organization. The private cloud can be physically present at your organizations on-site, or it can be hosted by a third-party service provider. In a private cloud, the services and infrastructure are always maintained on a private network, and the hardware and software are dedicated individually to one organization.

3. **Hybrid Cloud:** Hybrid clouds combine on-premises infrastructure, or private clouds, with public clouds so organizations can reap the advantages of both. In a hybrid cloud, data and applications can move between private and public clouds for greater flexibility and more deployment options.

Azure Cloud provides various cloud services:

1. **Infrastructure-as-a-service (IaaS):** With Infrastructure-as-a-service, Organization rent I T infrastructure—servers and virtual machines (VMs), storage, networks, operating systems—from a cloud provider on a pay-as-you-go basis. For example, VMs, Servers.

2. **Platform-as-a-service (PaaS):** Platform-as-a-service applies to cloud computing services that supply an on-demand environment for developing, testing, delivering, and managing software applications. Platform-as-a-service is designed to make it easier for developers to immediately develop and deploy web or mobile apps, without bothering about setting up or managing the underlying infrastructure of servers, storage, network, and databases needed for development. For example, App Service, Azure Function, Service Fabric.

3. **Software as a service (SaaS):** SaaS is a method for delivering software applications over the Internet, on demand and typically on a subscription basis. With SaaS, cloud provides host and manage the software application and underlying infrastructure and handle any maintenance, like software upgrades and security patching. For example, Dynamics 365, Office 365.

Microsoft gives these benefits for Dev Essential members, Join Visual Studio Dev Essential Program << https://www.visualstudio.com/dev-essentials/?campaign=VSBlog_AzureXamAnnoucement_VSDE >> to get the following benefits.

$300 in Azure Credit – You can now enjoy $25/month credit for 12 months.

Visual studio access – get all important applications and learning tutorial access like Pluralsight and other.

Required Prerequisites to get this membership:

* You need one Microsoft account.
* You will need credit card for your identity verification.

Once you complete this process and verification, you will be ready to use your Azure subscription.

## Dockers (Containers)

It is very necessary to understand the concept of Dockers for better Microservices usage. A Docker opens source container software platform that packages applications in "containers", allowing them to be portable with any Operating system. Docker is primarily developed for Linux. Docker is all about system Virtualization.

As per docker.com overview on (https://www.docker.com/what-docker).

*"Docker is the company driving the container movement and the only container platform provider to address every application across the hybrid cloud. Today's businesses are under pressure to transform digitally but are compelled by real applications and infrastructure while deliberating an increasingly diverse portfolio of clouds, data centers, and application architectures. Docker enables true autonomy between applications, infrastructure and developers and Dev ops to open their potential and creates a model for larger collaboration and innovation."*

Nowadays App-Modernization is a buzzword; let's understand what it is and how it is related with Docker. You must have heard about Any OS, Any Cloud, Any App, Anywhere - which is a terminology used by many enterprises nowadays.

Docker containers are lightweight by design and ideal for enabling microservices application development. Accelerate development, deployment, and rollback of tens or hundreds of containers composed as a single application.

## Adopting Microservices

In case you are accountable for driving advancement at your association, the microservices suggestion should sound attractive. Chances are you confront expanding weight to enhance the variability of the product you write keeping in mind the end goal to adjust better to a business group that needs to be more imaginative. It is hard to make a system more agreeable to change, yet the microservice revolve around building replaceable parts offers some desire.

In any case, when we've conversed with individuals inspired by receiving microservice-style designs they regularly have a few places. Behind the excitement for a new way of addressing their problem is a set of rising uncertainties about the possible damage that this approach strength cause to their systems. In particular, in the wake of adopting more about microservices methodologies, potential adopters frequently identify the following issues:

- They have already adhered to microservices architecture principles, but they didn't know it had a name.
- The organization, coordination, and control of a microservices structure would be exorbitantly troublesome.
- Collaborating with the Cross-functional team for development might be time-consuming.
- Orchestrating services would be very difficult.

While we don't trust that microservices are the response to each inquiry regarding a potential design decision, we do feel that these specific feelings of dread ought to be better comprehended before expelling a chance to enhance a framework. Let's understand at each of these obstacles to adoption of Microservices in more detail.

## Why Microservices?

With the often changes in Customer demand, unrelenting expansion of customer and partner ecosystem, organizations are looking forward to the better ways to strengthen the relationship with them. Microservices enables the business to fulfill customer demand quickly by adding new functionality, making changes to and maintaining existing functions by reducing speed to market. With a microservices architecture, the application monitors each functional component.

In a traditional monolithic app, it is quite difficult to make changes as it needs entire system deployment which requires downtime. In a traditional web application, client (a browser) posts a request. The business tier executes the business logic, the database collects/stores application-specific persistence data, and the UI shows the data to the user. If customer demands to modify existing function or to scale a particular function, it is exorbitantly troublesome to make those changes.

As discussed in previous chapter, Microservices are modular and serves a specific business function, it is to make changes as per customer demand and deploy the particular module without bringing down or impacting other services.

- **Agility:** Allows organizations to deliver new products, functions, and features more quickly and pivot more easily if needed.
- **Reusability:** Reduces development time and provides a compound benefit through reusability over time.
- **Independent deployability** of components get new features into production more quickly and provides more flexible options for piloting and prototyping.
- **Organizational alignment** of services to teams reduces ramp-up time and encourages teams to build more complex products and features iteratively.

- **Autonomous manageability** offers improved efficiency, and also overcomes the need for scheduled downtime.
- **Replaceability** of components reduces the technical debt that can lead to aging, unreliable environments.

## When to Use?

We discussed monolithic architecture and challenges in the previous section. In monolithic architecture, as your application grows, the code base grows within it, which can overload to adopt any functionality changes. If any single application function or component fails, then the entire application goes down. Just think if you have an application with separate functions handling tasks like booking, login, and account, and for some purpose, a particular function starts occupying more memory or CPU. The whole application will feel the burn, even though the obstacle is really only based on a single component.

**The problem in continuous delivery:** In case of bigger monolithic applications, deployment times can be annoyingly long and slow. If a single change to the system would require the whole application to be redeployed, then this could become an obstacle to regular deployments, and thus an impediment to continuous delivery.

**Difficult to manage team and project:** Project management has its own challenges in monolithic application development. Even a modularized application has reciprocality in terms of preparation and unharness. It takes a toll in terms of your time and energy to set up the discharge and manage tightly coupled dependent standard development.

Scaling such monolithic application is a huge pain, as everything is packaged as published code in a single .NET assembly. Each instance of the application in various servers will utilize the same am ount of underlying resources, which is often not an adequate way to design.

This can have an impact on the development stage as much as an application deployment grows. As applications get bigger, it's even more important that developers should be able to break things down into smaller and more workable units. Because everything in the monolithic approach is tied together, developers cannot work independently to develop/deploy their own modules. And because developers remain totally dependent on others, development time increases.

The solution of all proceeding is Microservices, building microservice architecture has its clear benefits for enterprises.

- **It's easy to scale based on real-world bottlenecks:** You can identify the bottlenecks in your services and replicate or fix them there without massive rewrites.
- **Its way easier to test:** test surface is smaller, and they don't do that much as big monolithic applications, so developers can test services locally - without having to deploy them to a test environment.
- **It's easier to deploy:** applications are smaller, so they deploy very quickly.

- **Easier monitoring:** services are limited, so it's obvious to monitor each of these instances.
- **Services can be versioned individually:** there's no need to add support for multiple versions in the same instances, so they don't end up joining multiple versions to the identical binary.
- Microservices are less susceptible to large failures.

## Benefits of Microservices

Building a microservices architecture in an enterprise environment has numerous benefits. Microservice is an architectural pattern, a proposal to software development in which a large application is built as a suite of modular services; small, autonomously versioned, and scalable customer-focused services with specific business goals, which interact with each other over standard protocols with well-defined interfaces. The main idea of following microservices architecture is that some types of applications become simpler to build and maintain when they are divided down into less, composable pieces which work together.

Following are the few advantages of using Microservices Architecture:

- Microservices is the process of breaking large applications into loosely coupled modules, which communicate with each other through small APIs.
- Teams do not require rewriting the whole application if they want to add new features for microservices based application.
- Smaller codebases make maintenance simpler and faster. This saves a huge development effort and time, therefore enhances overall productivity.
- The parts of an application can be scaled separately and are easier to deploy.
- Better fault isolation; if one microservice fails, the others will still continue to run.
- Code for various services can be written in multiple languages. It eliminates long-term commitment to a single technology stack.
- The microservice architecture facilitates continuous delivery.
- Easy to understand since they serve a small piece of functionality, and easy to modify for developers. Thus they can help a new team member become productive sooner.
- Each service serves a specific business context.
- Microservices are pure agile and works hand in hand with DevOps.

## Microservices versus SOA

SOA is a design pattern, where multiple services collaborate to produce some end set of capabilities. A service here typically means an entirely separate operating system process. Communication between these services occurs through calls across a network rather than method calls within a process boundary.

SOA is an architecture pattern, which application components provide services to other components via a communications protocol over a network. The communication can involve either simple message, or it could involve two or more services coordinating connecting services to each other.

There are two main parts in SOA, a service provider, and a consumer.

**Microservice architecture (MSA)** is a method of designing software systems which divides big software applications into many small services that can run independently. Each of the microservices has its own team working on it, so they are completely separated from each other. This allows every service to run its own unique process and communicate autonomously without having to rely on other services or the application as a whole. The ability for each microservice to be separated and recombined protects the system against architecture decay and better facilitates scalability and agile processes.

In Martin Fowler's classic definition, a microservices application is composed of "a suite of small services, each running in its individual process and interacting with lightweight mechanisms, often an HTTP resource API."

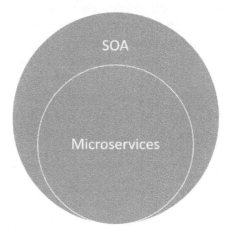

The differences between microservices and SOA

- **Microservices apps tend to involve more services:** Whereas an SOA app might involve just two or three services—a storage service and a front-end service, for example—a microservices app could have dozens of services, each handling different aspects of storage, compute, networking and other functionality.

- **Microservices apps are often deployed using containers:** It is not mandatory that you have to use containers to deploy microservices, but containers and microservices tend to go hand in hand. The popularization of Docker over the past several years has helped drive massive interest in microservices. In contrast, SOA apps existed long before most people were thinking about or using containers.

- **Microservices use complex APIs for communication:** Communication between different services in an SOA app tends to use a relatively simple approach, like basic sockets. Microservices use complex APIs that permit fine-grained configuration and more rigorous security.

- **Middleware versus API:** Microservices architecture approach generally termed as API layer whereas SOA as Middleware. The messaging middleware in SOA offers a host of additional capabilities not found in MSA, including mediation and routing, message enhancement, message, and protocol transformation. MSA has an API layer between services and service consumers.

- **Microservices are ease for deployment.** In microservices, services can operate and be deployed independently of other services, unlike SOA. So, it is simpler to deploy new versions of services frequently or scale a service independently.

- **Microservices are better for fault tolerance.** In SOA, ESB could turn into a single purpose of disappointment which impacts the whole application. Since each microservice is imparting through ESB, on the off chance that one of the service back off, could make the ESB be terminated with demands for that microservice. Then again, microservices are significantly improved in adaptation to internal failure. For instance, if there is a memory spill in one microservice, at that point just that microservice will be influenced. Alternate microservices will keep on handling demands.

To wrap things up, the first contrast amongst SOA and microservices lies in the size and degree. Microservice must be essentially littler than what SOA tends to be and for the most part is a littler freely deployable service.

## Summary

In this chapter, we discussed about the monolithic and SOA with the help of our demo application. We discussed various aspects of architectural style based on SOA. Then we went through Microservices, need and how to adapt it in the existing application.

In next chapter, we will discuss complete architecture of microservices application with the help of our demo applications and will start transitioning to microservices.

# CHAPTER 2

# Understanding Microservices Architecture

Earlier in this guide, you read about basic concepts of Microservices Architecture, Advantages of microservices and history of Microservice. In this chapter, we will emphasize more on Microservices architecture, Challenges of adapting and high-level Architecture of our demo application (Online Hotel Reservation). Microservices offer great benefits but also raise huge new challenges. Microservice architecture patterns are fundamental pillars when creating a microservice-based application.

You will learn the following topics:

- Understanding microservices architecture
- Understanding the layered approach
- Modularized Microservices Architecture
- Cohesive Microservices Architecture
- Microservices Boundaries
- Domain Driven Design
- Maturity Model of Micro Services

## Introduction

To recap a microservices architecture is an approach to building a server application as a set of small services. That means a microservices architecture is mainly oriented to the back-end, although the method is also being used for the front-end. Each API runs in its process and communicates with other processes using protocols such as HTTP/HTTPS, WebSocket, or AMQP. Each microservice executes a specific end-to-end domain or business direction within a particular context boundary, and each service must be developed autonomously and can be deployable independently.

What size should a microservice be? When building up a microservice, size ought not to be the essential point. Rather, the imperative point ought to be to make inexactly coupled services, so you have self-rule of autonomy of development, deployment, and scale, for each service. Obviously, while designing and planning microservices, you should try to keep microservices as small as possible, as long as there is not too many direct dependencies with other microservices. More significant than the size of the microservice is the internal cohesion it must have and its autonomy from other services.

Each of these small business units will correspond to each other using different protocols to deliver thriving business to the client. Question might be striking to your mind already that, how **Microservice Architecture (MSA)** varies from SOA? In layman term, SOA is a designing pattern, and Microservice is an implementation strategy to achieve SOA, or in other way Microservice is a type of SOA.

Below are some principles that you need to remember while developing a Microservice based system:

1. **Independent:** Each microservice should be autonomously deployable.

2. **Coupling:** Microservices must be loosely coupled with one another such that modification in one will not influence the other.

3. **Business Goal:** Each service package of the entire application must be smallest and capable of delivering one particular business goal.

## Characteristics of Microservices

In previous section you learned what microservices applications are.

Following are few characteristics of Microservices:

- Small in size
- Messaging enabled
- Bounded by contexts
- Autonomously developed
- Independently deployable
- Decentralized
- Built and released with automated processes

## How Microservice Architecture Works?

Microservices Architecture provides long-term agility. Microservices facilitate better maintainability in complex, large, and highly-scalable systems by making you create applications based on many autonomously deployable services that each has granular and individual life cycles.

As an added benefit, microservices can scale out separately. Instead of having a monolithic application that you must scale out as a package, you can instead scale out particular microservices. That way, you can scale just the specific service that needs more computing resource or network bandwidth to support huge request, rather than scaling out services that do not need to be scaled. That means cost savings on infrastructure because you need less hardware.

Following is the key differentiation between how Microservices deployment varies from Monolithic implementation.

| Monolithic Deployment | Microservices Deployment |
|---|---|
| Difficult to manage operational agility in the huge deployment of monolithic application artifacts. | Developing services discretely enables developers to use the relevant development framework for the task at hand. |
| Limited re-use. | Services are small and developed to solve a particular business problem. Can be exposed to any consumer with different supported protocol. |
| Packaged as a single unit. | Independent deployment. |
| Scaling is hard. | Easier to scale as services are encouraged to be small. Services exist as autonomous deployment artifacts and can be scaled separately of other services. |
| Large Codebase. | Codebase will be easier to manage. |
| Ease for deployment. | Deployment becomes more complicated with many functions, scripts, transfer areas, and config files for deployment. |
| Less infrastructure provisioning Cost. | Require more infrastructure cost, as services deployed independently. |
| Single team work on entire application and application relies on unique technology. | Design autonomy; the team has the freedom to employ different technologies, frameworks, and patterns to design and implement each microservice, and can change and redeploy each microservice independently. |

Architecting fine-grained microservices-based applications enable continuous integration and continuous delivery practices. It also expedites delivery of new functions into the application. Fine-grained presentation of applications also allows you to run and test microservices in isolation, and to evolve them autonomously while supporting clear contracts between them. As long as it is not needed to modify the interfaces or contracts, you can change the internal implementation of any service or add new functionality without destroying other microservices.

You've reasonably heard some of those tales already—Netflix, SoundCloud, and Spotify have all gone public about their microservices experiences. In any case, on the off chance that you are in head of the innovation division of a bank, hospital, or hotel network, you may assert that none of these organizations resemble yours. The microservices tales we hear the most about are from organizations that give streamed content. While this is a space with unimaginable pressure to stay flexible and perform at extraordinary scale, the business effect of an individual stream fizzling is basically exceptional to a hotel booking a reservation, a single dollar being lost, or a misstep in a therapeutic report. Does the greater part of this imply microservices is certifiably not a solid match for hotels, banks, and hospitals? However, the particular way your organization requires to implement a microservice system is possible vary from the idea that Netflix implements theirs. The deal is in having a clear goal and understanding where the controls are to move your organization toward it. Later in this chapter, we'll sprinkle some light on the principles and practices that help microservices companies succeed.

## Pre-requisites of Microservices Architecture

It is necessary to know the resulting ecosystem from the microservice architecture implementation. When you decide to adopt microservices, you must be ready with changes required to overcome the challenges of Microservices adaption. You are explicitly running away from having just one or a few components to a more complex system. In this new world, the many moving components act in inconstant ways as teams and services are created, altered, and destroyed continuously.

System's ability to change and adapt swiftly can provide significant benefits for your organization.

Following are few pre-requisites which need to be in place before adaption:

### *Rapid provisioning of computing resources*

Martin Fowler states:

*"You should be able to fire up a new server in a matter of hours. Naturally, this fits in with Cloud Computing, but it's also which can be done without a full cloud service. To be able to do such rapid provisioning, you'll need a lot of automation - it may not have to be fully automated to start with, but to do severe microservices later it will need to get that way."*

Consider this architecture style for:

1. Large applications that require a high release capacity.
2. Complex applications that require being extremely scalable.
3. Applications with strong domains or multiple subdomains.
4. An organization that have small development teams.

## Microservices Architecture of Online Hotel Reservation

Let us consider an example of online Hotel Reservation portal to understanding microservice in depth. Now, let us break this entire Hotel Booking portal into small business units such as user management, Room Inventory service, Room Booking Service, payment management, Booking management, and so on. One successful booking needs to proceed through all of these modules within a specific time frame.

Following is the consolidated image of different business units associated with the online Hotel Reservation system:

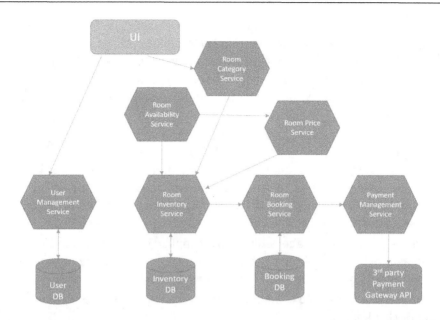

## Architecting Microservice-Based Applications using Azure Container Service

In this section, we discuss Docker as it is the container toolset most widely deployed in production today. However, as we already mentioned, alternative container solutions exist in varying stages of production readiness. Therefore, most things in this section should be understood as relevant to containers in general, not just Docker specifically.

Most microservices deployments are practically unthinkable without utilizing Docker containers. We have discussed some of the practical reasons for this. That said, we shouldn't think of Docker or containers as tools designed just for the microservice architecture. Containers in general, and Docker specifically, certainly exist outside microservice architecture. As a matter of fact, if we glance at the current systems operations landscape, we can see that the number of individuals and companies using containers many times exceeds those implementing the microservice architecture. Docker in and of itself is significantly more common than the microservice architecture.

### Docker Terminologies

*Docker is a container management service. The keywords of Docker are developed, ship, and run anywhere. Docker is an instrument intended to make it less demanding to create, send, and run applications by utilizing compartments. Containers enable developers to bundle up an application with the greater part of the parts it needs, for example, libraries and other dependencies and ship everything out as one bundle which can then be deployed anywhere.*

- **Container image:** Container Image is a set of packages with all the dependencies and data needed to build a container. An image incorporates all the dependencies (such as frameworks) plus deployment and execution configuration to be managed by a container runtime. Usually, an image obtains from various base images that are layers accumulated on top of each other to form the container's filesystem. An image is stable once it has been created.

- **Container:** An instance of a Docker image. A container generally performs execution of a single system, process, or service. It includes contents of a Docker image, an execution environment, and a standard set of guidance. When scaling a service, it is required to generate many instances of a container from the related image. Or a batch job can create various containers from the same image, passing several parameters to each instance.

- **Tag:** Tag is a mark or label which can be applied to the images so that several images or versions of the corresponding image can be recognized depending on the version number or the target environment.

- **Dockerfile:** Dockerfile is the text file that includes guidance on how to build a Docker image.

- The action of creating a container image based on the data and context provided by its Dockerfile, plus added files in the folder where the image is built. You can make images with the Docker "docker" build command.

- **Repository:** A set of similar Docker images, labeled with a tag that intimates the image version. Few repos holds multiple variants of a particular image, such as an image containing SDKs, an image containing only runtimes which is lighter, etc. Those modifications can be identified with tags. A single repo can include platform alternatives, such as a Linux image and a Windows image.

- **Registry:** Registry is a service that offers access to repositories. The default registry for public images is Docker Hub (owned by Docker). A registry usually has repositories from multiple teams. Organizations often have private registries to store and manage images they've built. Azure Container Registry is one example.

- **Docker Hub:** Docker Hub is a public registry to upload images and work with them. Docker Hub offers Docker image hosting, public or private registries, build triggers and web hooks, and integration with GitHub and Bitbucket.

- **Azure Container Registry:** Container registry provides a registry that is close to deployments in Azure and that provides control over access, making it possible to use Azure Active Directory groups and permissions. It is a public resource for working with Docker images and its components in Azure.

- **Cluster:** A set of Docker hosts exposed as a single virtual Docker host so that the application can scale to several instances of the services spread across various hosts within the cluster. Docker clusters can be built with Docker Swarm, Kubernetes, and Azure Service Fabric.

- **Orchestrator:** A tool that explains control of clusters and Docker hosts. Orchestrators enable you to manage images, containers, and hosts through a graphical UI or a command line interface (CLI). You can control container networking, load balancing, configurations, service discovery, availability, Docker host configuration, and more.

## When to choose .NET Core for Docker Containers

The modularity and lightweight nature of .NET Core makes microservices ideal for containers. When you deploy your microservice and start a container, its image is much smaller with .NET Core than with .NET Framework. Indifference, to use .NET Framework for a container, you must keep your image on the Windows Server Core image, which is a much heavier than the Windows Nano Server or Linux images.

.NET Core is cross-platform, so for deployment of server apps are feasible with Linux or Windows container images.

If your aim is to have an application that can run on cross platforms supported by Docker (Linux and Windows), .NET Core is the best choice, because .NET Framework only supports Windows.

.NET Core also promotes macOS as a development platform. However, when you deploy containers to a Docker host, that host must (currently) be based on Linux or Windows. For example, in a development environment, you could use a Linux VM running on a Mac.

Use .NET Core, with Windows or Linux Containers, for containerized Docker server application when:

There is a need of cross-platform application. For example, application needs to run on both Linux and Windows Containers. Your application architecture is designing on microservices. You need to use containers fast and want a small step per container to achieve better density or more containers per hardware unit in order to lower your costs.

In short, when you consider to create new containerized .NET applications, you should consider.NET Core as the default choice. It has many advantages and fits best with the containers opinion and style of working.

*An additional benefit of using .NET Core is that you can run side by side .NET versions for applications within the same machine. This benefit is more important for servers or VMs that do not use containers because containers isolate the versions of .NET that the application needs. Creating and deploying microservices on containers*

Containers were not designed for microservices. They emerged as a powerful response to a practical need: technology teams needed a capable toolset for universal and predictable deployment of complex applications. Indeed, by packaging our application as a Docker container, which assumes pre-bundling all the required dependencies at the correct version numbers, we can enable others to reliably deploy it to any cloud or on-premise hosting facility, without worrying about target environment and compatibility. The only remaining deployment requirement is that the servers should be Docker-enabled—a pretty low bar, in most cases. In comparison, if we just gave somebody our application as an executable, without pre-bundled environmental dependencies, we would be setting them up for a load of dependency pain. Alternatively, if we wanted to package the same software as a VM image, we would have to create multiple VM images for several major platforms, since there is no single, dominant VM standard currently adopted by major players.

You could also use the traditional .NET Framework for developing microservices-based applications without containers by using conventional processes. That way, because the .NET Framework is installed and shared across processes, processes are lightweight and faster. However, if you are planning to use containers, the image for the traditional .NET Framework is based on Windows Server Core, and that makes it much heavier for a microservices-on-containers approach.

In opposition, .NET Core is the best applicant if you are adopting a microservices-oriented system that is based on containers because .NET Core is lightweight. In addition, its related container images, either the Linux image or the Windows Nano image, are lean and small making containers light and fast to start.

## Modularized Microservices Architecture

Microservices are smaller and modular in nature. Each service solves specific business need and independent. It is modular in nature for ease development, deployment, and to invoke by the client depends on requirement.

"Modularity is to a technological economy what the division of labor is to a manufacturing one. —W. Brian Arthur, author of The Nature of Technology".

Much has been said in regards to moving from monolithic application to microservices. Other than moving off the language pleasantly, it additionally appears like an easy decision to hack up a monolithic into microservices. In any case, is this approach extremely the best decision for your organization? It's valid that there are numerous downsides to keeping up a single muddled application. In any case, there is a possible chance which is frequently ignored: isolated application improvement. In this section, we'll review what this elective involves and show how it identifies with building microservices.

At its most fundamental level, microservice architecture is about developing up an application or system into smaller parts. A software system that is modularized in nature will certainly have some limitations, but there is still a potential upside. Network accessible modularization facilitates automation and provides a concrete means of abstraction. Beyond that, some of the usage of microservice architecture advantages discussed earlier already apply at this base layer. To help application delivery speed, modularized services are independently deployable.

It is also reasonable to take a polyglot approach to tool and platform selection for individual services, regardless of what the service limits are. With respect to safety, services can be controlled individually at this layer. Also, the abstracted service interfaces offers for more granular testing.

## Modularity in Microservices

With microservices we can definitely have teams, work independently. These phrases are just a few of the many reasons that lead development teams down the path of microservices. Another one is necessary for scalability and resilience. Developers collectively seem to be a desire for is a modular approach to system design and development.

Modularity in software development can be bubbled into three guiding principles:

1. **Encapsulation:** Hiding implementation details within components, leading to low coupling between different components. Teams can work in isolation on decoupled components of the system.

2. **Well-defined Interfaces:** Sometime you can't hide everything (or else your system won't do anything meaningful), so well-defined and solid APIs between components is a must. A component can be followed by an implementation that conforms to the interface specification.

3. **High Cohesive:** having a modular system means distinct components must work together. You'd better have a good way of displaying (and verifying) their relationships.

Many of these principles can be accomplished with microservices. A microservice can be executed in any way, as long as it exposes a well-defined interface (oftentimes a REST API) for other services. Its implementation parts are internal to the service and can change without system-wide impact or coordination.

So, microservices obtain significant modularity principles, leading to major benefits:

- Teams can work and scale independently.
- Microservices are small and focused, reducing complexity.
- Services can be internally modified or replaced without global impact.

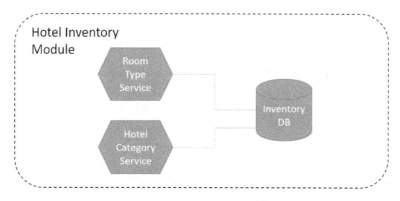

Let's see how Modularity in microservices falls under our demo application. As discussed earlier Microservices means each service has its own boundary. Following image describes modularity and bounded context of a domain.

Creating strong modules requires the same design difficulty as building good microservices. A class should model (part of) a single bounded context of the domain. Choosing microservice boundaries is an architecturally important decision with costly ramifications when done wrong. Module boundaries in a modular system are easier to change. Refactoring across modules is typically maintained by the type-system and the compiler. Redrawing microservice boundaries involves a lot of interpersonal communication not to let things blow up at run-time Inventory module in the above picture each service has its own set of functionalities and each service are independent. Each service Room Type and Hotel category service can be developed individually by different teams with different languages without any dependencies.

It is possible there is as much complexity in the connections between microservices as there is in the blended business logic of all unique microservices.

To help improving software delivery speed, modularized services are individually deployable. It is also reasonable to take a polyglot pattern to tool and platform selection for individual services, despite of what the service boundaries are. With respect to safety, services can be controlled individually at this layer. Also, the abstracted service interfaces allow for more granular testing.

It is better to have a set of high-level goals to use as a guide when making conclusions about what to do and how to go about doing it. Our final goal in building applications in a microservices way: finding the right harmony of speed and safety at scale. This ultimate goal gives you a destination to aim for and given enough time, iterations, and persistence, will tell you to build a system that hits the right notes for your own organization.

Adopting the point of view that microservice components should be "early Adoption" fits well with the notion of continuous delivery and the desire to have speed as a goal for your implementations.

## Cohesive Microservices Architecture

Cohesion indicates the level of intra-dependency amongst the elements of a software module. In other terms, Cohesion is a measure of the degree to which the responsibilities of a single module or a component form a meaningful unit.

Software development is time-consuming and expensive. Under the best cases, one goes from an idea to requirements, design, coding, testing, deployment, and then a maintenance phase. More or less, this is the traditional software development model.

Cohesion is described as the degree to which all elements of a module, class, or component work together as a functional unit. High cohesion is best, and low cohesion is inadequate. The ideal example is one where a module, class, or component provides only one function or, at most, a very closely related set of functions.

Components must be modularized in order to have better cohesive. Achieving cohesion in component comes from setting the right service boundaries and analyzing the semantics of the system. The idea of domains is useful at this layer, whether they are business-oriented or defined by some other axis. Cohesive microservice architecture can facilitate software speed by aligning the system's services with the supporting organization's structure. It can also produce composable services that are permitted to change at the pace the business dictates, rather than through unnecessary dependencies. Reducing the dependencies of a system emphasizing cohesive services also facilitates replaceability of services. Moreover, service cohesion reduces the need for highly orchestrated message exchanges between components, thereby creating a more efficient system.

High cohesion means related logic is kept in one service. Otherwise, different services need to be chatty with each other across the service boundary.

## Benefits of Microservices based Solution

Microservices architecture provides many advantages. Some of the important benefits are as follows:

Microservices tackles the problem of complexity by the decomposing application into a set of manageable services which are much quicker to develop, and much easier to understand and maintain.

It enables each service to be built independently by a team that is focused on that service.

It reduces the barrier of adopting new technologies since the developers are free to choose whatever technologies make sense for their application development and not bounded to the choices made at the start of the project.

Microservices architecture has become a popular approach for enterprises to achieve agility and the Continuous Delivery of applications to meet the increasing demand of their users, as well as to gain a competitive advantage.

- **Scaling:** In general, we create Microservices to build a system. It is easier to scale up the Microservice that is being used more. E.g. Let say, you have a Product Lookup service and Product Buy service. The frequency of calling Product Lookup service is much higher than that of Product Buy service. In this case, scale up the Product lookup service to run on powerful hardware with multiple servers. Whereas, Product Buy service can be deployed on less powerful hardware.

- **Resilience:** In Microservice architecture, if one service goes down, it may not affect the rest of the system. The other parts can keep functioning.

- **Technology-Independent:** These days technology is changing every day. With the Microservices approach, you can keep using the latest technology for your new Microservices. You can choose new technologies with less risk in Microservices architecture compared to Monolithic architecture. One of the greatest advantages of Microservices architecture. Moreover, you only need to add the infrastructure you need. Besides, no long-term commitment to single technology stack is required. This enables modular, polyglot and multi-framework applications.

- **Reuse:** Microservices enables reusing the models received from one service to another.

- **Easy Deployment:** If you have followed Microservices architecture correctly, helps in making the deployment process smooth. If anything goes incorrect, it can be rolled back easily and quickly in Microservices.

- **Independent:** Easy and frequent deployment. One service or module can be developed, tested and deployed without doing this for all services (or the whole application). The deployment unit is smaller. This explains and speeds up the build and release workflow. In turn, you can deploy more frequently. Due to the expanded build speed you get feedback faster from the continuous integration server after a commit of code changes.

  Moreover, the release of one module is not blocked by incomplete work in another service. Besides, the risk of deployment becomes less, because we only deploy a small part of the system and not the whole one.

  With microservices, you can make a change to a single service and deploy it independently of the rest of the system. This allows us to get code deployment faster. If an error does occur, it can be separated quickly to an individual service, making fast rollback easy to achieve.

- **Organizational Alignment:** Microservices allow us to align our architecture to our organization better, helping us minimize the number of people working on anyone codebase to hit the sweet spot of team size and productivity. You can also change ownership of services between teams to try to keep people working on one service located.

- **Composability:** One of the key commitments of distributed systems and service-oriented architectures is that we open up opportunities for reuse of functionality. With microservices, it is allowed that functionality to be consumed in different ways for different purposes. This can be especially important when you think about how consumers use our software.

- **High testability** due to the independence of the services and a well-defined contract between them (a few coarse-grained REST calls are easier to test than a lot of fine-grained in-process-calls).

## Downside of Microservices based Solution

For smaller projects microservices impose a management overhead that simply isn't necessary - you can compose into a monolithic chunk and have it not been a problem. Microservices also add latency to the application in question so even if the capacity of the system increases, it's performance as witnessed by the end user will not. And finally, microservices reintroduce version dependency hell - exactly the thing we were trying to avoid by using containers in the first place. API's that evolve (yes, they will) need to be versioned and work needs to go into either ensuring that a microservice is always teamed with the right version of the service that uses it, or that the microservice remains backward compatible.

Following points are some of the drawback of Microservices.

- **Operations and Infrastructure:** The development team has to work closely with operations more than ever before. Otherwise, things will spin off control due to the multitude of operations going on at once.

- **Support:** It is significantly difficult to support and maintain a microservices setup than a monolithic app. Each one may be made from a broad variety of frameworks and languages. The immense complexities of support influence decisions on adding services. If a team member needs to create a new service in an esoteric language, it impacts the whole team because they have to ensure it can work with the existing setup.

- **Monitoring:** When you create new services, your ability to maintain and configure monitoring for them becomes a challenge. You will have to place on automation to make sure monitoring can keep up with the changes in the scale of services. An increased effort for operations, deployment and monitoring. Each service is a separate deployment unit, which has to be released, tested and monitored.

- **Security of Application:** The increase of services in this architecture creates more soft targets for hackers, crackers and criminals. With a mixture of operating systems, frameworks and languages to keep track of, the security group has their hands full ensuring the system is not vulnerable. It's sometimes difficult to know where microservices reside, which can make securing them a headache. And with different microservices interacting with each other, this gives hackers more opportunities to penetrate the system.

- **Requests:** One way to transfer data between services is using request headers. Request headers can hold details like authentication that ultimately reduce the number of requests you need to make. However, when this is happening across a bunch services, it can increase the need for coordination with members of other teams.

- **Increased configuration management.** For each microservice it is require to create a dedicated build and delivery pipeline. This includes an MSBuild build configuration, a Git project, a Build job, a setup for tests, a release mechanism and a deployment approach.

## Microservices Boundaries

When you are starting off with Microservices, it is quite difficult for the team to identify what exactly constitutes a well-designed microservice. What is the correct size for a microservice? You mostly hear something to the effect of, "not too big and not too small" — and while that's absolutely correct, it's not very helpful in practice. But if you start from a beginning designed domain model, it's much easier to reason about microservices.

One of the difficulties with designing and developing a distributed software system using microservices implementation technique is figuring out the boundaries of microservices. And, indirectly, the size of these artifacts. What happens if the boundaries are incorrect? You get coupling between various microservices – both spatial and temporal. Such coupling can threaten a lot of implementation and delivery aspects. Some of these include failure for one team to fully implement a feature due to a dependency on some other service that performs something they require, inability to release without coordination with other teams, issues when delivering interdependent components may and will result in instability, loss or corruption of data, emergence of distributed transactions, etc.

## The Challenges of Drawing Boundaries

When you develop microservices, you need to consider carefully about where to draw the boundaries between services. Once services are developed and deployed in production, it can be hard to refactor across those boundaries. Choosing the right service limits is one of the biggest challenges when designing a microservices architecture. How big should each service be? When should methods be factored across several services, and when should it be kept inside the same service?

One of the major benefits of developing new systems with microservices is that the architecture allows developers to create and modify individual components independently — but problems can arise when it comes to reducing the number of callbacks between each API. The solution according to McFadden, is to apply the appropriate service boundaries.

But in other hand, sometimes difficult-to-grasp and abstract concept of **domain driven design (DDD)** — a framework for microservices. In DDD, Bounded Contexts are a way of managing the complexity involved in modeling large Domains. They serve to group closely related concepts and operations. Bounded Context is a best pattern in Domain-Driven Design. It is the center of DDD's strategic design section which is all about dealing with large models and teams. Determining microservice boundaries from a bounded context viewpoint can be a good start. Relying only on bounded context viewpoint may not always suffice. Other viewpoints are also vital to determine microservice boundaries. Viewpoints like non-functional requirements Scaling, Changeability, Deploy-ability, Testability, Business Process, and Organization Communication Structure. DDD is nothing but Domain Driven Design.

Major features of DDD are as follows:

- **Data consistency and integrity:** A primary principle of microservices is that each service manages its own data. This keeps services decoupled but can lead to difficulties with data integrity or redundancy.

- **Complexity:** A microservices application has more moving parts. Each service may be easy, but the services have to work together as a whole. A single user operation may involve multiple services.

- **Integration:** A Microservices defined as small, self-contained and fine-grained into small modules. The defining boundary of services is a huge pain for Integration and for interposes communication.

## Hotel Booking APP: Defining the Microservices Boundaries

Bounded context decides to represent boundaries of our complex domain into a business context. Bounded contexts are essential because they allow us to define a ubiquitous language that is shared and valid within a boundary. The meaning of a product for the Hotel Inventory bounded context is not the same as for the Room Booking bounded context.

The domain expert of the Hotel Inventory may not understand anything about Booking Context the Check-in, check-out rules or which room has assigned to the customer. However, this information is part of a day to day activity of the front office domain expert and she/he may even be able to help you to automate part of the system.

Using a bounded context is a great way to keep your system with high cohesion.

Following image explains how to define bounded context based on the domain model.

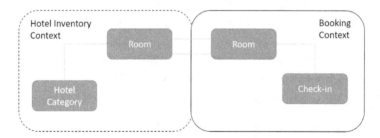

Now that you have heard about the bounded context you may be asking yourself what the difference between this is and what we did with the Inventory service and Booking service. To be honest, there is not much of a difference.

In the preceding example you might have to design to Microservices, one for Hotel Inventory service and other for Booking service. If you choose to have the room information on the Inventory service, then the booking service would need to acquire this information from the inventory service in order to do the booking logic to find available rooms, either by having the booking service calling Inventory service or by having a layer of orchestration between them.

Let's assume now few of the hotel rooms booking price varies depends on the facilities provided upon, so in this scenario now we need to change the logic in both the places, to categorize hotels based on facilities they provide and on Booking service to change price logic.

This may not be the central design for our architecture. Booking and Inventory have a high coupling, but also a low cohesion. The necessary data for the Booking service to work correctly is on the Inventory service. That is one of the reasons some organizations are struggling with microservices and the cost of changing anything in the system is huge. One easy change and you may need to change at least two services.

So, is the concept flawed? Is there something that can help deal with such issues? As always, you need to start with the base. In this case main foundational idea comes from Domain Driven Design – an *Aggregate*.

To overcome this, you will read more on Domain analysis and DDD approach in the next section. Following is a suggestion that you can use to inherit microservices from the domain model.

Start with a bounded context. In general, the methods in a microservice should not span more than one bounded context. By definition, a bounded context highlights the boundary of a particular domain model. If you find that a microservice combines different domain models together, that's a sign that you may need to relook and refine your domain analysis.

With the concepts of DDD Aggregate, you can now approach the sizing of a microservice and define its boundaries. Approaching the design thinking about the business rules that drives the implementation we really localize the scope of change, encapsulate the logic and state. The implementation becomes autonomous, we remove any potential for cross-service requests, complex orchestration goes away, an unnecessary generalization of code is not key point nowadays. The Source code becomes simpler, more robust, and easier to reason about. It is very simple to test, easier to maintain all of which really yields greater business agility – exactly what business asks of developing.

## Identifying Domain-Model Boundaries for Each Microservice

DDD promotes modeling based on the reality of business as relevant to your use cases. In the context of building applications, DDD explains about problems as domains. It defines independent problem areas as Bounded Contexts (each Bounded Context correlates to a microservice) and emphasizes a common language to speak about these problems.

As mentioned earlier, in microservices are defined as small services to serve only one thing and do one thing well. Each service is also independent and separated from the others. DDD principles can help you to keep the scope of the service small through what it calls "bounded context".

Subsequently, DDD is going to help you review and know your domain and all subdomains well through the communication you build with the business experts. By understanding your domain and subdomains well, you will know the map contexts and how all the subdomains interact with each other, which can be referred in designing and determining the type of your microservices architecture and what are the approaches you can consider to implement them, whether a reactive approach, orchestration approach, or hybrid. It depends on your learning about the domain you're working on. There are pros and cons for each approach that need to be evaluated based on the project and your domain knowledge.

Identifying the boundaries is the primary task when designing and defining a microservice. DDD patterns help you understand the complexity of the domain. To define the domain model for each Bounded Context, recognize and define the entities, value objects, and aggregates that model your domain. You develop and refine a domain model that is contained within a boundary that defines your context. And that is very precise in the form of a microservice. The components within those boundaries arrived being your microservices, although in some cases a boundary context or microservices can be composed of several physical services. DDD is about boundaries and hence are microservices.

The architectural style you will learn is very similar to microservices. It is about departing the monolithic applications into multiple standalone service applications or developing them separately from the origin with the help of bounded contexts, a DDD concept.

There are many resources which highlight the pros of having more granular services explained part of microservices narratives.

## Understanding Layered Architecture in Domain Driven Design

When we design the entire system, we need to choose few architecture patterns. One of them is the layered architecture style; this pattern seems to be generic enough to fit in all other architecture styles but with a separate scale.

For example, if we opt Microservice architecture, each service still needs its own layers. Service either in SOA or Microservice needs a persistence, service, and application layer.

In terms of more "classical" DDD, domain objects are typically not allowed anywhere outside of the domain. But it is not an arbitrary rule that domain objects are not used in the presentation layer. For example, Simple Objects represents a school of thought where domain objects are used directly.

Business logic is assumed to be implemented in the domain model; so much of what is in the application layer is connected with coordinating various services, typically to bring the data to and from the client applications. Many people use some part of SOA or at least web services for this. These call the repositories but also need other components such as assemblers to take the domain objects returned from repository calls and copy the property values into DTOs, which are then serializable and returned to the caller. The caller is usually a presenter or controller but if you are not using MVC or MVVM the caller would still be in the UI/Presentation layer. The reverse trip is more complex - the UI may send back DTOs that represent updates or DTOs that represent new objects to be added. Mediating this back and forth activities is primarily the purpose of the application layer.

The following image is representing a pictorial view of an architecture of microservices based on requirement to make HotelBooking application above. This is divided into the following parts:

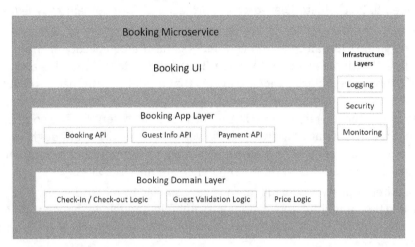

1. **UI (User Interface):** UI layer is responsible for displaying information to the user, and accept new data. It could be implemented for the web, desktop, or any presentation technology, present or future.

2. **Application Layer:** Application Layer is responsible for coordinating the actions to be performed on the domain. A microservice's application layer in .NET is usually developed as an ASP.NET Core Web API project. The project implements the microservice's communication, remote network access, and the external Web APIs used from the UI or client apps. It incorporates queries if using a CQRS approach, commands accepted by the microservice, and even the event-driven communication between microservices (integration events). The ASP.NET Core Web API that describes the application layer must not contain business rules or domain knowledge particularly domain rules for transactions or updates, these should be owned by the domain model class library. The application layer must only organize tasks and must not hold or define any domain state (domain model).

   Basically, the application logic is where you perform all use cases that depend on a given front end. For example, the implementation for a particular Web API.

3. **Domain Layer:** In this layer resides the heart of software, according to Evans. Business rules and logic lives inside this layer. Business entity state and behavior is defined and used here. Communication with other systems, persistence details, is forwarded to the infrastructure layer. Delegates the implementation of business rules to the domain model classes themselves (aggregate roots and domain entities), which will eventually update the data within those domain entities. Responsible for describing concepts of the

business, information about the business situation, and business rules. State that reflects the business rule is controlled and used here, even though the technical details of saving it are delegated to the infrastructure. This layer is the heart of business.

The domain model layer is a layer where the business is expressed. When implementing a microservice domain model layer in .NET, that layer is coded as a class library with the domain entities that carry data plus behavior (methods with logic).

Following is the persistence ignorance and the Infrastructure ignorance principles, this layer must completely ignore data persistence details. These persistence methods should be performed by the infrastructure layer. Therefore, this layer should not carry direct dependencies on the infrastructure, which means that an important rule is that domain model entity classes should be POCOs.

The purpose is that the domain logic in the domain model layer, its invariants, the data model, and related business rules must be entirely independent of the presentation and application layers. Most of all, the domain model layer should not directly depend on any infrastructure framework.

4.  **Infrastructure Layer:** The infrastructure layer described data is initially held in domain entities (in memory) are persisted in databases or another persistent store. An instance is using "Entity Framework Core" code to implement the Repository pattern classes that use a DBContext to persist data in SQL or any relational database.

## Designing a Microservice Domain Model

Let's take the same example of our OnlineHotelReservation APP to learn DDD.

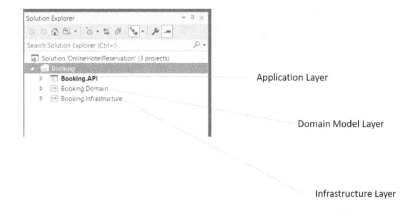

The previous image is depicting the overall folder structure of our microservices application – 'Online Hotel Reservation'. Following are the main components or projects of this architecture:

1. **Booking.API:** Booking.API is an App layer which is generally an ASP.NET core API layer which contains all the services and contracts of API. It includes commands and command handlers.

2. **Booking.Domain:** It is a class library which contains Domain model entities, POCO entity classes. It has dependencies only on the .NET Core libraries or NuGet packages, but not on any other custom library, e.g. data library or persistence library. When taking complexity, it is important to have a domain model controlled by aggregate roots that make sure that all the logics and rules related to that group of entities (aggregate) are performed through a single entry-point, the aggregate root.

3. **Booking.Infrastructure:** It is data persistence repository Which has Entity Framework core to connect to the data access layer. It also contains other infrastructure modules like Logging, Security, and Monitoring etc.

Using layers is the vertical way to organize source code. And that is the same with organizing team. You have to spend more time organizing them if you have more people in a team.

*One thing to microservices:*

They do not address layers, they address the horizontal way (functional way) to organize code mass. Here again: More code, more separation. But be careful, Microservices may give up consistency if they are missing the "bigger" context of your whole domain. So, if I design microservices they are an outbound view of parts of my business domain model considering global consistency.

So, most of the time I would not divide the business layer into smaller pieces as you may lose the possibility to check global constraints OR you will have to consider these consistency constraints in your microservice protocol, making them a lot more complex.

# Communication Between Services

Communication between microservices should be efficient and robust. With lots of small services interacting to perform a single transaction, this can be a challenge. In this chapter, you learn the tradeoffs between asynchronous messaging versus synchronous APIs. Then you look at some of the challenges in designing resilient interservice communication, and the role that a service mesh can play.

In the earlier section, we separated our Inventory module into Room services and discussed how we could break down the relationship between ROOM and BOOKING tables. In a monolithic application, we have one repository that queries the database to fetch the records from both ROOM Inventory and Booking tables. However, in our demo microservice application, we will segregate repositories between Inventory service and Booking service. With each service having its corresponding database, each one would access its own database only. Room service would only be able to access Inventory Database, whereas Booking service would be able to access Booking Database only. Room service should not be allowed to access Booking Database and vice versa.

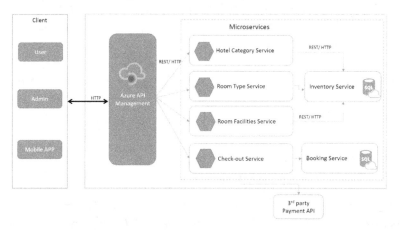

## Understanding High-level design of Online Booking Application

Let's understand the high-level architecture of Online hotel reservation App which has depicted in the above figure. There are three major components which have been used for this architecture, Microservices, API Management, Client and, the communication protocol used as REST/HTTP.

*Microservices*

- **Inventory Service:** It is a backend service which maintains all the hotel inventories e.g. Hotels, Room details, Facilities, address, rating etc. The idea behind creating Inventory as a backend API is Hotel inventory can be loaded from any channel partner or from database.

- **Hotel Category Service:** Hotel category service is a public API which will have hotel categories or type of hotel e.g. Premium, Heritage, Resorts, Budget Hotel, Motel etc. Hotel service will read hotel related information like Hotel address, Hotel Name, description, No. of visitors visited / last visited etc.

Hotel Policy can be managed by creating another service to make it more coupling, remember the core point each service has to be defined for serving only one business solution at a time and must bounded with a context.

- **Room Type Service:** Room type is another dependent service which has master child relationship with hotel, each hotel has multiple rooms and each room has been again categorized based upon certain parameter e.g. Double suite, Single room, Super deluxe room.

- **Room Facilities Service:** Room Facilities is again a dependent service which has foreign key relationship with Room Type Service, each room has different facilities, that is the reason Room facilities is a different service to maintain modularity. If at all the requirement got changed in future not to show Room facilities in the portal then it can be easily manageable.

- **Check-Out Service:** Before coming to check-out Room availability service needs to be consumed from inventory to see if there are any rooms available or not, If rooms are available it will connect to Booking service to maintain Booking transactions and then call 3rd party payment gateway to proceed with Payment and Confirm.
- **Booking Service:** Booking Service will allow the users to confirm the room and make the payment. This service also sends notification to both hotel manager and user that the particular room is booked during the given dates.

This chapter covers pure designing part of the Microservices, Source code would be defined on the Chapter 4.

## Role of API Management

API management controls all the APIs and a single entry point to all the services, it generally takes care of off-loading, routing, security of APIs. APIs, too, require management and policies to ensure that an API program reaches its fullest potential. A cloud-based application integration platform centralizes the development and administrative functions that pertain to APIs. It also ensures a consistent development environment to provide a centralized place for creating, managing, and monitoring APIs and their performance.

## Client

Client is the end user or customer who are the customer in our application. Client or presentation layer will have all the UI related stuffs, validation and service consumer.

It's important to differentiate between two types of API:

- Public APIs that client applications call.
- Backend APIs that are used for inter-service communication.

These two use cases have moderately different requirements. A public API should be compatible with client applications, typically browser applications or native mobile applications. Mostly, the public API will use REST over HTTP. For the backend APIs, but, you need to take network performance into account. Depending on the granularity of your services, inter-service communication can result in a lot of network traffic. Services can quickly become I/O bound. For that purpose, considerations such as serialization speed and payload size become more important.

- **Synchronous:** For web application communication, the HTTP protocol has been the standard for many years, and that is no different for microservices. In a synchronous, stateless protocol, this does have its drawbacks. However, they do not have an adverse impact on its popularity. In synchronous communication, generally the client sends a request and waits for a response from the service. Interestingly, using that protocol, the client can interact asynchronously with a server, which means that a thread is not molded, and the response will reach a callback eventually. An example of such a library, which offers the most common pattern for synchronous REST communication, is Spring Cloud Netflix. For asynchronous callback, there are frameworks like Node.js platform.

- **Asynchronous:** The key point here is that the client should not have blocked a thread while waiting for a response. In most cases, such communication is obtained with messaging brokers. The message producer normally does not wait for a response. It just waits for a response that the message has been received by the broker. The most used protocol for this kind of communication is **Advanced Message Queuing Protocol (AMQP),** which is recommended by many operating systems and cloud providers. An asynchronous messaging system may be achieved in a one-to-one (queue) or one-to-many (topic) mode. The most common message brokers are RabbitMQ and Azure Service Bus, and Apache Kafka. An impressive framework which offers mechanisms for building message-driven microservices based on those brokers is Spring Cloud Stream.

While doing design of Microservices architecture we need to consider following things

- **REST vs RPC.** Consider the balance achieved between using a REST-style interface versus an RPC-style interface.

  o REST model's resources, which can be a natural way, express your domain model. It defines a unique interface based on HTTP verbs, which encourages evolvability. It has well-defined definition in terms of idempotency, side effects, and response codes. And it implements stateless communication, which improves scalability.

  o RPC is more suitable around operations or commands. Because RPC interfaces look similar local method calls, it may lead you to design overly chatty APIs. However, that doesn't mean RPC must be familiar. It just mean you need to take care while designing the interface.

For a RESTful interface, the most popular choice is REST over HTTP using JSON. For an RPC-style interface, there are several popular frameworks, including gRPC, Apache Avro, and Apache Thrift.

## Maturity Model of Micro Services

A Maturity Model is a pre-defined set of parameters that describe certain aspects of Maturity in an enterprise. As the Microservices Architecture grows, predictability, process controls and effectiveness also increase. Development of the Enterprise-wide Microservices Architecture is critical because it provides the rules and definition necessary for the combination of information and services at the operation level over the Enterprise boundaries.

These layered characteristics—modularized and cohesive—help to define a maturity model that serves a number of purposes. First, it incorporates the benefits according to phase and goal (speed or safety) as discussed previously. Secondly, it explains the relative impact and priority of benefits as scale and complexity increase.

There is a desire to have an agile, nimble and lightweight architecture so that they can keep up the pace with fin-techs, who are on the verge of disrupting some of the other business model. As a result many organizations are adopting or rather migrating to a microservices based architecture fronted by an API management solution.

An organization's microservice architecture can be at various phases for different goals. Many organizations have become established in their approach to safety— through automation and other operational considerations—without seeking the speed-aligned system-level benefits.

In essence organizations need to adopt three things to move to a microservices based architecture.

Adopt Domain-Driven design by carving out vertical slices of the business functionality. This for me, is the most vital and the hardest thing to achieve.

Adopt DevOps to have the right infrastructure in place for provisioning, for monitoring, for treating infrastructure as code.

As a part of DevOps adoption, form full stack cross-functional teams who can own those vertical slices end to end following the paradigm – "you build it, you Run it".

The Microservices Maturity Model and its levels are explained in the following table. The model takes after the way of an endeavor as their Microservices reception develops and sets benchmarks to measure the execution and way that is a characteristic movement in the improvement of big business design.

| Level | Description |
| --- | --- |
| Level 0: No Microservices | Organizations still developing applications in a monolithic approach. There is no Microservices in place at this level of maturity. While solutions are developed and performed, done with no identified standards or base practices. |
| Level 1: Initial | The base Microservices architecture framework and standards established, typically performed informally. |
| Level 2: Inception | Define hybrid monolithic and Microservices. New Microservices were developed. Manage Governance Centrally. |
| Level 3: Established | Define enterprise Microservices Reference Architecture using recognized standard and/or customized versions of the templates. Initiate decentralized governance. |

| Level 4: Expanding | Collect Microservices performance metrics, analyze and acted upon. Metrics used to predict the performance and offer better understanding of the Microservices across the enterprise. Fully decentralized governance. |
|---|---|
| Level 5: Optimizing | The Microservices architecture processes are mature. Domain-based views, event-driven Data management are established. There are ongoing clarifications and improvements based on the understanding of the impact changes have to these processes. |

Microservices Maturity within the architecture framework will differ across the business capability, technology architecture, deployment, testing, infrastructure and monitoring as well as the architecture blueprint. This is an ever-evolving process of Enterprise that leads to an efficient, effective responsive development, and support organization.

To complete breakthrough with Microservices, enterprises must first build a well-designed application according to existing platform standards, refactor the system into a collection of Microservices as necessary to meet business needs. With the right team, processes, and tools, Microservices can deliver faster development and deployment, easier maintenance, improved scalability, and freedom from technology locking.

The microservices application architecture needs various approaches to design. To get the best return from the microservices approach, you might need to accept eventual consistency models, rather than the transactional interactions.

Ensure that your logic is state free if it needs to take advantage of the significant rapid scalability benefits.

Become familiar with the complex potential side effects of asynchronous communication if you decouple yourself from downstream components.

Microservices require a mature delivery capability. Continuous integration, deployment, and automated tests are a must. The developers who write code must be accountable for it in production. Build and deployment chains need significant changes to provide the right separation of concerns for a microservices environment.

As per Wikipedia << https://en.wikipedia.org/wiki/Conway%27s_law>>

"Conway's law is an adage named after computer programmer Melvin Conway, who introduced the idea in 1967.[1] It states that

"organizations which design systems ... are constrained to produce designs which are copies of the communication structures of these organizations." — M. Conway[2]"

The law is based on the thought that in order for a software module to function, multiple organizers must communicate frequently with each other. Therefore, the software interface structure of a system will reflect the social boundaries of the organization(s) that produced it, across which communication is more difficult. Conway's law was intended as a valid sociological observation, although sometimes it's used in a humorous context. It was dubbed Conway's law by participants at the 1968 National Symposium on Modular Programming.

Following figure depicts the definite parameter required to major Microservices maturity model .

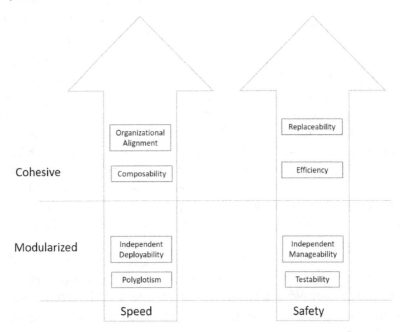

*Microservices Maturity Model*

## Benefits of Modularization and Cohesion

Modularization and Cohesion both are interlinked. Both bring easy development, deployment, and testing of the application. Following are the few key points which explain Why Modularization and Cohesion are primary aspect of any Microservices Architecture.

- **Continuous Integration:** Each service has their own Continuous Integration pipeline which deploys and tests them in dev/testing environments on each check-in.

- **Automated Deploys:** Deploying a service is a completely automated task that requires minimal manual interaction.

- **Independent Deploys:** Every service can be deployed autonomously, providing backward compatibility.

- **Continuous Delivery:** Services are always in a releasable state and releasing a feature is solely a business decision that can be taken without extra effort from the team.

- **Phased deployment:** When releasing new features, the deployment can be rolled back/forward as needed with minor impact to customers.

- **Configuration Management:** Configuring is easy with Microservices, If require to enhance to another protocol it can be configured easily. Hosts configurations and dependencies are automated and the code is under source control.

- **Replaceable services:** A service can be replaced without major changes to the architecture, as long as the business boundaries remain the same and good citizenship standards are followed.

- **Integrated testing:** Services are tested considering the communication paths and interaction between components, including their contracts.

- **Consumer-driven Contract testing:** Services are continuously tested against the contract provided by their consumers, ensuring they work as expected by external clients.

- **Cross-functional testing:** Traits like response time, availability, load, security are tested across all services ensuring the cross-functional requirements are met.

Above points are the primary aspects which you need to remember before designing any Microservices based application.

## Summary

In this chapter, we discussed about different Microservices Architecture. We discussed various aspects of architectural style like Modularized, cohesive, layered Microservices. Then we went through Microservice Boundaries, Domain model and communication between Microservices.

In next chapter, we will discuss high level design of microservices application with the help of our demo applications and will start transitioning to microservices.

# CHAPTER 3

# Designing the Microservice Application Layer

This chapter covers the basics of how to design an application, the steps to identify the problems in the use case with the help of a hands-on example. The problem use case that we will refer to is the same Online Hotel Booking application like the one we have used in our demo application. Before we jump into the intricacies of solution design, let us revisit some of the basic concepts that we already know or have already understood in the previous chapters.

Since we will be building the application within the scope of the microservices paradigm with the help of OOPS we have to brush up our basics about –

- OOPS
- Solid Principles
- Design Patterns
- Microservices Basics

## OOPS Basic

OOP is a programming methodology in which you conceive the problem in hand as small units of data, with defined behaviour, interacting with each other. And these interactions are what help us deliver a solution to our problem.

In OOPs, we look at the problem and do the following –

- Identify the different types of units of information and what will be their behaviour.
- Identify how and what the individual units will interact with each other and external entities
- What will be the outcome of those interactions?

Once the above has been understood in any problem, creating a basic object-oriented design is a step closer. So, based on the problem we have already defined in our demo application we have identified the following for our "Online Booking System" –

- Hotels are having rooms available for booking.
- They are rated with stars between 1 to 5 based on services they offer.
- Hotels may offer various facilities like Car parking, Lobby, Meeting rooms, Dine-in etc. But not all facilities are available in all the hotels.
- Hotels can be searched based on ratings, facilities, location and price at which the rooms are available.

- A hotel may have various categories of rooms.
- Rooms can be booked for one or more nights.
- A Hotel may offer various facilities for the Rooms like complimentary breakfast, mini-bar, wi-fi, tv, room services.
- Some of these facilities are available at a price while others may be free.
- Guests need to check in and check out of the room.
- Check out process involves the final bill generation.

Based on the above problem walkthrough, we have identified the entities that we need to replicate in our solution. The next step is to correlate the concepts of OOPs with these entities. When we want to work with OOPs we need to understand the following –

- **Class:** It can be described as the template for the programmable unit in OOPs. A class provides the basic definition of the unit with the help of properties and methods. So, for our problem, we may need to define classes for Hotel, Rooms, Services, and Facilities etc.

- **Objects:** An instance of the class, objects are actual instances of the class that contains business-related data and performs business functions on themselves or other objects or external systems. During programming, the instances of Hotels or Rooms will be created to contain critical information and perform necessary functions.

- **Encapsulation:** With encapsulation, the intent is to bundle up information into single units. So, when creating a Hotel class, we are trying to bundle information about the hotel like – Hotel Name, Address, Location, Phone number, Facilities, Hotel Type etc.

- **Abstraction:** The main goal of abstraction is to hide unnecessary details from the user that may complicate user understanding. In our example, we want to "abstract" the actual steps involved in Booking a room and expose a simpler interface with which it interacts. Booking may involve various steps like Check Room Type, Check Room Availability, and Change Status of Room to Blocked, Make Payment, change status to Booked on Payment Success or Change status to Available on Payment Failure, Generate Invoice, and Send Invoice Email etc.

- **Inheritance:** In Wiki, Inheritance is defined as - "Inheritance is the mechanism of basing an object or class upon another object (prototypical inheritance) or class (class-based inheritance), retaining similar implementation". Thus, with inheritance, we create a one more or classes basing off another class, so that its properties and behaviors are carried forward without duplicating the effort. Here the base class is mostly called the parent, whereas the classes created with inheritance are called child classes. The intent of inheritance is to create groups of classes that share similar traits. In our problem, we may choose to create a parent class of Room, having basic properties like

Bed, Rate, Facing, Status etc. We may now need to create 3 room classes inheriting the Room class, one is the SingleRoom, DoubleRoom, and Suite. By default, all the 3 child classes will have the properties from the Room class. For SingleRoom, we may choose to fix the value of Bed to 1, for DoubleRoom it can be set to 2, and for Suite it could be 4. Since child classes are classes on their own. So, they can have specific properties like NosOfRooms and ConciergeServices.

- **Polymorphism:** The Greek word polymorphism means to exist in multiple forms. While inheritance helps us extend and share similar behaviour. It introduces a problem. What if the class displays the same behaviour in 2 ways? For example, say the Room Booking can be done in 2 ways, like either online or offline or what if for Single and Double Room, the checkout involves Billing for all the services that have been taken as an add-on. But for Suites, the billing logic remains same for all regular guests but involves heavy discounts for privilege members, along with the allocation of discount coupons. Thus, billing for Suite should exist in multiple forms, all of which are unique.

- **Association:** Association is a relationship between two objects. Association can be of many types but at the end, it defines the multiplicity among the objects. The name of an association defines the nature of the relationship between objects. In diagrams, it is mostly represented as a solid line like the given as follows:

In our solution of Hotel Booking application, Hotel and Hotel Reviews are associated with each other. Hotel Review is associated with the Hotel. A hotel can be associated with multiple reviews. Both have a separate lifecycle.

| **Hotel** | | **Hotel Reviews** |
|---|---|---|

- **Aggregation:** Aggregation is a special form of association. Like association it represents a relationship between two classes, however, it's a directional association, which means it is strictly a one-way association. It is a containment relationship and is basically a HAS-A relationship. Thus, once class contains the other class. But the relationship will not make sense if it is reversed. This is represented with a solid line that has a diamond at end of the class that contains the other. The ends of the association may have numbers or 'n' representing 1 to 1, 1 to many, many to 1, and many to many relationships.

N             1

In our problems, Hotels may have Car Parking. Hotels and Car Parking can exist individually too. However, Car Parking can never have Hotels. Thus, the aggregation relationship between Hotels and Car Parking should be represented as –

- **Composition:** The Composition is another form of association. Like association, it represents a relationship between two classes and is a strictly one-way directional association. It is another form of containment relationship. In this relationship, one class cannot exist independent of the other class and will not make any sense if it is reversed. This is represented, in UML, with a solid line that has a solid diamond at end of the class that contains the other. The ends of the association may have numbers or 'n' representing 1 to 1, 1 to many, many to 1, and many to many relationships.

In our problems, Hotels will have Rooms. But Rooms cannot exist without Hotels and Rooms can never have Hotels. Thus, the composition relationship between Hotels and Rooms should be represented as follows:

- **Generalization & Specialization:** Generalization is a way to represents an inheritance relationship between two classes. The idea that drives generalization is in a way to take the most common features all the subclass. The contents of the superclass are driven by the common properties that are shared amongst the subclasses. Specialization is another way representing an inheritance relationship. In this form, you have a well-defined superclass available. You start implementing subclass by introducing specific behavior only and nothing else. Thus, while designing a specialization inheritance, you already know the superclass behavior, you start creating subclass on a need basis and adding specific properties or behavior. In UML, the generalization and specialization are represented by a solid line and arrow at the end. The arrow points to the superclass and connects to the subclass with the solid line.

In our example, Room may be of different types and can be represented by a Generalization of SingleRoom, DoubleRoom, and Suite.

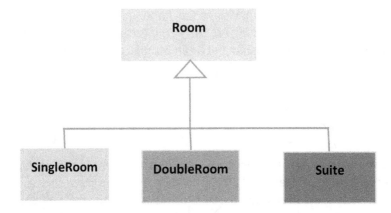

So, once we have an idea about which classes to form, next we move on to the next, which is, the principles that will guide us into creating basic classes when we have an understanding what they are supposed to do.

## Solid Principles

Once we know that we need to go OOPs, it is important to keep in mind certain principles or thumb-rules of when we are creating the classes for any solution. These principles guide us to create a solution that is manageable and extensible. The idea is to create meaningful classes that work the way we want. The benefits of SOLID Principles are many as they make system reusable, robust, maintainable, scalable, testable and more. So why are they known as SOLID? Well, simply because it is an acronym of the five principles that it represents. These are -

- **S — Single responsibility principle** - A class must have one and only one reason to change, meaning that a class should only be meant for one purpose. If functionality changes lead to a change of class definition, this may further lead to one or more changes in other related classes. In that case, if a class is doing too many things, then it may have to repeatedly undergo changes and will later lead to the creation of a big messy code. In our problem, a Booking class should only be responsible for making hotel booking and should not own the responsibility of sending out notifications.

- **O — Open, closed principle** - Open Closed Principle states that one can extend classes' behavior, without modifying it. This principle is the base for building code that is maintainable and reusable. This principle says Objects should be Open for Extension but Closed for Modification.

  - **Open for extension** - This assures that the class behavior can be extended. It should be possible to add fields to the classes, or new elements to the set of functions it performs. This can be done via inheritance or dependency injection techniques.

  - **Closed for modification** - The functionalities of such class are set to solve a requirement, and no one can make changes to the code. Once a structure has been given to the class, it should undergo minimalistic and corrective changes only.

Thus, we should create a Room class that should be stable enough functionality to be a generic parent for SingleRoom, DoubleRoom, and Suite. It should be extended with specific features for these 3 room type concrete implementation.

- **L — Liskov substitution principle** - The Liskov Substitution Principle (LSP) is one of the unique principles to object-oriented programming. The LSP says that any child type of a parent type should be able to hold in for that parent without things leaving up. It means is that every subclass/derived class should be substitutable for their base/parent class.

  In other words, if there is a class called "Notification," with a SendNotification() method, then any subclass of Notification should logically implement SendNotification (). So, EmailNotification should send email, SMSNotification should send SMS etc. Once must not define a BulletinBoard class that throws INotificationSendingNotRequiredException. This violates the LSP, and the argument would be that this class has no business inheriting from Notification.

- **I — Interface segregation principle** - A client should never be forced to implement an interface that it doesn't use, or clients shouldn't be forced to depend on methods which is not mandatory or what it does not need. We should avoid creating bulky, monolithic, do it all interfaces and instead of it create lightweight functionality specific interfaces that can be implemented in need to know basis. This is meant not to bind clients to depend on things they don't need. Just think your code consuming some big, heavy interface and having to re-compile or deploy with annoying repetition because some method you don't even worry about got a new signature.

- **D — Dependency Inversion principle** - The Dependency Inversion Principle (DIP) encourages to write code that depends upon abstractions rather than upon strong details.
  - o  A. High-level modules should not depend upon low-level modules. Both should depend upon abstractions.
  - o  B. Abstractions should not depend upon details. Details should depend upon abstractions.

You can identify abstractions in the code yourself by looking for a class or method that takes something generic like "Logging" and performs operations on it, as opposed to instantiating a specific FileLogging or database logging or whatever. Abstraction gives the code in question a lot more flexibility - you can exchange in anything that corresponds to the Stream abstraction, and it will work. By depending on higher-level abstractions, you can easily change one instance with another instance to change the behavior. Dependency Inversion improves the reusability and flexibility in code.

## Design Patterns

While we can create good, functional classes and hence a solution with SOLID principles, we are bound to face problems that are bound to creep in whenever we are creating a big solution. And in software development, thankfully, re-inventing the wheel is not required. With design patterns, we get the means to solve recurring problems.

**Design Patterns are general, repeatable solutions to commonly recurring problems in software development."** [From Wikipedia, the free encyclopedia, "Design pattern (computer science)"].

Explaining all the design patterns is beyond the scope of this book. However, whenever we will choose a pattern in our examples, we will walk you through the design decision that led to our choice.

## Microservices

From the first 2 chapters, we have understood the following: -

- **Modular and Independent:** Microservices are created each service are small and designed to solve specific business function and work independently of other microservices in the same suite. They are designed to be loosely coupled.

- **Decentralized and Cross-Functional:** The ideal organization for microservices has small, engaged team where each team oversees a business function made from various microservices which can be Independently deployed.

- **Resilient:** Microservices are better for fault isolation. This way If one of the services in the solution fails others will continue to work. This is one of the benefits of building distributed systems as microservices is that the ability of the system as a full to resist faults and surprising failures of elements, networks, computer resources, etc. These systems are resilient even within the face of faults.

- **Highly Scalable:** Scalability is the utmost importance of any distributed system and Microservices are meant for scaling. Thus, an individual service can be scaled or the entire application.

## Online Hotel Booking App Requirements

Now lets first understand the basic requirements of our Online Hotel Booking App that we will cover in our application examples. The requirements are given as follows:

- The system supports guests to book hotel rooms online. They will also be able to modify their booking.

- Guests can search the hotels based on Room Category (ex. Radisson, Delhi (Luxury))

- When a customer searches for hotels, the search result must contain hotel information, (address, Ratings, and Price) its availability within a chosen a check in and check out date.

- Customers can cancel their booking from their account.
- Customers can book online and make payment Online.
- The system must send booking confirmation email after successful payment.
- Customers can write reviews about hotels and apartment they have booked and stayed in and rate them.
- Customers can check their booking status from their account.

Based on the application needs and driven by the microservice architecture guidelines, we have identified the following main modules:

1. User
2. Room Category
3. Hotels
4. Price
5. Facilities
6. Booking
7. Review and Ratings

We have also identified that the application as a whole will have different types of access, thus we need to have different roles to manage the application end to end. These roles are -

## Roles

1. Admin
2. Hotel (Hotel Management)
3. User

The process of booking that we have finalized will have the following steps -

## Booking Process

1. Details required are City, Check-in/Check-out and Guest details
2. Select Hotels from category
3. View Hotel details
4. Room Details and facilities
5. Book Room
6. Confirmation message
7. Payment (online/Cash)

The functions that are possible from the admin panel of the application are as follows:-

## Admin Panel

1. Manage User and Hotel data

2. Manage transaction and payment— Payout for Hotels (Payment Terms)

3. Manage Booking

4. Manage reservation & cancellation

5. Generate invoice

6. Manage History

The functions that are possible from the user panel of the application are as follows:

## User Panel

1. Register/Login

2. Home (view nearby hotel)

3. Map & List View with Hotels Title, basic Description, Images, Rating etc

4. Reserve Hotel Room Type.

5. Book Room.

6. View invoice

7. Notification (booking confirmation)

8. Manage Upcoming, Completed and cancelled booking

9. Payment (Online/Cash)

10. Review Hotel

The functions that are possible from the hotel panel of the application are as follows:

## Hotel Panel

1. Register/Login

2. User Info (can view Guest profile who had booked the hotel)

3. Manage Hotel (Photo, Policies)

4. Payment (Online/Cash)

5. Manage Rooms and Facilities.

6. View invoice

7. Manage booking and cancellations

8. View User Review

9. History

## State Diagram of Online Hotel Booking

Following is the state diagram of the Online Hotel Booking system as per requirement that we have given above.

Customer inquiries about hotel based on city, Check-in/Check-out date. The application checks for availability and suggests room details-based on details mentioned in the inquiry. Next, the User enters the room details and Logs in and enters details of the guest who will be occupying the room. Please note that the user/customer/guests are one and the same thing. Customer next proceeds to book the room, the application processes the request by assigning the room and generating the Invoice for a successful payment.

The Hotel Admin takes care of adding room details into the system.

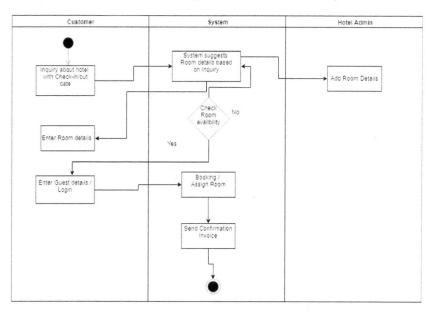

## Pre-Requisites to Build Online Hotel Booking Application

Before we proceed with our activity let us check our development pre-requisites. We would need the latest version of Visual Studio 2017. You can download the community edition for learning propose which is free. If you have an existing Visual Studio 2017, you can update by following the below steps.

### Update Visual Studio 2017 version 15.6 or Later

It is straightforward now, the installation and update experience to use directly from within the IDE. Below is how to update from version 15.6 and later to newer versions of Visual Studio.

### Use the Notifications Hub

When there is an update, there's a similar notification flag in Visual Studio.

1.  Save your work.
2.  Choose the notification flag to open the **Notifications** hub, and then choose the update that you need to install.

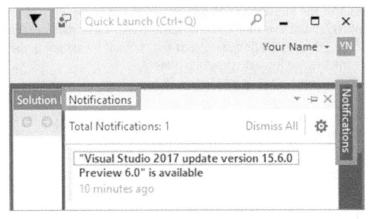

3.  When the Update dialog box opens, choose Update Now.

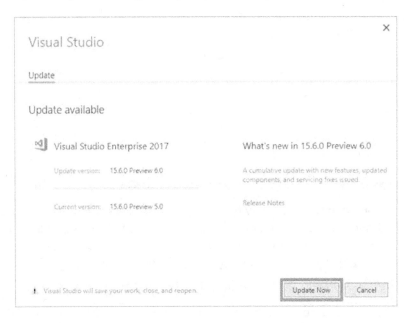

If a User Access Control dialog box opens, choose Yes. Next, a ", Please wait" dialogue might open for a moment, and then the Visual Studio Installer opens to start the update.

## Install .NET Core 2.1.x

To build this application .NET core 2.1 being used but you always can update SDK with the latest version available.

### Step 1: Run Installer

Download Core SDK2.1 from this path << https://www.microsoft.com/net/download/thank-you/dotnet-sdk-2.1.300-rc1-windows-x64-installer>>

When your download completes, run the installer and complete the steps to install .NET on your machine.

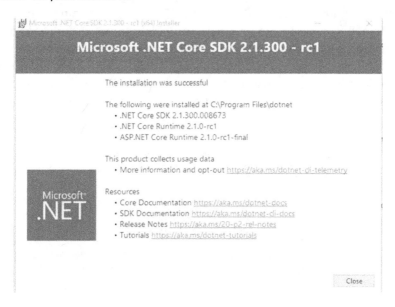

## Step 2: Verify Installation

When the installer completes, open a new command prompt and run the **dotnet** command. This will verify .NET is correctly installed and ready to use.

Online Hotel Booking requirements which have already been discussed in Chapter 1 as stated.

## Patterns for Data management in Microservices

Once we have a clear understanding as to what we need from different users and how we want to process the information collected from different users. It is important to understand how this information would be stored in our application backend. Hence finalizing the DB Design is very important.

As per the requirement, we need to design a DB with all Constraints and foreign key relationship. But it has a huge underlying problem that we may tend to overlook. Microservices architecture is more autonomous. Microservices architecture suggests that each service should handle its own data. Hence any service (Service A) dependent on data owned by other services (service B) should access such data not by making direct DB calls but through the API provided by the second service (service B).

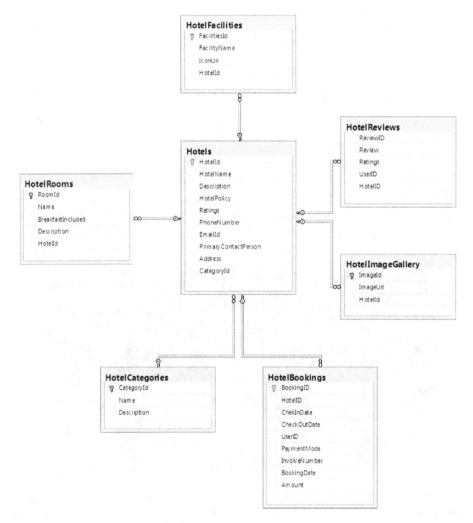

So, what do microservices best practices suggest on checking foreign key constraints?

There are several ways to keep a service's persistent data private. One may not need to assign a database server for each service. If you are handling a relational database below are the options that we have for our DB design needs:

- **Private-tables-per-service:** In this design approach, each service has a set of tables that must only be accessed by that service.

- **Schema-per-service:** In this design approach, each service owns a database schema that's controlled by that service.

- **Database-server-per-service:** In this design approach, each service has its database server.

Private-tables-per-service and schema-per-service have the lowest overhead. Using a schema per service is interesting since it makes ownership clearer. Some high throughput services might need their database server.

Based on the requirement it forces that some transactions require to fetch data that is owned by multiple services. For example, the View Bookings must use the query the Customer to find the No. Of. Rooms and number of Guests to calculate the total amount of the open Bookings.

Some queries may need to join data that is controlled by multiple services. For example, finding customers in a location and their current bookings requires a join between customers and bookings.

Different services have different data storage requirements. Some service SQL and for few Redis Cache is required. (You can get more details on Redis Cache at https://redis.io/ )

## Getting a Solution to the Problems

It is a good idea to create restrictions that force the modularity. For example, assign a separate database user id to each service and use a database access control mechanism such as permissions. Without restriction to enforcing encapsulation, developers will always be motivated to bypass a service's API and access it's data directly. The reference application (Online HotelBooking) is cross-platform at the server and client side, that is the reason to use .NET Core services which can run on Linux or Windows containers depending on Docker host, and to Xamarin for hybrid mobile apps running on Android, iOS or Windows plus any browser for the web apps.

The architecture offers a microservice oriented architecture implementation with multiple independent microservices (each one owning its DB) and implementing different approaches within each microservice (simple CRUD vs. DDD/CQRS patterns) using Http as the communication protocol connecting the client apps and the microservices and supports asynchronous communication for data updates spread across multiple services based on Integration Events and an Event Bus e.g. Azure Service Bus/ RabbitMQ.

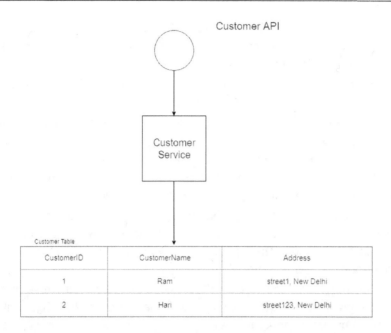

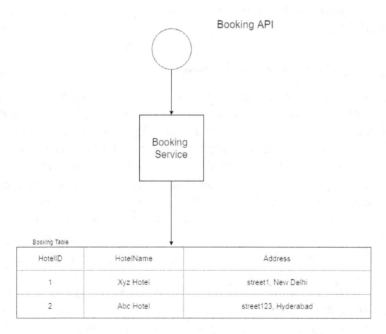

Now let us take a look at the various aspects of this proposed architecture -

API Composition - The application interface implements the join rather than the database. For example, a service (or the API gateway) could fetch a customer and their bookings by first querying the customer from the customer service and then querying the Booking service to return the customer's most recent bookings.

Command Query Responsibility Segregation (CQRS) – In CQRS, we split the application DB needs into two parts: the command-side and the query-side. The command-side will handle the data manipulation activities like create, update, and delete requests and exposes public events when data changes. On the other hand, the query-side handles queries by executing them against one or more materialized views. Thus, we ensure that the application maintains one or more materialized views that contain data from multiple services. The views are kept by services that subscribe to events that each service publishes when it updates its data. For example, online Booking could implement a query that finds customers in a region and their recent bookings by maintaining a view that joins customers and bookings. The view is updated by a service that subscribes to customer and booking events. We will cover CQRS pattern in-details on next section.

## CQRS Pattern and Domain Driven Design (DDD)

CQRS means Command Query Responsibility Segregation. Many people think that CQRS is a full-fledged DB architecture, but that is not correct. CQRS is just a pattern in which identify and segregate our data manipulation and data reading activities and expose them differently.

This pattern was first introduced by Greg Young and Udi Dahan. They took inspiration from a pattern called Command Query Separation which was defined by Bertrand Meyer in his book "Object-Oriented Software Construction." The main idea behind CQS is: "A method should either change the state of an object, or return a result, but not both." CQRS is an architectural pattern that groups the models for reading and writing data separately. The stated term Command Query Separation (CQS) was originally defined by Bertrand Meyer in his book "Object-Oriented Software Construction."

The primary idea is that you can divide a system's operations into two distinctly classified categories:

- **Queries** - These deliver a result and do not change the nature of the system, and they are free of side effects.
- **Commands** -These change the state of a system.

CQS is a simply a concept. CQRS is about methods within a single object being either queries or commands. Each method either returns state or mutates state, but not both. Even a single repository pattern object can comply with CQS. CQS can be considered a foundational principle for CQRS.

The separation aspect of CQRS is achieved by grouping query operations in one layer and commands in another layer. Each layer has its data model (note that we say, model, not necessarily a different database) and is built using its aggregate of patterns and technologies. Also, importantly, the two layers can be in the same tier or microservice, as in the example (Hotel microservice) used for this example. Or they could be performed on different microservices or methods, so they can be optimized and scaled out independently without affecting one another.

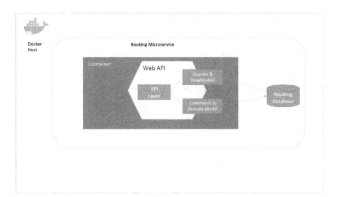

CQRS means having separate objects for a read/write operation wherein the other context there is one. There are reasons to have a denormalized reads database, which you can learn about in more advanced CQRS literature. But we are not using that approach here, where the goal is to have more flexibility in the queries instead of limiting the queries with constraints from DDD patterns like aggregates.

The idea of requesting microservice at the hotel booking reference application depends on CQRS standards. However, it utilizes the least difficult approach, which is simply isolating the inquiries from the bookings and utilizing a similar database for the two activities.

One such example is the Aggregate example, which we inspect more in later segments. Quickly, in the Aggregate example, you regard numerous space questions as a solitary unit because of their relationship in the area. You may not generally pick up focal points from this example in inquiries; it can build the many-sided quality of question rationale. For read-just inquiries, you don't get the upsides of regarding various questions as a solitary Aggregate. You just get the unpredictability.

On the other hand, commands which trigger transactions and updates data, change state in the system. With commands, it is extremely important to be careful when dealing with complexity and changes in business rules. This is the where DDD techniques are required to have a better-modeled system.

The DDD patterns shown in this guide should not be applied everywhere. They propose constraints on design. Those constraints give benefits such as higher quality over time, particularly in commands and other code that modifies system state. However, those constraints add complexity with lesser benefits for reading and querying data.

Before we get into the in-depth understanding of DDD, we must understand its importance:

- In DDD as we have discussed earlier, development is more domain oriented not UI/Database oriented.
- Domain layer captures most of the business logic, creating a very light service layer, i.e., just a gateway into your domain via DTO's.

- The domain-oriented development offers you to execute real service-oriented architecture i.e. making services more reusable as they are not specific to UI/Presentation layer.
- Unit tests are quite easy to formulate as code scales horizontally and not vertically, making methods light and quickly testable.
- DDD is a collection of Principles and Patterns, this offers developers a framework to work with, and most importantly supporting everyone in the development team to go in the same direction.

## Bounded Contexts

It is easier to identify which ones could be a microservices in this system, a bounded context marks the boundary of a domain model and we already know a microservice only has one specific responsibility. So, the functionality in a microservice should not span more than one bounded context. If you find that a microservice combines different domain models, that's an indication that there is something wrong with the domain and solution analysis and you may need to relook and refine it.

## Source Code: Booking.API

### HotelCatgeroies.cs

```
using System;
using System.Collections.Generic;

namespace OnlineHotel.Infra.Domain.Models
{
    public partial class HotelCategories
    {
        public HotelCategories()
        {
            Hotels = new HashSet<Hotels>();
        }
        public int CategoryId { get; set; }
        public string Name { get; set; }
        public string Description { get; set; }
        public ICollection<Hotels> Hotels { get; set; }
    }
}
```

### Hotels.cs

```
using System;
using System.Collections.Generic;

namespace OnlineHotel.Infra.Domain.Models
{
    public partial class Hotels
```

```
    {
        public Hotels()
        {
            HotelBookingDdds = new HashSet<HotelBookingDdds>();
            HotelFacilities = new HashSet<HotelFacilities>();
            HotelImageGallery = new
            HashSet<HotelImageGallery>();
            HotelRooms = new HashSet<HotelRooms>();
        }
        public int HotelId { get; set; }
        public string HotelName { get; set; }
        public string Description { get; set; }
        public string HotelPolicy { get; set; }
        public int? Ratings { get; set; }
        public string PhoneNumber { get; set; }
        public string EmailId { get; set; }
        public string PrimaryContactPerson { get; set; }
        public string Address { get; set; }
        public int? CategoryId { get; set; }

        public HotelCategories Category { get; set; }
        public ICollection<HotelBookingDdds>
        HotelBookingDdds { get; set; }
        public ICollection<HotelFacilities> HotelFacilities
        { get; set; }
        public ICollection<HotelImageGallery>
        HotelImageGallery { get; set; }
        public ICollection<HotelRooms> HotelRooms
        { get; set; }
    }
}
```

### HotelRooms.cs

```
using System;
using System.Collections.Generic;

namespace OnlineHotel.Infra.Domain.Models
{
    public partial class HotelRooms
    {
        public int RoomId { get; set; }
        public string Name { get; set; }
        public bool? BreakfastIncluded { get; set; }
        public string Description { get; set; }
        public int? HotelId { get; set; }

        public Hotels Hotel { get; set; }
    }
}
```

## Facilities.cs

```
using System;
using System.Collections.Generic;

namespace OnlineHotel.Infra.Domain.Models
{
    public partial class HotelFacilities
    {
        public int FacilitiesId { get; set; }
        public string FacilityName { get; set; }
        public string IconUrl { get; set; }
        public int? HotelId { get; set; }

        public Hotels Hotel { get; set; }
    }
}
```

## Booking.cs

```
using System;
using System.Collections.Generic;

namespace OnlineHotel.Infra.Domain.Models
{
    public partial class HotelBookings
    {
        public int BookingId { get; set; }
        public int? HotelId { get; set; }
        public DateTime? ChekInDate { get; set; }
        public DateTime? CheckOutDate { get; set; }
        public int? UserId { get; set; }
        public string PaymentMode { get; set; }
        public string InvoiveNumber { get; set; }
        public DateTime? BookingDate { get; set; }
        public decimal? Amount { get; set; }

        public Hotels Hotel { get; set; }
    }
}
```

## Customer.cs

```
using System;
using OnlineHotel.Infra.Domain.Core.Models;

namespace OnlineHotel.Infra.Domain.Models
{
    public class Customer: Entity
    {
        public Customer(Guid id, string name, string email,
        DateTime birthDate)
        {
```

```
        Id = id;
        Name = name;
        Email = email;
        BirthDate = birthDate;
    }
    // Empty constructor for EF
    protected Customer() { }

    public string Name { get; private set; }

    public string Email { get; private set; }

    public DateTime BirthDate { get; private set; }
}
}
```

## Breaking the Code

The above code represents a set of anemic classes. Some developers may stop here and use these classes to pass data to service and then bind this data to the UI. But we should not stop here and try to make our models more matured.

When a customer searches for hotels online, they choose hotels first, then they navigate around the search results and eventually they will book a room. So, we need something that will book hotels, this object will have no identity and it will be transient.

Hotels will simply contain nos. of rooms, facilities, images, and bookings.

In the source code, we have taken customer class, created value and entity object and added certain details of the customer.

## Interservice Communication

One of the essential aspects of developing microservices than a monolithic application is inter-service communication. Usually, in a monolithic application, which runs on single process calls between components are realized by programming-level method calls. If you want to follow the MVC design pattern during development, you generally have model classes which map relational databases to an object model. Then, you need to components which expose methods that help to perform standard (CRUD) operations on database tables e.g. create, read, update, and delete. The components generally are known as Data Access Object (DAO) or data repository objects which should not be straight called from a controller, but through an additional layer which can also add some part of business logic if required.

Decisions related to such a system needs information about the business aspects of a system, but communication standards can be simply defined, and they are fixed no matter which approach to architecture we decide to implement. If we are talking about communication styles, it is possible to classify them in two parts. The primary step is to determine whether a protocol is synchronous or asynchronous. Communication between services is exciting, you have so many options to select from.

As mentioned above, inter-service communication is of 2 types:

- Synchronous
- Asynchronous

## Synchronous - REST HTTP

We have explained about synchronous: Rest HTTP in detail in later chapters, but it is good to understand that the easiest viable solution for synchronous communication between services is to apply the same strategy for communication as to end clients - JSON over HTTP. And reasonably it's fine to pay the price of a small cost for the ability to re-use endpoints by different services and distribute them with clients. And of course, if you need something more performant for "service to service" requests (i.e. user's authentication token verification).

For one-to-one synchronous services, the same can be achieved with a load-balancing mechanism performed on the client side. Each service has information about the location addresses of all instances that are calling services. This information can be taken from a service discovery server or may be provided manually in configuration properties.

## Asynchronous - Lightweight Messaging

While we can implement asynchronous messaging on our own, but the reliability of such messaging cannot be sure shot unless we are very thorough and are backed with rigorous testing. So, what is the easier way out? As of now, there are many out of the box framework that helps us do exactly that. To support lightweight messaging, we need to select a software package that will act as lightweight message broker delivering your messages to consumers running on respective microservices. There's a great variety of tools to support that, amongst them are as follows:

- RabbitMQ
- Redis
- Azure Service Bus

RESTful HTTP has many benefits like decoupling client and server and scaling through caching. The other solution is using Kafka or another persistent queue.

Non-blocking technologies to work with TCP and HTTP are there but still many popular stacks are blocking threads while doing I/O which can lead to instability and inability to answer some requests because of just a few hundred requests that wait for upstream services to respond. Also, the back-pressure problem exists - one can use only A.K.K.A-HTTP clients and servers but services are supposed to be decoupled and you cannot be sure if backpressure is considered all over. With Kafka, you don't have this concern.

HTTP, at the connection level, is blocking (until one response comes, or timeouts, the next request cannot be issued on the same connection) - this is changing with HTTP-2. Even if ensuring that neither threads nor connections are blocked for each request-response cycle, the number of open file descriptors or other resources are used by applications more extensively than by using Kafka.

## Application Lifecycle

Unlike software development life cycle (SDLC), it is necessary to understand the features of the microservice development life cycle processes for a successful implementation of the microservices architecture. Microservices are smaller and autonomous in nature, hence each microservice has its own code base, deployment pipeline, and independent lifecycle.

### Independent Life Cycles Boosts Developer Productivity

Speed to market isn't the only reason that it is required to go with an independent life cycle for a module. It can increase developer productivity too.

Very few developers would say monoliths help them be productive. They work hard through dictionary-length developer setup guides. Build times are very lengthy. It can take longer for a developer to get up to speed on a project. With a smaller codebase, a developer can get their head wrapped around a microservice in a day or two. Builds finish in a few minutes. If the build gets broken, developers know instantly, and they can take immediate action to fix the issue.

Smaller code bases also mean testing a microservice can be simpler and be focused. Microservices are all about flexibility, including customized deployment pipelines. You are no longer forced to push every line of code through the exact same sieve. In the same way, microservices offer to choose the best technology for the system, you also have the liberty to use the right mix of tests, and code quality scans for each microservice.

### Tools Used

1.   Visual Studio 2017
2.   .NET Core 2.1
3.   Mediatr
4.   AspNet.Core.Identity

## Summary

In this chapter, we discussed the `OOPs concept, SOLID principles, CQRS and DDD patterns with the help of our demo application. We discussed various aspects of architectural styles, flow diagram. Then we went through Microservices, need and how to adapt it in the existing application.

In the next chapter, we will discuss complete hands-on development of the microservices application with the help of our demo applications and will start transitioning to microservices.

# CHAPTER 4

# Hands on Microservices Development of Online Hotel Reservation App

## Introduction

In the previous chapter, we have walkthrough the basic design concepts that we will apply in our application development. We have breezed through the OOPs, SOLID Design Principles and retouched Microservices basics. We have introduced our DB design challenges and what are the options we have, to tackle the problems or challenges that we may face.

In this chapter, we will use those concepts and create a solution around it.

## High-level Architecture of Online Hotel Reservation App

So, the first step to designing and developing an application, is to create a high-level design (HLD). Based on our application needs, the high-level architecture of the demo app Online Hotel Reservation is given below. We have made the following design decisions –

- UI/client layer to be developed using Angular SPA
- Middleware will have API management details of which are given in the following chapter
- Backend layer is in .NET core for Microservices development.
- APP to be developed as a multi-container architecture pattern with each service will be having its own DB running on the separate container.
- RabbitMQ is used for Event-driven architecture (you may choose something else too).

The Service layers and angular based SPA App source code and its explanation can be found in the following sections. The application will consist of following types of components:

- **Presentation components.** This component responsible for handling the UI and consuming remote services (Angular SPA).
- **Domain or business logic.** This component holds the application's domain logic. (.NET Core Microservices)
- **Database access logic.** This layer consists of data access components responsible for accessing databases (SQL).
- **Application integration logic.** This component includes a messaging channel, largely based on message brokers (RabbitMQ/ Azure Service Bus).

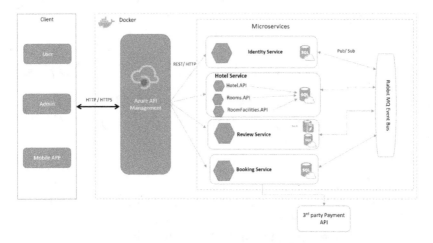

## Development Environment setup of Online Hotel Reservation App

While development is the most important part of the solution lifecycle, but to reap the benefits of a good design, the application should be backed with a great deployment. And planning it is also important. For our application, we have chosen the following development environment -

- OS: Windows 10
- Database: SQL Server Express 2017 & SQL Server Management Studio 2017
- Either Visual Studio 2017 or Visual Studio Code
- .NET Core 2.1 SDK
- Redis Cache
- RabbitMQ
- Docker
- Service Fabric
- Microsoft Azure

Node 8.9.4 & NPM 6.4.1

- NPM CLI -> npm install -g @angular/cli

## Implementing Authentication and Authorization in Microservices

Microservices Architecture carries many advantages to software applications, including small development teams, quicker development cycles, versatility in language selection, and enhanced service scalability.

At the same time, many complicated problems of distributed systems have also been added. One of the difficulties is how to implement a flexible, secure and effective authentication and authorization scheme in the Microservices Architecture.

Let us first understand the difference between authentication and authorization. Though it may appear confusing but, it is very simple –

**Authentication:** It verifies who you are, so one may use several techniques to authenticate oneself, the simplest being use of username and password for authentication.

**Authorization:** This is more about what action once can perform, for example, access, edit or delete permissions to some documents, and this occurs only after the system has authenticated you.

Then how does the Monolithic authentication and authorization differ from that of Microservices?

## Monolithic Application Authentication and Authorization

In the monolithic design, the entire application is a single process. In the application, a security module is usually implemented for user authentication and authorization.

When the user logs in to the application, the security module of the application verifies the identity of the user. After authenticating that the user is the one that is recognized by the systems, a session is created for the user, and a unique session ID is mapped with the session. A session stores login user data such as Username, Role, and Permission. The server replies the Session Id to the client. The client stores the Session-Id as a cookie and sends it to the application in the following requests. The application can then pass the Session Id to verify the user's identity, without asking to enter a username and password for authentication each time.

## Microservices Authentication and Authorization Problems

Under the microservice architecture, an application is divided into multiple microservice processes, and each microservice executes the business logic of module in the initial single application. After the application is divided, the access request for each microservice needs to be authenticated and authorized.

Authentication and authorization logic is required to be handled in each microservice, and this part of the global logic requires to be implemented frequently in each microservice.

Since Microservices are designed to deliver a single functionality as per the principle of single responsibility. A microservice only manages a unique business logic. The business logic of authentication and authorization should not be put in the microservice implementation.

The authentication and authorization mechanism in the microservices architecture involves cases that are more complex, including users accessing microservice applications, third-party applications obtaining microservice applications, and multiple microservice applications accessing other microservices, and in each scenario, the subsequent authentication and authorization schemes require to be considered to guarantee the security of the application. One may create a separate authentication service that authenticates the user and creates a session that can be accessed by other services.

## Authenticating Using .NET Core Identity

Once the authentication is completed, ASP.NET Core Web APIs must authorize access. This process permits a service to make APIs available to some authenticated users, but not to all the users.

Authorization is done based on the users' roles or based on custom policy, which might include examining claims. ASP.NET Core Identity has a built-in concept of roles. In addition to users, ASP.NET Core Identity also saves information about different roles used by the application and keeps the record of which users are assigned to which roles. ASP.NET Core Identity comes with a membership system which enables you to add login functionality to your application. Users either need to create an account and login with a credential (username and password) or can choose from various external login providers such as Facebook, Google, Microsoft account, or others.

You can always configure ASP.NET Core Identity to use a SQL Server database to store usernames, passwords, and profile data. The original reference assembly for the Identity system is Microsoft.AspNetCore.Identity. This package includes the core set of interfaces for ASP.NET Core Identity and is added through Microsoft. AspNetCore.Identity.EntityFrameworkCore. These dependencies are required to practice the Identity system in ASP.NET Core applications. So, let us look a little deeper and understand what they do:

- **Microsoft.AspNetCore.Identity.EntityFrameworkCore:** It holds the necessary types to use Identity with Entity Framework Core.

- **Microsoft.EntityFrameworkCore.SqlServer:** Entity Framework Core is Microsoft's suggested data access technology for any relational databases like SQL Server.

- **Microsoft.AspNetCore.Authentication.Cookies:** Middleware that enables an app to use cookie-based authentication.

In the demo Online Hotel Reservation application, we need to authenticate Users before they can proceed for booking and Admin Role that is required to manage Hotels, Rooms, and Bookings (mostly CRUD operations). The things that we need to do are as follows:

- We need to lock Booking API so that it can only be accessed by authenticated users and users will be locating the API via your client-side (Angular SPA) application.

- You need to create new ASP.NET Core Identity to add functionality to register, log in, and log out a user.

Let's move on and start implementing the user registration and login functionality using ASP.NET Core 2 Web API. A few basic details before we start the actual implementation:

- Token authentication is the method of attaching a token (also termed as a bearer or access token) to HTTP requests to authenticate the user. It's normally used with APIs that helped mobile or SPA (JavaScript) clients to communicate with.
- Each request that comes at the API is examined. If a valid token is detected, the request is passed. If no token is encountered, or the token is not valid, the request is denied with a 401 Unauthorized response.

First, create a New project and choose API with no Authentication.

## Data model

The user is the key to our application, and luckily the ASP.NET Core Identity provider offers the IdentityUser class which offers a useful entity to store all our user-related data. Also, it can be extended to add custom properties you may need all the users to maintain in your application. This class maps straight to the AspNetUsers table in the database.

**AppUser.cs**

```
using Microsoft.AspNetCore.Identity;

namespace UserIdentity.Api.Models
{
    public class AppUser : IdentityUser
    {
        // Extended Properties
        public string FirstName { get; set; }
        public string LastName { get; set; }
        public long? FacebookId { get; set; }
        public string PictureUrl { get; set; }
    }
}
```

Customer class is a custom class which has custom properties and a reference to AppUser through the Identity property. The IdentityId is the foreign key relationship in the database (SQL) which is used by Entity Framework Core, uses to map the relationship among two.

**Customer.cs**

```
namespace UserIdentity.Api.Models
{
    public class Customer
    {
        public int Id { get; set; }
        public string IdentityId { get; set; }
        public AppUser Identity { get; set; }
        public string Location { get; set; }
        public string Gender { get; set; }
    }
}
```

## Database Context

We need to complete the database and object graph in the application by creating a new DatabaseContext class which is used by Entity Framework Core to communicate with the database and our application objects. ApplicationDbContext which is simple as we only have to add the Customers mapping. It inherits from IdentityDbContext, and it is already implicated of IdentityUser and the other identity-related classes/tables, so we don't need to map them explicitly again.

### ApplicationDbContext.cs

```
using Microsoft.AspNetCore.Identity.EntityFrameworkCore;
using Microsoft.EntityFrameworkCore;

namespace UserIdentity.Api.Models
{
    public class ApplicationDbContext :
    IdentityDbContext<AppUser>
    {
        public ApplicationDbContext(DbContextOptions options)
        : base(options)
        {
        }

        public DbSet<Customer> Customers { get; set; }
    }
}
```

The Entity Framework tool is available from the .NET Core CLI so that you can create a first migration file by running this from, the command line in the project root folder.

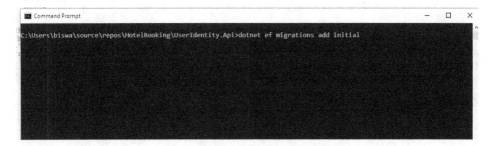

You can change the Database configuration settings in appsettings.json. Change the Database server name to your local SQL server name.

```
{
    "ConnectionStrings": {
        "DefaultConnection": "Server=DESKTOP-
        TTCGSA2;Database=Ho telUsers;Trusted_Connection=T
        rue;;MultipleActiveResultSets=true"
    },
```

```
"Logging": {
    "LogLevel": {
        "Default": "Warning"
    }
},
}
```

This command will fetch the connection string from the project's appsettings.json file, connect to SQL Server and generate a new database based on the previously created migrations.

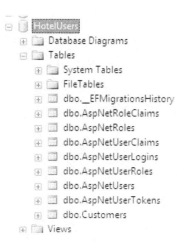

## User Registration

The API for adding new users through email registration will be the ability of the AccountsController.

There's a single action method here to accept a POST request with the user registration details. It's reasonably candid as we are using Identity's UserManager to create a new user in the database. Then we are using the context to create the related customer entity as described before. There is also certain mapping and validation occurring here using AutoMapper and FluentValidation to help keep our code in more organized manner.

```
PM> install-package automapper
PM> install-package AutoMapper.Extensions.Microsoft.
DependencyInjection
PM> Install-Package FluentValidation.AspNetCore
```

### AccountsController.cs

```
using System.Threading.Tasks;
using UserIdentity.Api.Helpers;
using AutoMapper;
using Microsoft.AspNetCore.Identity;
using Microsoft.AspNetCore.Mvc;
```

```csharp
using UserIdentity.Api.Models;
using UserIdentity.Api.ViewModels;

namespace UserIdentity.Api.Controllers
{
    [Route("api/[controller]")]
    public class AccountsController : Controller
    {
        private readonly ApplicationDbContext _appDbContext;
        private readonly UserManager<AppUser> _userManager;
        private readonly IMapper _mapper;

        public AccountsController(UserManager<AppUser>
        userManager, IMapper mapper,
        ApplicationDbContext appDbContext)
        {
            _userManager = userManager;
            _mapper = mapper;
            _appDbContext = appDbContext;
        }

        // POST api/accounts
        [HttpPost]
        public async Task<IActionResult> Post([FromBody]
        RegistrationViewModel model)
        {
            if (!ModelState.IsValid)
            {
                return BadRequest(ModelState);
            }

            var userIdentity = _mapper.Map<AppUser>(model);

            var result = await _userManager.
            CreateAsync(userIdentity, model.Password);

            if (!result.Succeeded) return new
            BadRequestObjectResult
            (Errors.AddErrorsToModelState(result,
            ModelState));

            await _appDbContext.Customers.AddAsync
            (new Customer { IdentityId = userIdentity.Id,
            Location = model.Location });
            await _appDbContext.SaveChangesAsync();

            return new OkObjectResult("Account created");
        }
    }
}
```

## Login

There is one POST method login which will validate user credentials with database and send the response.

```csharp
using System.Security.Claims;
using System.Threading.Tasks;
using UserIdentity.Api.Auth;
using UserIdentity.Api.Helpers;
using UserIdentity.Api.Models;
using UserIdentity.Api.ViewModels;
using Microsoft.AspNetCore.Identity;
using Microsoft.AspNetCore.Mvc;
using Microsoft.Extensions.Options;
using Newtonsoft.Json;

namespace UserIdentity.Api.Controllers
{
    [Route("api/[controller]")]
    public class AuthController : Controller
    {
        private readonly UserManager<AppUser> _userManager;
        private readonly IJwtFactory _jwtFactory;
        private readonly JwtIssuerOptions _jwtOptions;

        public AuthController(UserManager<AppUser>
        userManager,
        IJwtFactory jwtFactory, IOptions<JwtIssuerOptions>
        jwtOptions)
        {
            _userManager = userManager;
            _jwtFactory = jwtFactory;
            _jwtOptions = jwtOptions.Value;
        }

        // POST api/auth/login
        [HttpPost("login")]
        public async Task<IActionResult> Post([FromBody]
        CredentialsViewModel credentials)
        {
            if (!ModelState.IsValid)
            {
                return BadRequest(ModelState);
            }

            var identity = await
            GetClaimsIdentity(credentials.
            UserName,credentials.Password);
            if (identity == null)
            {
```

```
            return BadRequest(Errors.AddErrorToModelState
            ("login_failure", "Invalid username or
            password.", ModelState));
        }

        var jwt = await Tokens.GenerateJwt(identity,
        _jwtFactory, credentials.UserName,
        _jwtOptions, new JsonSerializerSettings {
        Formatting = Formatting.Indented });
        return new OkObjectResult(jwt);
    }

    private async Task<ClaimsIdentity> GetClaimsIdentity
    (string userName, string password)
    {
        if (string.IsNullOrEmpty(userName) || string.
        IsNullOrEmpty(password))
        return await Task.FromResult<ClaimsIdentity>
        (null);

        // get the user to verifty
        var userToVerify = await _userManager.
        FindByNameAsync(userName);

        if (userToVerify == null) return await Task.
        FromResult<ClaimsIdentity>(null);

        // check the credentials
        if (await _userManager.CheckPasswordAsync
        (userToVerify, password))
        {
            return await Task.FromResult(_jwtFactory.
            GenerateClaimsIdentity
            (userName, userToVerify.Id));
        }

        // Credentials are invalid, or account doesn't
        exist
        return await Task.FromResult<ClaimsIdentity>
        (null);
    }
  }
}
```

## JWT Token

The **JSON Web Token (JWT)** is a standard that defines a way to securely transmit information between two parties as a JSON object.

It consists of three parts.

HEADER.PAYLOAD.SIGNATURE

The header means the token is JWT and which hashing algorithm, has been used while creating the Token. This is Base64Url encoded.

The payload is the piece that is an application-specific part which contains claims, you want to transfer (also Base64Url encoded).

Finally, using the algorithm mentioned in the header, the server will combine the encoded header and payload, then sign them using a secret.

That signature is then added to the end of the token and can be used by anyone who holds the secret to authenticate that the sender of the JWT is validated and that means the token wasn't tampered with before it reached its destination.

Then add the configuration service and middleware in Startup.cs.

**Startup.cs**

```csharp
using System;
using System.Net;
using System.Text;
using AutoMapper;
using FluentValidation.AspNetCore;
using Microsoft.AspNetCore.Authentication.JwtBearer;
using Microsoft.AspNetCore.Builder;
using Microsoft.AspNetCore.Diagnostics;
using Microsoft.AspNetCore.Hosting;
using Microsoft.AspNetCore.Http;
using Microsoft.AspNetCore.HttpsPolicy;
using Microsoft.AspNetCore.Identity;
using Microsoft.AspNetCore.Mvc;
using Microsoft.EntityFrameworkCore;
using Microsoft.Extensions.Configuration;
using Microsoft.Extensions.DependencyInjection;
using Microsoft.Extensions.DependencyInjection.Extensions;
using Microsoft.Extensions.Logging;
using Microsoft.Extensions.Options;
using Microsoft.IdentityModel.Tokens;
using UserIdentity.Api.Auth;
using UserIdentity.Api.Extensions;
using UserIdentity.Api.Helpers;
using UserIdentity.Api.Models;

namespace UserIdentity.Api
{
    public class Startup
    {
        private const string SecretKey =
        "iNivDmHLpUA223sqsfhqGbMRdRj1PVkH";
        private readonly SymmetricSecurityKey _signingKey
        = new
        SymmetricSecurityKey(Encoding.ASCII.
```

```
GetBytes(SecretKey));
public Startup(IConfiguration configuration)
{
    Configuration = configuration;
}

public IConfiguration Configuration { get; }

// This method gets called by the runtime. Use this
method to add services to the container.
public void ConfigureServices(IServiceCollection
services)
{
    // services.AddDbContext<ApplicationDbContext>();
    services.AddDbContext<Models.
    ApplicationDbContext>(options =>
    options.UseSqlServer(Configuration.
    GetConnectionString
    ("DefaultConnection")));

    services.AddSingleton<IJwtFactory, JwtFactory>();

    services.TryAddTransient<IHttpContextAccessor,
    HttpContextAccessor>();

    // jwt wire up
    // Get options from app settings
    var jwtAppSettingOptions =
    Configuration.GetSection(nameof
    (JwtIssuerOptions));

    // Configure JwtIssuerOptions
    services.Configure<JwtIssuerOptions>(options =>
    {
        options.Issuer = jwtAppSettingOptions[nameof
        (JwtIssuerOptions.Issuer)];
        options.Audience =
        jwtAppSettingOptions[nameof(JwtIssuerOptions.
        Audience)];
        options.SigningCredentials = new
        SigningCredentials(_signingKey,
        SecurityAlgorithms.HmacSha256);
    });

    var tokenValidationParameters = new
    TokenValidationParameters
    {
        ValidateIssuer = true,
        ValidIssuer = jwtAppSettingOptions[nameof(Jwt
        IssuerOptions.Issuer)],

        ValidateAudience = true,
```

```
        ValidAudience = jwtAppSettingOptions[nameof
        (JwtIssuerOptions.Audience)],

        ValidateIssuerSigningKey = true,
        IssuerSigningKey = _signingKey,

        RequireExpirationTime = false,
        ValidateLifetime = true,
        ClockSkew = TimeSpan.Zero
};
services.AddAuthentication(options =>
{
    options.DefaultAuthenticateScheme =
    JwtBearerDefaults.AuthenticationScheme;
    options.DefaultChallengeScheme =
    JwtBearerDefaults.AuthenticationScheme;

}).AddJwtBearer(configureOptions =>
{
    configureOptions.ClaimsIssuer =
    jwtAppSettingOptions[nameof(JwtIssuerOptions.
    Issuer)];
    configureOptions.TokenValidationParameters =
    tokenValidationParameters;
    configureOptions.SaveToken = true;
});
// api user claim policy
services.AddAuthorization(options =>
{
    options.AddPolicy("ApiUser", policy =>
    policy.RequireClaim(Constants.Strings.
    JwtClaimIdentifiers.Rol,
    Constants.Strings.JwtClaims.ApiAccess));
});
// add identity
var builder = services.AddIdentityCore<AppUser>
(o =>
{
    // configure identity options
    o.Password.RequireDigit = false;
    o.Password.RequireLowercase = false;
    o.Password.RequireUppercase = false;
    o.Password.RequireNonAlphanumeric = false;
    o.Password.RequiredLength = 6;
});
builder = new IdentityBuilder(builder.UserType,
typeof(IdentityRole), builder.Services);
builder.AddEntityFrameworkStores
```

```
        <ApplicationDbContext>().
        AddDefaultTokenProviders();

        services.AddAutoMapper();
        services.AddMvc().AddFluentValidation(fv =>
        fv.RegisterValidatorsFromAssemblyContaining<
        Startup>());
    }

    // This method gets called by runtime. Use this
    method to setup the HTTP request.
    public void Configure(IApplicationBuilder app,
    IHostingEnvironment env, ApplicationDbContext
    dbContext)
    {
        if (env.IsDevelopment())
        {
            app.UseDeveloperExceptionPage();
        }
        else
        {
            app.UseHsts();
        }
        app.UseExceptionHandler(
        builder =>
        {
            builder.Run(
            async context =>
            {
                context.Response.StatusCode =
                    int)HttpStatusCode.InternalServerError;
                context.Response.Headers.Add
                ("Access-Control-Allow-Origin", "*");

                var error =
                context.Features.Get<IExceptionHandler
                Feature>();
                if (error != null)
                {
                    context.Response.
                    AddApplicationError(error.Error.
                    Message);
                    await
                    context.Response.WriteAsync(error.
                    Error.Message).ConfigureAwait(false);
                }
            });
        });
```

```
        app.UseAuthentication();
        app.UseDefaultFiles();
        app.UseStaticFiles();
        app.UseMvc();
        dbContext.Database.EnsureCreated();
    }
  }
}
```

In our source code, refer to the class JwtFactory, JwtFactory for JWT authentication. Achieving basic authentication with JSON web tokens on top of an ASP.NET Core Web API is reasonably straightforward. Most of what you need is in middleware given by the Microsoft.AspNetCore.Authentication.JwtBearer package.

To get started, refer to the class JwtIssuerOptions describing few of the claim properties our generated tokens will contain.

A new configuration section added to the appsettings.json file and then the Configuration API in ConfigureServices() being used to read these settings and wire up JwtIssuerOptions in the IoC container.

## Testing the API

In this chapter Postman used to test both register and Login API of accounts controller.

### Register API:

It needs RegistrationViewModel as an input in raw JSON format.

```
POST /api/accounts/ HTTP/1.1
Host: localhost:44379
Content-Type: application/json
Cache-Control: no-cache
Postman-Token: ca75ab8a-2af4-5518-8d13-dd5b483168ce
```

{"email" : "abc@gmail.com", "password" : "Test@123", "firstname" : "Puja", "lastname" :"Mohapatra", "location":"Hyderabad,India"}

**Login API:**

Postman being used to test these APIS to make sure we are getting the expected response when passing valid and invalid credentials to the authentication API. To send POST request to /API/auth/login bypassing CredentialsViewModel as an input.

```
POST /api/auth/login HTTP/1.1
Host: localhost:44379
Content-Type: application/json
Cache-Control: no-cache
Postman-Token: af1d91be-d097-2d66-054b-b4a9cb1e45f6

{"UserName" : "abc@gmail.com", "password" : "Test@123"}
```

## Authenticating Using External Providers

Allowing users to sign-in with their existing credentials is helpful for the users and transfers many of the challenges of managing the sign-in process onto a third party e.g. Facebook, Twitter etc. In this section, we will learn how to enable authentication of user using Facebook.

Before we deep dive into coding, we require a Facebook application with which to integrate. I have created OnlineHotelReservation APP which should work fine for you when you're executing the project but if you want to use your own application you will require to create a new application and configure it on Facebook's developer portal https://developers.facebook.com/.

Once you log in, click on Add New App.

You need to provide the following details:

**Display Name:** Give a proper name.

**Note:** Make sure not to use the word Facebook in the display name. It will throw an error.

**Contact Email:** Give your email ID. If you do not desire to provide your personal email ID then you can also use any arbitrary email id e.g. abc@gmail.com.

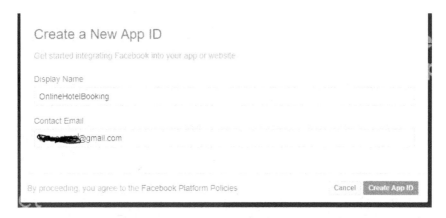

Once you have completed all the details, click on the **Create App ID** button. If there is no error in the form, your Facebook app will be created happily, and you will be redirected to the Dashboard.

Click on Facebook Login --> Settings from the navigation menu on the left. Now click on **Settings--> Basic**. You can now see the App ID and App Secret values for the Facebook app you have created. Click on show button inside App secret field to get the value. Take a note of both values as you will need them to configure Facebook authentication in the web app.

## JWT Tokens for Authenticated Facebook Users

To complete the Facebook login, process a new Web API controller named ExternalAuthController with a single action to handle Facebook logins has been added.

```
using System;
using System.Net.Http;
using System.Threading.Tasks;
using UserIdentity.Api.Auth;
using UserIdentity.Api.Helpers;
using UserIdentity.Api.Models;
using UserIdentity.Api.ViewModels;
using Microsoft.AspNetCore.Identity;
using Microsoft.AspNetCore.Mvc;
using Microsoft.Extensions.Options;
```

```csharp
using Newtonsoft.Json;

namespace UserIdentity.Api.Controllers
{
    [Route("api/[controller]/[action]")]
    public class ExternalAuthController : Controller
    {
        private readonly ApplicationDbContext _appDbContext;
        private readonly UserManager<AppUser> _userManager;
        private readonly FacebookAuthSettings _fbAuthSettings;
        private readonly IJwtFactory _jwtFactory;
        private readonly JwtIssuerOptions _jwtOptions;
        private static readonly HttpClient Client =
        new HttpClient();

        public ExternalAuthController(IOptions<
        FacebookAuthS    ettings> fbAuthSettingsAccessor,
        UserManager<AppUser> userManager,
        ApplicationDbContext appDbContext, IJwtFactory
        jwtFactory, IOptions<JwtIssuerOptions> jwtOptions)
        {
            _fbAuthSettings = fbAuthSettingsAccessor.Value;
            _userManager = userManager;
            _appDbContext = appDbContext;
            _jwtFactory = jwtFactory;
            _jwtOptions = jwtOptions.Value;
        }

        // POST api/externalauth/facebook
        [HttpPost]
        public async Task<IActionResult> Facebook([FromBody]
        FacebookAuthViewModel model)
        {
            // 1.generate an app access token
            var appAccessTokenResponse = awaitClient.
            GetStringAsync($"https://graph.facebook.
            com/oauth/access_token?client_id=
            {_fbAuthSettings.AppId}&client_secret=
            {_fbAuthSettings.AppSecret}&grant_type=client_
            credentials");
            var appAccessToken = JsonConvert.Deserialize
            Object<FacebookAppAccessToken>
            (appAccessTokenRes ponse);
            // 2. validate the user access token
            var userAccessTokenValidationResponse =
            await Client.GetStringAsync($"https://
            graph.facebook.com/debug_token?input_
            token={model.AccessToken}&access_
            token={appAccessToken.AccessToken}");
```

```
var userAccessTokenValidation =
JsonConvert.DeserializeObject<FacebookUserAccess
TokenValidation>(userAccessTokenValidation
Response);

if (!userAccessTokenValidation.Data.IsValid)
{
    return BadRequest(Errors.
    AddErrorToModelState("login_failure",
    "Invalidfacebook token.", ModelState));
}

// 3. we've got a valid token so we can request
user data from fb
var userInfoResponse = await Client.
GetStringAsync($"https://graph.facebook.
com/v2.8/me?fields=id,email,first_name,last_name
,name,gender,locale,birthday,picture&access_
token={model.AccessToken}");
var userInfo = JsonConvert.DeserializeObject<
FacebookUserData>(userInfoResponse);

// 4. ready to create the local user account (if
necessary) and jwt
var user = await _userManager.
FindByEmailAsync(userInfo.Email);

if (user == null)
{
    var appUser = new AppUser
    {
        FirstName = userInfo.FirstName,
        LastName = userInfo.LastName,
        FacebookId = userInfo.Id,
        Email = userInfo.Email,
        UserName = userInfo.Email,
        PictureUrl = userInfo.Picture.Data.Url
    };

    var result = await _userManager.
    CreateAsync(appUser,
    Convert.ToBase64String(Guid.NewGuid().
    ToByteArray()).Substring(0, 8));

    if (!result.Succeeded) return new
    BadRequestObjectResult(Errors.
    AddErrorsToModelState(result, ModelState));

    await _appDbContext.Customers.AddAsync(new
    Customer
    { IdentityId = appUser.Id, Location = "",
```

```
        Gender = userInfo.Gender});
        await _appDbContext.SaveChangesAsync();
    }
    // generate the jwt for the local user...
    var localUser = await _userManager.
    FindByNameAsync(userInfo.Email);

    if (localUser==null)
    {
        return BadRequest(Errors.AddErrorToModelState
        ("login_failure", "Failed to create local
        user account.", ModelState));
    }

    var jwt = await
    Tokens.GenerateJwt(_jwtFactory.
    GenerateClaimsIdentity
    (localUser.UserName, localUser.Id),
    _jwtFactory, localUser.UserName, _jwtOptions,
    new JsonSerializerSettings
    {Formatting = Formatting.Indented});

    return new OkObjectResult(jwt);
        }
    }
}
```

Above Code basically does the following:

1. Calls the Facebook API to create an app access token you need, to make the next request.
2. Make another call again to Facebook to authenticate the user access token which you received on the first login.
3. If the token is authentic, use it to request a message about the user from the Facebook API: email, name, picture, and so on.
4. Uses userManager to check if you have this user in your local database, if not, add all the users and add an associated customer entity, in exact same process, we followed while registering user using ASP.NET core Identity above.
5. Create a JWT token and return to the client as a response.
6. With a JWT token returned to the Angular app, the flow is complete.

## Implementation of Role-Based Authorization

The JWT middleware in ASP.NET Core understands how to represent roles claim inside JWT payload and will add the relevant claims to the ClaimsIdentity. This does use the [Authorize] attribute with Roles very easy.

```
services.AddAuthorization(options =>
{
    options.AddPolicy("ApiUser", policy => policy.
    RequireClaim(Constants.Strings.JwtClaimIdentifiers.Rol,
    Constants.Strings.JwtClaims.ApiAccess));
});
services.AddAuthorization(options =>
{
    options.AddPolicy("AdminRole", policy => policy.
    RequireRole("Admin"));
});
```

Then add claim policy for required controller e.g. User needs to be authenticated or logged in to the system before proceeding for booking.

```
[Authorize(Policy = "ApiUser")]
    [Route("api/[controller]")]
    [ApiController]
    public class BookingsController : ControllerBase
    {
}
```

Only Admin users can add/modify hotel.

```
[Authorize(Policy = "AdminRole")]
    [HttpPost]
    public async Task<IActionResult> PostHotels([FromBody]
    Models.Hotels hotels)
    {
}
```

## Development of Microservices for Hotel Reservation

In this section, we will cover all the source code of controllers of our Hotel Reservation microservices.

### Requirements for Hotels API access

HotelsInfoController has all the business logic for the basic CRUD functions and the Search functionalities which will return only specific hotel details based on the search criteria that is provided.

### HotelsInfoController.cs

```
using System;
using System.Collections.Generic;
using System.Linq;
using System.Threading.Tasks;
using Microsoft.AspNetCore.Http;
using Microsoft.AspNetCore.Mvc;
using Microsoft.EntityFrameworkCore;
```

```csharp
using Hotels.API.Models;
using Microsoft.AspNetCore.Authorization;

namespace Hotels.API.Controllers
{
    [Route("api/[controller]")]
    //[EnableCors("SiteCorsPolicy")]
    [ApiController]
    public class HotelsInfoController : ControllerBase
    {
        private readonly HotelsContext _context;
        public HotelsInfoController(HotelsContext context)
        {
            _context = context;
        }

        [HttpGet]
        public IEnumerable<HotelsInfo> FindHotelsInCity
        (string city, DateTime
         startDate, DateTime endDate)
        {
            var hotelNames = from hotels in _context.HotelsInfo
                join address in _context.HotelAddress on
                hotels.HotelId equals address.HotelId
                join room in _context.Rooms on hotels.HotelId
                equals room.HotelId
                where address.City.Equals(city) && room.
                Available == true
                select hotels;
            return hotelNames;
        }

        // GET: api/HotelsInfo/HotelsList
        [HttpGet("HotelsList")]
        public IActionResult GetHotelsInfo()
        {
            var hotels = _context.HotelsInfo;
            return Ok(hotels);
        }

        // GET: api/HotelsInfo/5
        [HttpGet("{id}")]
        public async Task<IActionResult>
        GetHotelsInfo([FromRoute] int id)
        {
            if (!ModelState.IsValid)
            {
                return BadRequest(ModelState);
            }
```

```csharp
        var hotelsInfo = await _context.HotelsInfo.
        FindAsync(id);
        if (hotelsInfo == null)
        {
            return NotFound();
        }
        return Ok(hotelsInfo);
}
// PUT: api/HotelsInfo/5
[HttpPut("{id}")]
[Authorize(Policy = "AdminRole")]
public async Task<IActionResult>
PutHotelsInfo([FromRoute]
int id, [FromBody] HotelsInfo hotelsInfo)
{
    if (!ModelState.IsValid)
    {
        return BadRequest(ModelState);
    }
    if (id != hotelsInfo.HotelId)
    {
        return BadRequest();
    }
    _context.Entry(hotelsInfo).State = EntityState.
    Modified;
    try
    {
        await _context.SaveChangesAsync();
    }
    catch (DbUpdateConcurrencyException)
    {
        if (!HotelsInfoExists(id))
        {
            return NotFound();
        }
        else
        {
            throw;
        }
    }
    return NoContent();
}
// POST: api/HotelsInfo
[HttpPost]
```

```
[Authorize(Policy = "AdminRole")]
public async Task<IActionResult>
PostHotelsInfo([FromBody]
HotelsInfo hotelsInfo)
{
    if (!ModelState.IsValid)
    {
        return BadRequest(ModelState);
    }

    _context.HotelsInfo.Add(hotelsInfo);
    await _context.SaveChangesAsync();

    return CreatedAtAction("GetHotelsInfo",
    new { id = hotelsInfo.HotelId }, hotelsInfo);
}
// DELETE: api/HotelsInfo/5
[HttpDelete("{id}")]
[Authorize(Policy = "AdminRole")]
public async Task<IActionResult>
DeleteHotelsInfo([FromRoute] int id)
{
    if (!ModelState.IsValid)
    {
        return BadRequest(ModelState);
    }

    var hotelsInfo = await _context.HotelsInfo.
    FindAsync(id);
    if (hotelsInfo == null)
    {
        return NotFound();
    }

    _context.HotelsInfo.Remove(hotelsInfo);
    await _context.SaveChangesAsync();

    return Ok(hotelsInfo);
}
private bool HotelsInfoExists(int id)
{
    return _context.HotelsInfo.Any(e => e.HotelId
    == id);
}

    }
}
```

Hotelsinfo API can be used by users to find a hotel, Fetch hotels info, whereas
Hotel Managers or Admins only has permission to Create, Edit, Update, or Delete a

Hotel. If you investigate the source code, the role specific access has been granted with the Authorize attribute at the method level. You can read more about the action filters and what all could be achieved by it.

## Hotels Search API

Search hotel will find hotels for which rooms are available. Following API join Hotels with rooms and fetch only those rooms which are available. Further, this API can be extended to search hotels in a particular location/city.

```
[HttpGet]
    public IEnumerable<HotelsInfo> FindHotelsInCity
    (string city, DateTime startDate, DateTime endDate)
    {
        var hotelNames = from hotels in _context.HotelsInfo
            join address in _context.HotelAddress
            on hotels.HotelId equals address.HotelId
            join room in _context.Rooms on
            hotels.HotelId equals room.HotelId
            where address.City.Equals(city) && room.
            Available == true
            select hotels;
        return hotelNames;
    }
```

## *Models*

```
public partial class HotelsInfo
    {
        public HotelsInfo()
        {
            HotelAddress = new HashSet<HotelAddress>();
            Rooms = new HashSet<Rooms>();
        }

        public int HotelId { get; set; }
        public string HotelName { get; set; }
        public string Description { get; set; }

        public ICollection<HotelAddress> HotelAddress
        { get; set; }
        public ICollection<Rooms> Rooms { get; set; }
    }
```

Models are the DB entity which has mapped EF Model with DB.

## Room Type API

RoomType Controller to create Room types e.g. Luxury, Deluxe, Single and to set the base price for each room. RoomType Entity is the Subset of a Hotel and Rooms with the room details mapped with each RoomType.

**RoomType.cs**

```csharp
using System;
using System.Collections.Generic;
using System.Linq;
using System.Threading.Tasks;
using Microsoft.AspNetCore.Http;
using Microsoft.AspNetCore.Mvc;
using Microsoft.EntityFrameworkCore;
using Hotels.API.Models;
namespace Hotels.API.Controllers
{
    [Route("api/[controller]")]
    [ApiController]
    public class RoomTypesController : ControllerBase
    {
        private readonly HotelsContext _context;
        public RoomTypesController(HotelsContext context)
        {
            _context = context;
        }

        // GET: api/RoomTypes
        [HttpGet]
        public IEnumerable<RoomTypes> GetRoomTypes()
        {
            return _context.RoomTypes;
        }

        // GET: api/RoomTypes/5
        [HttpGet("{id}")]
        public async Task<IActionResult>
        GetRoomTypes([FromRoute] string id)
        {
            if (!ModelState.IsValid)
            {
                return BadRequest(ModelState);
            }

            var roomTypes = await _context.RoomTypes.
            FindAsync(id);

            if (roomTypes == null)
            {
                return NotFound();
            }

            return Ok(roomTypes);
        }
```

```csharp
// PUT: api/RoomTypes/5
[HttpPut("{id}")]
public async Task<IActionResult>
PutRoomTypes([FromRoute]
string id, [FromBody] RoomTypes roomTypes)
{
    if (!ModelState.IsValid)
    {
        return BadRequest(ModelState);
    }

    if (id != roomTypes.Id)
    {
        return BadRequest();
    }

    _context.Entry(roomTypes).State = EntityState.
    Modified;

    try
    {
        await _context.SaveChangesAsync();
    }
    catch (DbUpdateConcurrencyException)
    {
        if (!RoomTypesExists(id))
        {
            return NotFound();
        }
        else
        {
            throw;
        }
    }

    return NoContent();
}
// POST: api/RoomTypes
[HttpPost]
public async Task<IActionResult>
PostRoomTypes([FromBody] RoomTypes roomTypes)
{
    if (!ModelState.IsValid)
    {
        return BadRequest(ModelState);
    }

    _context.RoomTypes.Add(roomTypes);
    try
    {
```

```
        await _context.SaveChangesAsync();
    }
    catch (DbUpdateException)
    {
        if (RoomTypesExists(roomTypes.Id))
        {
            return new StatusCodeResult(StatusCodes.
            Status409Conflict);
        }
        else
        {
            throw;
        }
    }

    return CreatedAtAction("GetRoomTypes", new { id
    = roomTypes.Id }, roomTypes);
}
// DELETE: api/RoomTypes/5
[HttpDelete("{id}")]
public async Task<IActionResult>
DeleteRoomTypes([FromRoute] string id)
{
    if (!ModelState.IsValid)
    {
        return BadRequest(ModelState);
    }

    var roomTypes = await _context.RoomTypes.
    FindAsync(id);
    if (roomTypes == null)
    {
        return NotFound();
    }

    _context.RoomTypes.Remove(roomTypes);
    await _context.SaveChangesAsync();

    return Ok(roomTypes);
}
private bool RoomTypesExists(string id)
{
    return _context.RoomTypes.Any(e => e.Id == id);
}
    }
}
```

## Models

```
using System;
using System.Collections.Generic;

namespace Hotels.API.Models
{
    public partial class RoomTypes
    {
        public RoomTypes()
        {
            Rooms = new HashSet<Rooms>();
        }

        public string Id { get; set; }
        public decimal BasePrice { get; set; }
        public string Description { get; set; }
        public string Name { get; set; }

        public ICollection<Rooms> Rooms { get; set; }
    }
}
```

## Rooms API

Rooms API contains all the room details like room no, maximum guests allowed, room price and whether the room is available or not, each room mapped with a Roomtype id and with a HotelID.

### RoomsController.cs

```
using System;
using System.Collections.Generic;
using System.Linq;
using System.Threading.Tasks;
using Microsoft.AspNetCore.Http;
using Microsoft.AspNetCore.Mvc;
using Microsoft.EntityFrameworkCore;
using Hotels.API.Models;
using Microsoft.AspNetCore.Cors;

namespace Hotels.API.Controllers
{
    [Route("api/[controller]")]
    //[EnableCors("AllowMyOrigin")]
    [ApiController]
    public class RoomsController : ControllerBase
    {
        private readonly HotelsContext _context;

        public RoomsController(HotelsContext context)
        {
```

```csharp
        _context = context;
}
// GET: api/Rooms
[HttpGet]
public IEnumerable<Rooms> GetRooms()
{
    return _context.Rooms;
}
// GET: api/Rooms/5
[HttpGet("{id}")]
public async Task<IActionResult> GetRooms
([FromRoute] string id)
{
    if (!ModelState.IsValid)
    {
        return BadRequest(ModelState);
    }

    var rooms = await _context.Rooms.FindAsync(id);
    if (rooms == null)
    {
        return NotFound();
    }

    return Ok(rooms);
}
[HttpGet("GetRoomsByHotel/{id}")]
// [Route("")]
public IEnumerable<Rooms> GetRoomsByHotel
([FromRoute] int id)
{
    return _context.Rooms.Where(p => p.HotelId == id);
}
// PUT: api/Rooms/5
[HttpPut("{id}")]
//[Authorize(Policy = "AdminRole")]
public async Task<IActionResult> PutRooms
([FromRoute] string id, [FromBody] Rooms rooms)
{
    if (!ModelState.IsValid)
    {
        return BadRequest(ModelState);
    }
    if (id != rooms.Id)
    {
        return BadRequest();
```

```
        }
    _context.Entry(rooms).State = EntityState.
    Modified;
    try
    {
        await _context.SaveChangesAsync();
    }
    catch (DbUpdateConcurrencyException)
    {
        if (!RoomsExists(id))
        {
            return NotFound();
        }
        else
        {
            throw;
        }
    }

    return NoContent();
}
// POST: api/Rooms
[HttpPost]
//[Authorize(Policy = "AdminRole")]
public async Task<IActionResult> PostRooms
([FromBody] Rooms rooms)
{
    if (!ModelState.IsValid)
    {
        return BadRequest(ModelState);
    }

    rooms.Id = Guid.NewGuid().ToString();
    _context.Rooms.Add(rooms);
    try
    {
        await _context.SaveChangesAsync();
    }
    catch (DbUpdateException)
    {
        if (RoomsExists(rooms.Id))
        {
            return new StatusCodeResult(StatusCodes.
            Status409Conflict);
        }
        else
        {
```

```
            throw;
        }
    }

    return CreatedAtAction("GetRooms", new
    { id = rooms.Id }, rooms);
}
// DELETE: api/Rooms/5
[HttpDelete("{id}")]
//[Authorize(Policy = "AdminRole")]
public async Task<IActionResult>
DeleteRooms([FromRoute] string id)
{
    if (!ModelState.IsValid)
    {
        return BadRequest(ModelState);
    }

    var rooms = await _context.Rooms.FindAsync(id);
    if (rooms == null)
    {
        return NotFound();
    }

    _context.Rooms.Remove(rooms);
    await _context.SaveChangesAsync();

    return Ok(rooms);
}
private bool RoomsExists(string id)
{
    return _context.Rooms.Any(e => e.Id == id);
}
    }
}
```

## Models

```
using System;
using System.Collections.Generic;

namespace Hotels.API.Models
{
    public partial class Rooms
    {
        public Rooms()
        {
            Images = new HashSet<Images>();
            RoomFacilitiesRelationships = new HashSet<
            RoomFacilitiesRelationships>();
```

```
        }
        public string Id { get; set; }
        public bool Available { get; set; }
        public string Description { get; set; }
        public int MaximumGuests { get; set; }
        public int Number { get; set; }
        public decimal Price { get; set; }
        public string RoomTypeId { get; set; }
        public int? HotelId { get; set; }

        public Hotels Hotel { get; set; }
        public RoomTypes RoomType { get; set; }
        public ICollection<Images> Images { get; set; }
        public ICollection<RoomFacilitiesRelationships>
        RoomFacilitiesRelationships { get; set; }
    }
}
```

## Room Facilities API

### FacilitiesController.cs

```
using System;
using System.Collections.Generic;
using System.Linq;
using System.Threading.Tasks;
using Microsoft.AspNetCore.Http;
using Microsoft.AspNetCore.Mvc;
using Microsoft.EntityFrameworkCore;
using Hotels.API.Models;

namespace Hotels.API.Controllers
{
    [Route("api/[controller]")]
    [ApiController]
    public class FacilitiesController : ControllerBase
    {
        private readonly HotelsContext _context;

        public FacilitiesController(HotelsContext context)
        {
            _context = context;
        }

        // GET: api/Facilities
        [HttpGet]
        public IEnumerable<Facilities> GetFacilities()
        {
            return _context.Facilities;
        }
```

```
// GET: api/Facilities/5
[HttpGet("{id}")]
public async Task<IActionResult>
GetFacilities([FromRoute] string id)
{
    if (!ModelState.IsValid)
    {
        return BadRequest(ModelState);
    }

    var facilities = await _context.Facilities.
    FindAsync(id);

    if (facilities == null)
    {
        return NotFound();
    }

    return Ok(facilities);
}
// PUT: api/Facilities/5
[HttpPut("{id}")]
public async Task<IActionResult>
PutFacilities([FromRoute]
string id, [FromBody] Facilities facilities)
{
    if (!ModelState.IsValid)
    {
        return BadRequest(ModelState);
    }

    if (id != facilities.Id)
    {
        return BadRequest();
    }

    _context.Entry(facilities).State = EntityState.
    Modified;

    try
    {
        await _context.SaveChangesAsync();
    }
    catch (DbUpdateConcurrencyException)
    {
        if (!FacilitiesExists(id))
        {
            return NotFound();
        }
        else
```

```csharp
        {
            throw;
        }
    }

    return NoContent();
}
// POST: api/Facilities
[HttpPost]
public async Task<IActionResult> PostFacilities
([FromBody] Facilities facilities)
{
    if (!ModelState.IsValid)
    {
        return BadRequest(ModelState);
    }

    _context.Facilities.Add(facilities);
    try
    {
        await _context.SaveChangesAsync();
    }
    catch (DbUpdateException)
    {
        if (FacilitiesExists(facilities.Id))
        {
            return new StatusCodeResult(StatusCodes.
            Status409Conflict);
        }
        else
        {
            throw;
        }
    }

    return CreatedAtAction("GetFacilities",
    new { id = facilities.Id }, facilities);
}
// DELETE: api/Facilities/5
[HttpDelete("{id}")]
public async Task<IActionResult>
DeleteFacilities([FromRoute] string id)
{
    if (!ModelState.IsValid)
    {
        return BadRequest(ModelState);
    }

    var facilities = await _context.Facilities.
```

```
            FindAsync(id);
            if (facilities == null)
            {
                return NotFound();
            }

            _context.Facilities.Remove(facilities);
            await _context.SaveChangesAsync();

            return Ok(facilities);
        }
        private bool FacilitiesExists(string id)
        {
            return _context.Facilities.Any(e => e.Id == id);
        }
    }
}
```

## Models

```
using System;
using System.Collections.Generic;

namespace Hotels.API.Models
{
    public partial class Facilities
    {
        public Facilities()
        {
            RoomFacilitiesRelationships = new HashSet
            <RoomFacilitiesRelationships>();
        }

        public string Id { get; set; }
        public string Icon { get; set; }
        public string Name { get; set; }

        public ICollection<RoomFacilitiesRelationships>
        RoomFacilitiesRelationships { get; set; }
    }
}
```

## Room Images API

### ImagesController.Cs

```
using System;
using System.Collections.Generic;
using System.Linq;
using System.Threading.Tasks;
using Microsoft.AspNetCore.Http;
using Microsoft.AspNetCore.Mvc;
```

```csharp
using Microsoft.EntityFrameworkCore;
using Hotels.API.Models;
namespace Hotels.API.Controllers
{
    [Route("api/[controller]")]
    [ApiController]
    public class ImagesController : ControllerBase
    {
        private readonly HotelsContext _context;
        public ImagesController(HotelsContext context)
        {
            _context = context;
        }
        // GET: api/Images
        [HttpGet]
        public IEnumerable<Images> GetImages()
        {
            return _context.Images;
        }
        // GET: api/Images/5
        [HttpGet("{id}")]
        public async Task<IActionResult> GetImages
        ([FromRoute] string id)
        {
            if (!ModelState.IsValid)
            {
                return BadRequest(ModelState);
            }
            var images = await _context.Images.FindAsync(id);
            if (images == null)
            {
                return NotFound();
            }
            return Ok(images);
        }
        // PUT: api/Images/5
        [HttpPut("{id}")]
        public async Task<IActionResult>
        PutImages([FromRoute] string id, [FromBody]
        Images images)
        {
            if (!ModelState.IsValid)
            {
                return BadRequest(ModelState);
```

```
        }
        if (id != images.Id)
        {
            return BadRequest();
        }

        _context.Entry(images).State = EntityState.
        Modified;

        try
        {
            await _context.SaveChangesAsync();
        }
        catch (DbUpdateConcurrencyException)
        {
            if (!ImagesExists(id))
            {
                return NotFound();
            }
            else
            {
                throw;
            }
        }

        return NoContent();
    }
    // POST: api/Images
    [HttpPost]
    public async Task<IActionResult> PostImages
    ([FromBody] Images images)
    {
        if (!ModelState.IsValid)
        {
            return BadRequest(ModelState);
        }

        _context.Images.Add(images);
        try
        {
            await _context.SaveChangesAsync();
        }
        catch (DbUpdateException)
        {
            if (ImagesExists(images.Id))
            {
                return new StatusCodeResult(StatusCodes.
                Status409Conflict);
            }
```

```csharp
            else
            {
                throw;
            }
        }
        return CreatedAtAction("GetImages", new { id =
        images.Id }, images);
    }
    // DELETE: api/Images/5
    [HttpDelete("{id}")]
    public async Task<IActionResult>
    DeleteImages([FromRoute] string id)
    {
        if (!ModelState.IsValid)
        {
            return BadRequest(ModelState);
        }
        var images = await _context.Images.FindAsync(id);
        if (images == null)
        {
            return NotFound();
        }
        _context.Images.Remove(images);
        await _context.SaveChangesAsync();

        return Ok(images);
    }
    private bool ImagesExists(string id)
    {
        return _context.Images.Any(e => e.Id == id);
    }
    }
}
```

## Models

```csharp
using System;
using System.Collections.Generic;

namespace Hotels.API.Models
{
    public partial class Images
    {
        public Images()
        {
            ItemImageRelationships = new HashSet
            <ItemImageRelationships>();
```

```
        }
        public string Id { get; set; }
        public string RoomId { get; set; }
        public string FilePath { get; set; }
        public string Size { get; set; }
        public string Name { get; set; }
        public string ImageUrl { get; set; }

        public Rooms Room { get; set; }
        public ICollection<ItemImageRelationships>
        ItemImageRelationships { get; set; }
    }
}
```

## Booking API

Booking API allows users to book a hotel and before proceeding with the booking, it does a check whether that particular room is available or not.

### BookingController.cs

```
using System;
using System.Collections.Generic;
using System.Linq;
using System.Threading.Tasks;
using Microsoft.AspNetCore.Http;
using Microsoft.AspNetCore.Mvc;
using Microsoft.EntityFrameworkCore;
using Booking.API.Models;
using Microsoft.AspNetCore.Authorization;
namespace Booking.API.Controllers
{
    [Authorize(Policy = "ApiUser")]
    [Route("api/[controller]")]
    [ApiController]
    public class BookingsController : ControllerBase
    {
        private readonly HotelBookingsContext _context;
        public BookingsController(HotelBookingsContext
        context)
        {
            _context = context;
        }
        // GET: api/Bookings
        [HttpGet]
        public IEnumerable<Bookings> GetBookings()
        {
            return _context.Bookings;
```

```
        }
        // GET: api/Bookings/5
        [HttpGet("{id}")]
        public async Task<IActionResult>
        GetBookings([FromRoute] string id)
        {
            if (!ModelState.IsValid)
            {
                return BadRequest(ModelState);
            }

            var bookings = await _context.Bookings.
            FindAsync(id);

            if (bookings == null)
            {
                return NotFound();
            }

            return Ok(bookings);
        }
        // PUT: api/Bookings/5
        [HttpPut("{id}")]
        public async Task<IActionResult> PutBookings
        ([FromRoute] string id, [FromBody] Bookings bookings)
        {
            if (!ModelState.IsValid)
            {
                return BadRequest(ModelState);
            }

            if (id != bookings.Id)
            {
                return BadRequest();
            }

            _context.Entry(bookings).State = EntityState.
            Modified;

            try
            {
                await _context.SaveChangesAsync();
            }
            catch (DbUpdateConcurrencyException)
            {
                if (!BookingsExists(id))
                {
                    return NotFound();
                }
                else
```

```
            {
                throw;
            }
        }

        return NoContent();
    }
// POST: api/Bookings
[HttpPost]
public async Task<IActionResult>
PostBookings([FromBody] Bookings bookings)
{
    if (!ModelState.IsValid)
    {
        return BadRequest(ModelState);
    }

    _context.Bookings.Add(bookings);
    try
    {
        await _context.SaveChangesAsync();
    }
    catch (DbUpdateException)
    {
        if (BookingsExists(bookings.Id))
        {
            return new StatusCodeResult(StatusCodes.
            Status409Conflict);
        }
        else
        {
            throw;
        }
    }

    return CreatedAtAction("GetBookings", new { id =
    bookings.Id }, bookings);
}
// DELETE: api/Bookings/5
[HttpDelete("{id}")]
public async Task<IActionResult>
DeleteBookings([FromRoute] string id)
{
    if (!ModelState.IsValid)
    {
        return BadRequest(ModelState);
    }

    var bookings = await _context.Bookings.
```

```
        FindAsync(id);
        if (bookings == null)
        {
            return NotFound();
        }

        _context.Bookings.Remove(bookings);
        await _context.SaveChangesAsync();

        return Ok(bookings);
    }

    private bool BookingsExists(string id)
    {
        return _context.Bookings.Any(e => e.Id == id);
    }
}
}
```

## Models

```
using System;
using System.Collections.Generic;

namespace Booking.API.Models
{
    public partial class Bookings
    {
        public string Id { get; set; }
        public DateTime CheckIn { get; set; }
        public DateTime CheckOut { get; set; }
        public bool Completed { get; set; }
        public string CustomerAddress { get; set; }
        public string CustomerCity { get; set; }
        public string CustomerEmail { get; set; }
        public string CustomerName { get; set; }
        public string CustomerPhone { get; set; }
        public DateTime DateCreated { get; set; }
        public int Guests { get; set; }
        public string OtherRequests { get; set; }
        public bool Paid { get; set; }
        public decimal TotalFee { get; set; }
        public string HotelId { get; set; }
    }
}
```

## Reviews API

Reviews API fetch all the reviews of a specific hotel.

**ReviewsController.cs**

```csharp
using System;
using System.Collections.Generic;
using System.Linq;
using System.Threading.Tasks;
using Microsoft.AspNetCore.Http;
using Microsoft.AspNetCore.Mvc;
using Microsoft.EntityFrameworkCore;
using Microsoft.Extensions.Caching.Distributed;
using Reviews.API.Models;
using Reviews.API.Extensions;
using Microsoft.AspNetCore.Authorization;
using Reviews.API.Services;

namespace Reviews.API.Controllers
{
    [Route("api/[controller]")]
    [ApiController]
    [Authorize]
    public class ReviewsController : ControllerBase
    {
        private readonly HotelreviewsContext _context;
        private readonly IDistributedCache _distributedCache;
        private readonly IIdentityService _identitySvc;
        private string Cachekey = "ReviewRedisCache";
        public ReviewsController(HotelreviewsContext context,
        IDistributedCache distributedCache)
        {
            _context = context;
            _distributedCache = distributedCache;

        }

        // GET: api/Reviews
        [HttpGet]
        public async Task<IEnumerable<Models.Reviews>>
        GetReviews([FromRoute] string hotelid)
        {
            IEnumerable<Models.Reviews> reviews = null;
            if (!string.IsNullOrEmpty(Cachekey))
            {
                reviews = await
                _distributedCache.    GetAsync
                <IEnumerable<Models.Reviews>>(Cachekey);
            }
            else
            {
                reviews = _context.Reviews.Where(p =>
```

```
                p.HotelId.Equals(hotelid));
            await _distributedCache.
            SetAsync<IEnumerable<Models.Reviews>>
            (Cachekey, reviews, new
            DistributedCacheEntryOptions() {
            AbsoluteExpirationRelativeToNow = TimeSpan.
            FromHours(2) });
        }
        return reviews;
    }

    // POST: api/Reviews
    [HttpPost]
    public async Task<IActionResult> PostReviews
    ([FromBody] Models.Reviews reviews)
    {
        if (!ModelState.IsValid)
        {
            return BadRequest(ModelState);
        }

        _context.Reviews.Add(reviews);

        try
        {
            await _context.SaveChangesAsync();
            //make cache null
            _distributedCache.Remove(Cachekey);
        }
        catch (DbUpdateException)
        {
            if (ReviewsExists(reviews.Id))
            {
                return new StatusCodeResult(StatusCodes.
                Status409Conflict);
            }
            else
            {
                throw;
            }
        }

        return CreatedAtAction("GetReviews", new { id =
        reviews.Id }, reviews);
    }
    // DELETE: api/Reviews/5
    [HttpDelete("{id}")]
    public async Task<IActionResult>
    DeleteReviews([FromRoute] string id)
```

```
        {
            if (!ModelState.IsValid)
            {
                return BadRequest(ModelState);
            }

            var reviews = await _context.Reviews.FindAsync(id);
            if (reviews == null)
            {
                return NotFound();
            }

            _context.Reviews.Remove(reviews);
            await _context.SaveChangesAsync();

            return Ok(reviews);
        }

        private bool ReviewsExists(string id)
        {
            return _context.Reviews.Any(e => e.Id == id);
        }
    }
}
```

## Models

```
using System;
using System.Collections.Generic;

namespace Reviews.API.Models
{
    public partial class Reviews
    {
        public string Id { get; set; }
        public string Description { get; set; }
        public string ReviewerEmail { get; set; }
        public string ReviewerName { get; set; }
        public string HotelId { get; set; }
    }
}
```

# Manage Distributed Transactions Using Redis Cache

In an Azure-based system with multiple cloud services communicating with each other and the outside world and that what shares a lot of data in between, there is bound to have issues. We need a distributed cache solution that could be accessed from all cloud services. For our solution, we feel Redis is the best-distributed cache solution for Azure based application.

What is Redis? Redis is an in-memory, high-performance server. Azure Redis Cache is based on the famous open-source Redis cache. It is generally used as a cache to enhance the performance and scalability of systems that rely heavily on backend data-stores. Performance is improved by temporarily copying frequently accessed data to fast storage found closer to the application.

The traffic progress of applications that need to access relational databases like SQL Server is increasingly using **Entity Framework (EF)** Core. In our code sample, we will be using Redis in Reviews API, the reason behind implementing Redis in Reviews API to reduce the load from DB, User rarely post a review but would surely like to go through the top reviews that have been recently posted. So, it is a good idea to cache the reviews.

We will configure Redis Cache in the Azure portal. For this, you will need to login to the Azure portal. Then choose to Create a resource > Databases > Redis Cache.

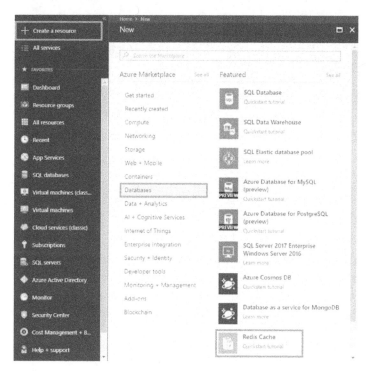

Fetch hostname, ports, and access keys by using the Azure portal. While connecting to an Azure Redis Cache instance, cache clients want the hostname, ports, and a key for the cache. Some clients might point to these items by somewhat different names.

To retrieve the hostname and ports, select **Properties** and get the hostname, Ports, and key for the cache.

Add Redis Cache settings in appsettings.json.

```
"CacheConnection":   "HotelTest.redis.cache.windows.net:9000,
abortConnect = false,ssl=true,password=<access-key>"
```

Replace < BookingTest > with the cache hostname you've created.

Replace <access-key> with the primary key for your cache.

To use Redis cache follow the following commands:

- First install NuGet package Tools > NuGet Package Manager > Package Manager Console. Microsoft.Extensions.Caching.Redis

```
PM> Install-Package Microsoft.Extensions.Caching.Redis
```

- In your startup.cs, you now need to add the following to your ConfigureServices method. It should look something like:

```
public void ConfigureServices(IServiceCollection services)
{
    services.AddMvc();
    //DB Connection
    services.AddDbContext<Models.
    HotelBookingsContext>(options =>

    options.UseSqlServer(Configuration.GetConnectionString
    ("DefaultConnection")));

    //Redis Cache Configuration
    services.AddDistributedRedisCache(option =>
    {
        option.Configuration =
        Configuration.GetConnectionString("CacheConnection");
        option.InstanceName = "HotelTest";
    });
}
```

- AddDistributedRedisCache actually adds an interface automatically to your service collection called IDistributedCache that you can then use to set and retrieve values. You can then use controller dependency injection to get this anywhere in your app. You can read more about controller dependency injection at - https://docs.microsoft.com/en-us/aspnet/core/mvc/controllers/dependency-injection?view=aspnetcore-2.1

**ReviewsController.cs**

```
private readonly IDistributedCache _distributedCache;
    private string cacheKey = "ReviewsCache";
    public ReviewsController(HotelreviewsContext context,
    IDistributedCache distributedCache)
    {
        _context = context;
        _distributedCache = distributedCache;
    }

    // GET: api/Reviews
    [HttpGet]
```

```
public async Task<IEnumerable<Models.Reviews>>
GetReviews([FromRoute] string hotelid)
{

    IEnumerable<Models.Reviews> reviews = null;
    if (!string.IsNullOrEmpty(cacheKey))
    {
        reviews = await
        _distributedCache.GetAsync<IEnumerable<Models.
        Reviews>>(cacheKey);

    }
    else
    {
        reviews = _context.Reviews.Where(p => p.HotelId.
        Equals(hotelid));
        await _distributedCache.
        SetAsync<IEnumerable<Models.Reviews>>
        (cacheKey, reviews, new
        DistributedCacheEntryOptions() {
        AbsoluteExpirationRelativeToNow = TimeSpan.
        FromHours(2) });
    }
    return reviews;
}
```

- **Reset Cache:** You will need to clear cache and reload it whenever a new review is posted.

```
// POST: api/Reviews
    [HttpPost]
    public async Task<IActionResult> PostReviews([FromBody]
    Models.Reviews reviews)
    {
        if (!ModelState.IsValid)
        {
            return BadRequest(ModelState);
        }

        _context.Reviews.Add(reviews);

        try
        {
            await _context.SaveChangesAsync();
            //make cache null
            _distributedCache.Remove(cacheKey);

        }
        catch (DbUpdateException)
        {
            if (ReviewsExists(reviews.Id))
```

```
    {
        return new StatusCodeResult(StatusCodes.
        Status409Conflict);
    }
    else
    {
        throw;
    }
    }
    return CreatedAtAction("GetReviews", new { id =
    reviews.Id }, reviews);
}
```

# Communication Between Microservices

One of the most significant aspects of using microservices rather than a monolithic application is an inter-service communication. With a monolithic application, which runs on single process requests between components are obtained on language-level method calls. A microservices-based application is a distributed system commanding on multiple processes or services, normally even across multiple servers or hosts. Each service instance is a process. Hence, services must communicate using an inter-process communication protocol such as HTTP, AMQP, or a binary protocol like TCP, depending on the characteristics of each service. The most used protocols are synchronous HTTP request/response with resource APIs, and lightweight asynchronous messaging when communicating across many microservices.

## Communication Types

Client and services can communicate via several types of communication, each one targeting a separate scenario and goals. Originally, those types of communications can be categorized into two types.

- **Synchronous protocol:** HTTP is a synchronous protocol. The client typically sends a request to the service and waits for a response from it. That is not dependent on the client code execution that could be synchronous (thread is prevented) or asynchronous; the thread is not obstructed, and the response will reach a callback ultimately. The primary point here is that the protocol (HTTP/HTTPS) is synchronous and the client-side task can only continue when it receives the HTTP server response. For web application communication, the standard HTTP protocol has been used, and it is the same for microservices as well. It is a synchronous, stateless protocol, which does have its disadvantages. However, they do not have an adverse impact on its demand. In synchronous communication, the client broadcasts a request and waits for a response. Interestingly, using the same protocol, the client can interact asynchronously with a server as well, which means that the thread is not blocked, and the response will reach callback ultimately.

- **Asynchronous protocol:** Other protocols like AMQP (Protocol recommended by many OS and cloud environments) use asynchronous messages. The client code or sender normally does not wait for a response. It just sends the message unlike sending a message to a RabbitMQ queue or any other message broker.

Building Microservices with REST principles with a JSON web service is one of the best ways of implementation of Microservices.

## Implementing Event-Based Communication Between Microservices

When you use event-based communication, a microservice declares an event when something important happens, such as when it updates an entity. Other microservices subscribe themselves to those events. When a microservice gets an event, it can update its own entities, which might lead to more events being declared. This publish/subscribe system is usually accomplished by implementing an event bus. The event bus can be produced as an interface with the API required to subscribe and unsubscribe to events and to host events. Event bus can also have individual or more implementations depends on an inter-process or messaging communication, unlike a messaging queue or a service bus that promotes asynchronous communication and a publish/subscribe model.

You can choose any one from various messaging technologies for achieving your abstract event bus. But these technologies are at various levels. For example, RabbitMQ, a messaging broker transport, is at a lower level than commercial products like Azure Service Bus, NServiceBus, or MassTransit. Most of these products can work on the addition of either RabbitMQ or Azure Service Bus.

## Integration Events

Following code used to create a Redis Repository for Reviews to Fetch and put reviews in a distributed in-memory cache instead of accessing the DB every time.

**RedisReviewRepository.cs**

```
using Microsoft.Extensions.Caching.Distributed;
using System.Threading;
using System.Threading.Tasks;

namespace Reviews.API.Extensions
{
    public static class RedisReviewRepository
    {
        public async static Task SetAsync<T>(this
        IDistributedCache distributedCache,
        string key, T value, DistributedCacheEntryOptions
        options,
        CancellationToken token = default(CancellationToken))
        {
```

```
        await distributedCache.SetAsync(key, value.
        ToByteArray(), options, token);
    }

    public async static Task<T> GetAsync<T>(this
    IDistributedCache distributedCache,
    string key, CancellationToken token =
    default(CancellationToken)) where T : class
    {
        var result = await distributedCache.GetAsync
        (key, token);
        return result.FromByteArray<T>();
    }

    }
}
```

Also, to authenticate the user before writing a Review, the user needs to login to the application and for that, in the code, we are calling Identity Service and Authoring the user before invoking any Reviews API method.

```
public class IdentityService : IIdentityService
    {
        private IHttpContextAccessor _context;
        public IdentityService(IHttpContextAccessor context)
        {
            _context = context ?? throw new
            ArgumentNullException(nameof(context));
        }
        public string GetUserIdentity()
        {
            return _context.HttpContext.User.
            FindFirst("sub").Value;
        }
    }
```

## Presentation Layer (Angular SPA)

Next, we need to learn how to invoke .NET core APIs (Microservices) from an Angular SPA application. At this point, we are almost done with the backend development. However, we may have to tweak here and there to add things like exception handling, logging etc.

These are the following modules for this demo App. Administrators role has all rights to Create, Update, Read, and Delete modules and customers can search hotel, see room details and book a room.

1.   Admin Role
     a.   Login

   b.   Manage Hotel (CRUD)

   c.   Manage Room Type (CRUD)

   d.   Manage Room (CRUD)

   e.   Manage Facilities (CRUD)

   f.   Manage Customers (Read-only)

   g.   List of Bookings (Read-only)

   h.   List of Reviews (Read-only)

2.   Customer Role

   a.   Sign-up/Login

   b.   Search Hotels

   c.   View Room details

   d.   View Facilities

   e.   Add Review

   f.   Booking

## Designing Functionality with Modules

This application has three major UI modules. UI modules in Angular SPA application are created as follows:

1.   Admin

   a.   Hotel

      i.    RoomType

      ii.   Room

      iii.  Room Facilities

      iv.   Reviews

2.   Home

   a.   Search

   b.   Fetch Hotels/Room/RoomType

   c.   Booking

   d.   Reviews

   e.   Checkout

3.   Login

   a.   Registration

   b.   Login

User Interface of Admin to Add/Update/Delete Rooms as shown in the following screenshot:

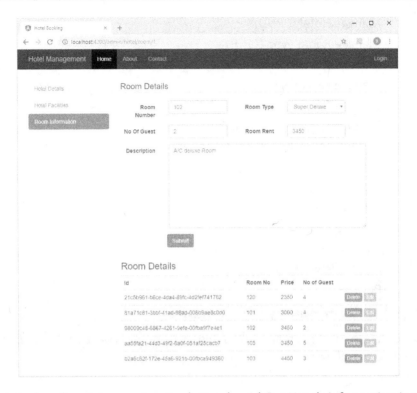

User Interface for customers to search Hotels and Get Hotels information is given as follows:

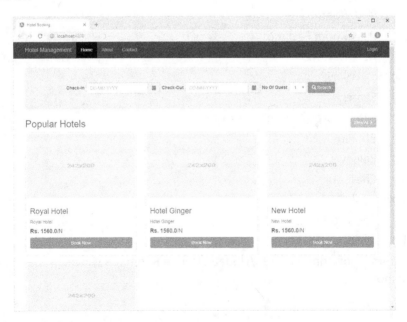

Interface to Get the Room details and Proceed to Booking as illustrated in the following screenshot. Once you download the source code and setup DB, you should be able to view all the following UI:

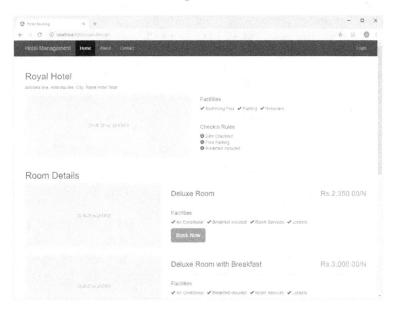

Angular modules give a super-effective way to classify related components, directives, and services, in a way that they can be merged with other modules to compile an application. For this app, the functions are grouped above into modules by using the Angular CLI to create them within the src\app folder. To create the modules, use the following NPM commands:

```
src\app\admin>ng g module hotel
```

## Creating Component

Then, we'll add a new form component for User Registration where users will create their account. Go to the command line to use the CLI once again within the src\app\account module folder.

```
src\app\admin\hotel>ng g component hotel-detail
```

Once we create a component under module Angular it create three files, one with .css for all stylesheets, .html to keep all your html tags and .ts which is a Typescript file to call service layer and for databinding propose.

**hotel-detail.component.html**

```
<div class="row">
    <div class="col-md-3">
        <ul class="nav nav-pills nav-stacked">
            <li class="active"><a >Hotel Details</a></li>
            <li><a href="#">Hotel Facilities</a></li>
            <li><a href="admin/hotel/room/1">Room
```

```
                Information</a></li>
        </ul>
    </div>
    <div class="col-md-9">
        <legend>Hotel Details</legend>
        <fieldset>
            <div class="form-horizontal">
                <div class="form-group">
                    <label for="hotelName" class="col-sm-2
                    control-label">Hotel Name</label>
                    <div class="col-sm-9">
                        <input type="text" class="form-control"
                        [(ngModel)]="hotelName"id="hotelName"
                        name="hotelName" placeholder="Name
                        of the Hotel" required>
                    </div>
                </div>
                <div class="form-group">
                    <label for="description" class="col-sm-2
                    control-label">Description</label>
                    <div class="col-sm-9">
                        <textarea class="form-control"
                        rows="10"
                        [(ngModel)]="description"
                        id="description"name="descript
                        ion" placeholder="Hotel Description"
                        required>
                        </textarea>
                    </div>
                </div>
                <div class="form-group">
                    <div class="col-sm-offset-2 col-sm-10">
                        <button type="submit" class="btn
                        btn-primary"
                        (click)='submit()'>Submit</button>
                    </div>
                </div>
            </div>
        </fieldset>
    </div>
</div>
```

**hotel-detail.component.ts**

```
import { Component, OnInit } from '@angular/core';
import { HotelService } from '../../../service/hotel.service';
import { ActivatedRoute, Router } from '@angular/router'
import { HttpErrorResponse } from '@angular/common/http';
```

```
@Component({
    selector: 'app-hotel-detail',
    templateUrl: './hotel-detail.component.html',
    styleUrls: ['./hotel-detail.component.css']
})
export class HotelDetailComponent implements OnInit {
    hotelId: number;
    hotelName: string = 'New Hotel';
    description: string;

    constructor(private route: ActivatedRoute, private
    router: Router, private hotelService: HotelService) {
        this.route.params.subscribe(res => {
            if(res.id)
            {
                this.hotelId = res.id;
                this.loadHotel();
            }
        });
    }

    ngOnInit() {
    }

    loadHotel()
    {
        this.hotelService.getHotelInfo(this.hotelId).
        subscribe(
            (response: any)=>{
                if (response) {
                    this.hotelName = response.hotelName;
                    this.description = response.description;
                }
                else
                {
                    this.router.navigate(['/admin/hotel/
                    add']);
                }
            },
            (err: HttpErrorResponse)=>{
                this.router.navigate(['/admin/hotel/add']);
            }
        )
    }

    submit()
    {
    var hotel: any = {
        HotelName: this.hotelName,
```

```
        Description : this.description
    }

    this.hotelService.addHotel(hotel).subscribe(
        (response: any)=>{
            if (response) {
                this.router.navigate(['/admin/hotel/edit/' +
                response.hotelId]);
            }
        },
        (err: HttpErrorResponse)=>{}
        )
    }

}
```

## Creating Service

Next up, we'll add service where Modules will connect to our service layer. Navigate to the command line to use the CLI once again within the src\app\ account module folder.

```
src\app>ng g service Hotel
```

This command will create .service.ts file where we need to define all service calls.

Following is the service call for hotelsinfo, follow the source code to see all other service calls.

```
import { Injectable } from '@angular/core';
import { HttpClient, HttpHeaders } from '@angular/common/
http';

@Injectable()
export class HotelService {
    //private headers: HttpHeaders;
    private accessPointUrl: string = 'https://localhost:
    44347/api';

    constructor(private http: HttpClient) {
        //this.headers = new HttpHeaders({'Content-Type':
        'application/json; charset=utf-8'});
    }

    getHotels() {
        return this.http.get(this.accessPointUrl + "/
        hotelsinfo/hotelslist");
    }

    getHotelInfo(id: number) {
        return this.http.get(this.accessPointUrl + "/
        hotelsinfo/" + id );
    }
```

```
addHotel(hotel: any)
{
    return this.http.post(this.accessPointUrl + "/
    hotelsinfo", hotel);
}
}
```

## Steps to Run Source Code

1.   Download and install all the pre-requisites software.
2.   Download the source code from Git link https://github.com/bpbpublications/Microservices-by-example
3.   Run or publish the API either on cloud or on-premises.
4.   Before publishing the API change the DB connection to your DB server in appsetting.json.
5.   Change the accessPointUrl from service folder of the Angular project and point to your API URLs.
6.   Deploy Angular APP either on cloud or on-premises.
7.   You are ready to Go!

## Summary

In this chapter, we discussed more on the hands-on development of API using core and Angular SPA application. Then we discussed on Security in API, how to use out of the box CoreIdentity to authenticate users. We also discussed on creating JWT tokens and validation.

In the next chapter, we will discuss how to deploy microservices and modernize using Docker?

# CHAPTER 5

# Deployment of Microservices for App Modernization at Scale with Docker

## Introduction to Docker

Docker is a container management service. The tagline of Docker is developed, ship, and run anywhere. Docker is an instrument intended to make it less demanding to make, send, and run applications by utilizing compartments. Containers enable developers to bundle up an application with the greater part of the parts it needs, for example, libraries and other dependencies and ship everything out as one bundle which can then be deployed anywhere.

### Docker Terminologies

Following is the list of terms and definitions with which you should become familiar with.

**Container image:** A set with all of the dependencies and information needed to create a container. An image covers all of the dependencies (such as frameworks) plus deployment and configuration to be used by a container runtime. Normally, an image determines from various base images that are layers stacked one atop the other to form the container's file system. An image is immutable once it is created.

Followings are the three methods for building or modifying a Docker image:

1. Pull or download from Docker registry.
2. Clean your Docker image using Docker file and the related directories.
3. Build by committing the modified container.

**Container:** An instance of a Docker image. A container describes a runtime for a single system, process, or service. It is a group of contents of a Docker image, a runtime environment, and a usual set of the guideline. When scaling a service, generally you create many instances of a container from the same image. Or, a batch job also can create many containers from the same image, passing various parameters to each instance.

**Tag:** Tag is a label that usually applied to images so that many images or versions of a particular image (depending on the version number or the destination environment) can be identified.

**Dockerfile:** Dockerfile is a text file that holds guidance on how to build a Docker image.

**Build:** Build is the action of creating a container image based on the information and context given by its Dockerfile as well as extra files in the folder where the image is created. You can build images by running the below docker build command .

```
docker build [OPTIONS] PATH | URL | -
```

**Repository (also known as a repo):** A group of related Docker images labeled with a tag that shows the image version. Some repositories hold multiple variants of a particular image, such as an image containing SDKs (heavier), an image including only runtimes (lighter), and so on. Those variants can be labeled with tags. A single repository can hold platform variants, such as a Windows and a Linux image.

**Registry:** A service that gives access to repositories. The default registry for most common images is Docker Hub (owned by Docker as an organization). A registry normally contains repositories from various teams. Organizations usually have private registries to store and handle images that they've built. Azure Container Registry is another example.

**Docker Hub:** Docker Hub is a collected resource mechanism while working with the components of Docker technology. Docker Hub is the best example for a public repository and it helps you in collaborating with your friends to make most from Docker. There are few services provided by Docker Hub like Docker's image hosting service for this. Docker Hub can act as both private and public storage media for Docker. A public registry to upload images and operate with them. Docker Hub gives Docker image hosting, public or private registries, build triggers and webhooks, and integration with GitHub and Bitbucket.

**Docker Swarm:** It is a domestic cluster for Docker. This will allow creation and access to a collection of Docker hosts with the help of Docker tools. As Docker Swarm acts as worthful API for Docker, any of Docker tools which are communicating with Docker daemon could use Swarm for transparently scaling different hosts.

**Azure Container Registry:** A public resource for Docker images and its components in Azure. This gives a registry that is close to your deployments in Azure and that provides you control beyond access, making it reasonable to use your Azure Active Directory groups and permissions.

**Compose:** A CLI tool and YAML file format with metadata for representing and running multi-container applications. You name a single application based on multiple images with one or more .yml files that can override values depending on the environment. After you have built the definitions, you can deploy the entire multi-container application by applying a single command (docker-compose up) that generates a container per image on the Docker host.

**Cluster:** A group of Docker hosts presented as if they were a single virtual Docker host, so that the system can scale to multiple occurrences of the services spread over various hosts within the cluster. You can build Docker clusters by using Docker Swarm, Kubernetes, Azure Service Fabric, and Mesosphere DC/OS.

**Orchestrator:** A tool that explains the administration of clusters and Docker hosts. Using orchestrators, you can control their images, containers, and hosts through a CLI or a graphical user interface. You can control container networking, load balancing, configuration, service discovery, high availability, Docker host configuration, and more. An orchestrator is capable of running, distributing, scaling, and healing workloads across a collection of nodes. Generally, orchestrator products are the corresponding products that present cluster infrastructure, like Mesosphere DC/OS, Kubernetes, Docker Swarm, and Azure Service Fabric.

## Features of Docker

Docker has the capacity to reduce the size of development by offering a smaller footstep of the operating system through containers.

With containers, it becomes obvious for teams across diverse units to work seamlessly over applications.

Docker containers can be used anywhere, on any physical, virtual machines, and even on the cloud.

Since the Docker containers are much lightweight, they are very easily scalable.

## Prerequisites

* Azure CLI [Refer: https://docs.microsoft.com/cli/azure/install-azure-cli]
* Docker for Windows [Refer: https://docs.docker.com/docker-for-windows/install/ ]

## Installation and Setup

Install Docker for Windows and for Docker installation, review the information at Docker for Windows: What to know before you install?

Shared Drives in Docker for Windows should be configured to maintain volume mapping and debugging. Right-click on the System Tray's Docker icon, then select Settings, and select Shared Drives. Select the drive where Docker stores files. Click on Apply.

## Dockerize ASP.NET Core Application

To containerize ASP.NET Core project, the project should target .NET Core. Both Windows and Linux containers are supported.

When creating Docker support for a project, you need to choose either a Windows or a Linux container.

Create a Dockerfile in your project folder.

Add the text below to Dockerfile for either Windows or Linux Containers. The tags below are multi-arch sense they pull either Linux or Windows containers depending on what mode is set in Docker for Windows. Read more on switching containers.

Dcokerfile assumed to be in the current directory of your application . You also need to modify to the Dockerfile to use the DLL file of your project.

## New app

When building a new app with the ASP.NET Core Web Application project templates, select the Enable Docker Support checkbox:

Check the Docker Support checkbox.

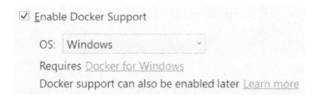

If the framework is .NET Core, the OS drop-down provides the choice of a container type.

## Existing Application

For existing ASP.NET Core projects targeting .NET Core, there are two choices for adding Docker support through the tooling. Open the project in Visual Studio, and select one of the following options:

Choose Docker Support on the Project menu.

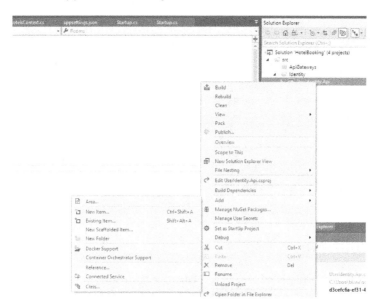

Right-click on the Solution Explorer and select Add > Docker Support. Choose the OS "Windows" or "Linux" of a container type.

## .NET Core for Docker Containers

The modularity and lightweight nature of .NET Core makes it perfect for containers. When you deploy and start a container, its image is far smaller with .NET Core than with .NET Framework. In contrast, to use .NET Framework for a container, you must base your image on the Windows Server Core image, which is a lot heavier than the Windows Nano Server or Linux images that you use for .NET Core.

Additionally, .NET Core is cross-platform, so you can deploy server apps with Linux or Windows container images.

- You have cross-platform needs. For example, you want to use both Linux and Windows Containers.
- Your application architecture is based on microservices.
- You need to start containers fast and want a small footprint per container to achieve better density or more containers per hardware unit in order to lower your costs.

## Dockerfile Overview

A Dockerfile is a Docker image which is added to the project root. This appropriate Dockerfile uses a multi-stage build with four different, named build stages:

```
FROM Microsoft/dotnet:2.1-aspnetcore-runtime-nano server-1709
AS base
WORKDIR /app
EXPOSE 55584
EXPOSE 44379

FROM microsoft/dotnet:2.1-sdk-nanoserver-1709 AS build
WORKDIR /src
COPY UserIdentity.Api/UserIdentity.Api.csproj UserIdentity.
Api/
RUN dotnet restore UserIdentity.Api/UserIdentity.Api.csproj
COPY . .
WORKDIR /src/UserIdentity.Api
RUN dotnet build UserIdentity.Api.csproj -c Release -o /app

FROM build AS publish
RUN dotnet publish UserIdentity.Api.csproj -c Release -o /app

FROM base AS final
WORKDIR /app
COPY --from=publish /app .
ENTRYPOINT ["dotnet", "UserIdentity.Api.dll"]
```

The following Dockerfile is based on the Microsoft/dotnet image. This base image holds the ASP.NET Core runtime and NuGet packages.

First line FROM Microsoft/dotnet:2.1-SDK-nano server-1709 AS build

is the base image of this application to run the Dot NET core application.

WORKDIR / src is the working directory of the image; it will store all DLLs inside the src folder.

ENTRYPOINT is bound to run the main application with the help of UserIdentity. Api.dll.

COPY generally copied the DLLs of the application to root directory of the image.

Before running the application, you need to build and call the publish command. Open the command prompt and go to the project folder where you have created the project.

Once you are in the project path, to execute, follow the following command:

```
"dotnet publish --configuration release --output hotebooking.
api/obj/Docker/publish"
```

When above command is complete, you can observe inside obj/Docker folder, then the publish folder gets created. This publish folder has all the DLLs of your project.

## Build and Run the Docker Image

The .NET Docker images are the images generated and optimized by Microsoft. They are openly available in the Microsoft repositories on Docker Hub << https:// hub.docker.com/u/microsoft/>>. Each repository can hold multiple images, depending on .NET versions, and depending on the OS and versions (Linux Debian, Linux Alpine, Windows Nano Server, Windows Server Core, etc.).

Since .NET Core 2.1, all the .NET Core images, including for ASP.NET Core are available at Docker Hub at the .NET Core image repo.

You can instantly run a container with a pre-built .NET Core Docker image. Open the command prompt and then go to your project folder. If your application only has a single container, you can run it by deploying it to your Docker host either VM or physical server. But, if your application contains multiple services, you can deploy it as a composed application, either using a single CLI command (docker-compose up), or with Visual Studio.

Use the following commands to create and run your Docker image:

Type the following Docker command:

```
docker run --name HotelBooking --rm -it -p 9000:80 src/
HotelBooking: UserIdentity.API
```

Before creating the image, make sure you need to switch to Windows container; only then can you make images on Docker because while creating dot net core application you have chosen Docker to support OS for Windows.

Navigate to your project folder where Dockerfile lives in command prompt and call the following command:

```
docker build -t HotelBooking: UserIdentity.API.
```

*   where build is docker command to create images
*   -t is the tag (name) of the application
*   Here image name is HotelBooking: UserIdentity.API
*   . (dot) represents the current directory where Dockerfile exists

After building the image, you should run the image with the help of the command.

```
docker run -p 9000:80 HotelBooking: UserIdentity.API
```

- Where "run" is the command to run image
- -p is the port assigned to the application
- HotelBooking: UserIdentity.API is the image name.

## Defining Your Container Orchestrator with docker-compose. yml

The Visual Studio Tools for Docker attach a docker-compose project to the solution with the following files:

**docker-compose.dcproj:** This file representing the project which Includes a <DockerTargetOS> element specifying the OS to be used.

**.dockerignore:** It lists the file and directory patterns to exclude when making a build context.

**docker-compose.yml:** The Docker Compose file is used to define the collection of images built and run with docker-compose build and docker-compose run, individually.

**docker-compose.override.yml:** It is an optional file, read by Docker Compose, with configuration overrides for services. Visual Studio performs docker-compose -f "docker-compose.yml" -f "docker-compose.override.yml" to merge these files.

### Publishing a Single-Container Based Application to Docker

**docker-compose.yml**

```
version: '3.4'
services:
    useridentity.api:
        image: ${DOCKER_REGISTRY}useridentityapi
        build:
            context: .
            dockerfile: UserIdentity.Api\Dockerfile
            docker-compose.override.yml
version: '3.4'
services:
    useridentity.api:
        environment:
            - ASPNETCORE_ENVIRONMENT=Development
            - ASPNETCORE_URLS=https://+:443;http://+:80
        ports:
            - "55584:80"
            - "44379:443"
        volumes:
            - ${APPDATA}/ASP.NET/Https:C:\Users\ContainerUser
```

```
            \AppData\Roaming\ASP.NET\Https:ro
            - ${APPDATA}/Microsoft/UserSecrets:C:\Users
            \ContainerUser\AppData\Roaming\Microsoft
            \UserSecrets:ro
networks:
    default:
        external:
            name: nat
```

In the above example, image: useridentityapi generates the image useridentityapi: dev when the app runs in Debug mode. The useridentityapi:latest image is generated when the app runs in Release mode.

Prefix the image name with the Docker Hub username (e.g., dockerhubusername/ useridentityapi) if the image is pushed to the registry. Alternatively, change the image name to add the private registry URL (for example, privateregistry.domain. com/ useridentityapi) depending on the configuration.

## Publishing Multi-Container Based Application to Docker

The root key here in the file is services. Under that key, you add the services you want to deploy and run when you execute the docker-compose up command or when it is needed to deploy from Visual Studio by using this docker-compose.yml file. In this scenario, the docker-compose.yml file has many services defined, as described in the following list.

useridentity.api container including the Identity ASP.NET Core Web API microservice

hotels.api container including the hotel's information ASP.NET Core Web API microservice

sql.data container running SQL Server for Linux, containing the microservices databases

booking.api container with the booking engine ASP.NET Core Web API microservice

reviews.api container with the user reviews ASP.NET Core Web API microservice

reviews.data container managing the REDIS cache service, with the reviews database as a REDIS cache

```
version: '3.4'

services:
    useridentity.api:
        image: ${DOCKER_REGISTRY}useridentity.api
        build:
            context: .
            dockerfile: UserIdentity.Api\Dockerfile
    booking.api:
        image:${DOCKER_REGISTRY}booking.api
        build:
```

```
            context:  .
            dockerfile:  booking.Api\Dockerfile
        depends_on:
            - sql.data
            - identity.api
            - rabbitmq
    hotels.api:
        image:${DOCKER_REGISTRY}hotels.api
        build:
            context:  .
            dockerfile:  hotels.Api\Dockerfile
        depends_on:
            - sql.data
            - identity.api
    reviews.api:
        image:${DOCKER_REGISTRY}reviews.api
        build:
            context:  .
            dockerfile:  reviews.Api\Dockerfile
        depends_on:
            - sql.data
            - identity.api
            - reviews.data
    sql.data:
        image:  microsoft/mssql-server-linux:2017-latest
    reviews.data:
        image:  redis
    rabbitmq:
        image:  rabbitmq:3-management
```

It defines an environment variable called ConnectionString with the connection string to be used by Entity Framework to obtain the SQL Server instance that holds the hotel's data model. In this case, the corresponding SQL Server container is supporting multiple databases. Therefore, you require less memory in your development machine for Docker. However, you can also deploy one SQL Server container for each microservice database.

The SQL Server name is SQL.data, (same name used for the container that is running the SQL Server case for Linux). This is acceptable; being able to use this name resolution which is internal to the Docker host will solve the network address so you don't need to know the internal IP for the containers which is accessible from other containers.

## Configuring CI/CD pipeline for DevOps Using MS Build

Developing and releasing application can be a complex process, especially as applications, teams, and deployment infrastructure grow in complexity themselves. Often, challenges become more obvious as projects grow. To develop, test, and deploy software in a quick and consistent way, developers and organizations have created three related but separate strategies to manage and automate these processes.

Continuous integration weighs on integrating work from individual developers into the main repository multiple times a day to catch integration bugs early and stimulate collaborative development. Continuous delivery is concerned with decreasing conflict in the deployment or release process, automating the steps required to deploy a build hence that code can be released safely at any time. Continuous deployment brings this one step further by automatically deploying code base every time a code change is done.

**Visual Studio Team Services (VSTS)** offers a highly customizable **continuous integration (CI)** and **continuous deployment (CD)** pipeline which automatically deploy ASP.NET Core web app to a Windows **virtual machine (VM)** in Azure.

Continuous integration is a method that encourages developers to integrate their code into a main branch of a shared repository early and often. Instead of developing features in isolation and integrating them at the end of a development cycle, code is combined with the shared repository by each developer multiple times during the day.

The idea is to reduce the cost of integration by making it an early consideration. Developers can detect conflicts at the boundaries between new and existing code early, while conflicts are still relatively easy to reconcile. Once the conflict is solved, work can continue with confidence that the new code honors the requirements of the existing codebase.

### Prerequisites

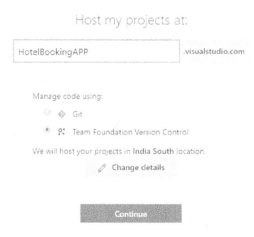

You just need a VSTS organization. If you don't have a VSTS organization before, you can create one for free. If your team has one already, then make sure you are an administrator of the project you want to use. To create a free VSTS account follow the following link and login with your Microsoft credential.

```
https://app.vsaex.visualstudio.com
```

Once signed in, provide name of your project codebase. Choose either Git/TFS as source control. It takes a while to create Project.

You need to keep ready of a Windows virtual machine that has a default web site running in IIS. Create a Windows VM with the Azure CLI for instructions to create a virtual machine in Azure, to install IIS, and to get its publicIpAddress.

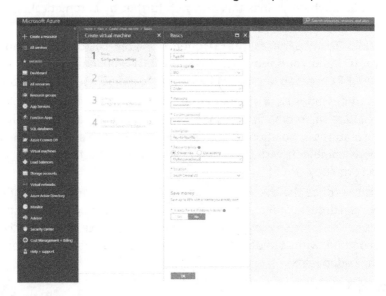

## Install Web Server

To see your VM in action, install the IIS web server. Open a PowerShell prompt on the VM and run the following command:

**PowerShell**

```
Install-WindowsFeature -name Web-Server -IncludeManagement
Tools
```

## Prepare the Windows VM

Running an ASP.NET Core app on Windows requires some of the dependencies.

**On** your VM, open as an Administrator: Windows PowerShell console. Install IIS and the required .NET features:

**PowerShell**

```
# Install IIS
Install-WindowsFeature Web-Server,Web-Asp-Net45,NET-
Framework-Features
```

```
# Install the .NET Core SDK
Invoke-WebRequest "https://go.microsoft.com/
fwlink/?linkid=848827 -outfile $env:temp\dotnet-dev-win-
x64.1.0.4.exe."
Start-Process $env:temp\dotnet-dev-win-x64.1.0.4.exe
-ArgumentList '/quiet' -Wait

# Install the .NET Core Windows Server Hosting package
Invoke-WebRequest https://go.microsoft.com/
fwlink/?LinkId=817246 -outfile $env:temp\DotNetCore.
WindowsHosting.exe
Start-Process $env:temp\DotNetCore.WindowsHosting.exe
-ArgumentList '/quiet' -Wait

# Restart the web server so that system PATH updates take
effect
net stop was /y
net start w3svc
```

## Create a Deployment Group

Deployment groups in VSTS make it simpler to organize the servers that you want to use to host your app. A deployment group is a group of machines including a VSTS agent on each of them. Each machine communicates with VSTS to organize deployment of your app.

Open the VSTS web portal, go to the Build and Release hub, and then click Deployment groups.

Click Add Deployment group or New if there are current deployment groups in place.

## Steps to Configure VM for Build Agent

1.  Enter a name for the group, e.g. for our demo app HotelBookingIIS, and then click Create.

2.  In the Register machine section, check that Windows is selected, and that use a personal access token in the script for authentication is selected. Click copy script to clipboard.

3.  The script that copied to your clipboard will download and configure an agent on the VM so that it can get new web deployment packages and apply them to IIS.

4.  On your VM, paste and run the script in PowerShell console as Admin.

5.  When you're advised to configure tags for the agent and press Enter.

6.  The account under which the agent runs requires Manage permissions for the C:\Windows\system32\inetsrv\ directory. Adding non-admin users to mentioned directory is not advised. In addition, if you need to have a custom user identity for application pools, the custom identity needs permission to read the crypto-keys. Local service accounts and user accounts are necessary to provide read access for this.

7.  When the script is executed, it shows the message service vstsagent.account. computername started successfully.

8.  On the Deployment groups page of the Build & Release tab in VSTS, open the HotelBookingIIS deployment group. On the Targets tab, verify that VM you are using is listed.

9.  Import your source code to VSTS.

## Set up Continuous Integration

A CI process builds and tests code every time a team member commits changes to version control automatically. You'll need to create a CI pipeline that helps your team to keep the master branch clean.

CI emerged as a conventional practice because software developers often work in isolation, and then they need to integrate their modifications with the rest of the team's code base. Waiting days or weeks to integrate codebase creates many merge conflicts, hard to fix bugs, diverging code strategies, and duplicated efforts. CI requires the development team's code be merged to a shared version control branch continuously to avoid these problems.

Go to << https://visualstudio.microsoft.com/team-services/continuous-integration/>> click on@Get started for free.

Choose the source control where you want to map or store your code base.

This is the Build and Release hub in VSTS, required to choose a template.

In the right panel, click on the ASP.NET Core, and then click on Apply.

You now observe all the tasks that were automatically added to the build pipeline by the template. These are the jobs that will automatically run each time you push code changes.

For the Agent queue, select Hosted VS2017. This is how you can use pool of agents that have the software you need to build your application.

Click on the Triggers tab in the build pipeline. Enable the Continuous Integration trigger. This will assure that the build process is automatically triggered every time you commit a change to your repository.

Click on Save, now your first build is ready to queue. Click on Save & queue, on the build pipeline and queue dialog Save box.

A new build is started. You'll find a link to the new build on the top of the page. Click on the link to see the new build as it happens. Wait for the build to finish and succeed before proceeding to the next section.

## Set up Continuous Deployment

**Continuous deployment (CD)** is a strong practice that your team can use to keep production fresh. Here you generally set up a short automatic path from the availability of new code in version control to deployment. Specifically, you'll determine a CD release management process that picks up the artifacts from your CI build and deploys application to the IIS web server hosted in your Windows VM. Continuous delivery is an addition of continuous integration. It focuses on automating the software deployment process so that teams can easily and confidently deploy their code to production at any time. By ensuring that the codebase is always ready in a deployable state, releasing software becomes an unremarkable event without complicated ritual. Teams can be certain that they can release whenever they need to without complex coordination or late-stage testing. Like continuous integration, continuous delivery is a discipline that requires a mixture of technical and organizational improvements to be effective.

On the technology side, continuous delivery relies heavily on deployment pipelines to automate the testing and deployment processes. A deployment pipeline is an automated operation that runs frequently rigorous test suites against a build as a series of sequential stages. This picks up where continuous integration drops off, so a reliable continuous integration setup is a prerequisite to implementing continuous delivery.

Once the build succeeds, click on the **Release action** on build summary page.

In the Create release pipeline wizard, choose IIS Website Deployment template, and then click **Apply**.

Click the **Tasks** tab, then click on the **IIS Deployment**. For the Deployment Group, open the deployment group you created earlier, such as HotelBookingIIS which we created under IIS deployment group in the release pipeline.

Click **Save**. On the **Save** dialog box, click **OK**.

Now, you can deploy to any machine, whether Windows, Linux, cloud-hosted, or on-premises. Deploy applications to VMs that have complex network topology. Perform rolling updates while making sure the high availability of the application.

To test the release pipeline, click **Release | Create Release**.

On the "**Create new release** dialog box, click on **Queue**" to create the release queue.

Note that a new release was created. Click on the link to go to the release, New release created message.

Click the **Logs** tab to view the logs from the deployment as it happens. Wait for the release to be deployed to the Azure web application.

Once deployment has been finished, open your web browser and test the web application by following the link: *http://<publicIpAddress>*

## DevOps Culture

Now, once you have defined CI/CD for your enterprise, you can say Our enterprise has adopted Devops Culture. Good luck!!

CI/CD, DevOps these are the buzz words in Industry and almost all the organizations are part of the show to adopt DevOps to make customer experience better to say we are in pure Agile model.

DevOps culture stresses small, multidisciplinary teams, who work autonomously and take collective accountability for how actual users experience their software. For a DevOps team, production environment is the best place. Everything they do is, providing customers' with better live experience.

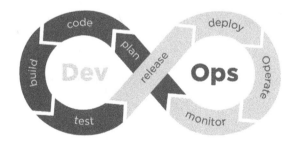

*<<picture copied: Source : Medium, https://medium.com/@neonrocket/devops-is-a-culture-not-a-role-be1bed149b0>>*

DevOps teams apply agile methods and include operations in the team responsibility. Teams work in small groups, focus on improving the end-to-end delivery of customer value, and strive to eliminate loss and difficulties along the way. There are no silos and no criticism, because the team is mutually accountable.

When you are working on Microservices Architecture you need to closely work with DevOps team to deliver in faster pace. DevOps teams encapsulate individual pieces of functionality in microservices and build larger systems by composing the microservices like building blocks.

DevOps is a new term arising from the impact of two major related trends. The first was also called *agile infrastructure* or *agile operations*; it sprang from applying Agile and Lean approaches to operations work. The second is an extremely expanded understanding of the value of collaboration between development and operations staff during all stages of the software development lifecycle when creating and operating a service, and how important operations has become in our increasingly service-oriented world.

## Summary

In this chapter we started with the basics of Azure Container Service. Deployment of Microservices for app-modernization with Docker and discussed about the deployment and covered the DevOps.

In coming the chapter we will discuss about microservices in details and then we will do indepth discussion of Service fabric – Why one should consider Service Fabric for microservices?

# CHAPTER 6

# Service Orchestration of Microservices Using Azure Service Fabric

## What is Service Fabric

Other cloud services similar to Azure are the fundamental large distributed systems, Cloud service providers hosts all manner of services. Some of them are presented infrastructure, containers, and microservices, some are development platforms, and some take benefit of serverless architecture.

They all require one thing: a management and orchestration platform. General-purpose cross-cloud tools like Kubernetes offer one road to delivering a managed container environment, but there's also a place for custom environments that focus on the needs of a specific cloud platform. For Azure, that's handled by a tool that's been there since the earliest days of Microsoft's public cloud: Azure Service Fabric.

Azure Service Fabric is a **Platform-as-a-Service (PaaS)** presented by Microsoft. Azure SQL Database, Azure Document DB, Azure IoT, Cortana, Power BI, Event Hubs and Skype for Business are some of the other PaaS products from Microsoft that leverage Service Fabric.

Service Fabric provides the infrastructure to run massive scale, reliable, stateless or stateful services. It offers end-to-end application lifecycle management and provides a container and process orchestration services and health monitoring.

Ability to deploy applications either running in containers or as processes:

- Programming APIs, to build applications as microservices: ASP.NET Core, Reliable Actors, and Reliable Services.
- Health Monitoring
- High Availability
- Reliability
- Service Discovery
- Resource Optimization using Higher Density – multiple services can be hosted on a single node
- End-to-End Lifecycle Management

Azure Service Fabric is a distributed systems platform that makes it easy to package, deploy, and manage scalable and reliable microservices and containers. Service Fabric also addresses the significant challenges in developing and managing cloud-native applications. Developers and administrators can avoid complex infrastructure problems and focus on implementing mission-critical, demanding workloads that are scalable, reliable, and manageable.

*"By using Service Fabric developers and administrators can avoid solving complex infrastructure problems and focus instead on implementing mission-critical, demanding workloads knowing that they are scalable, reliable, and manageable."*

*— Mark Fussel, principal program manager at Microsoft*

## Service Fabric Architecture

Service Fabric is made with Layered Architecture. These subsystems allow you to write applications that are as follows:

- Highly available
- Scalable
- Manageable
- Testable

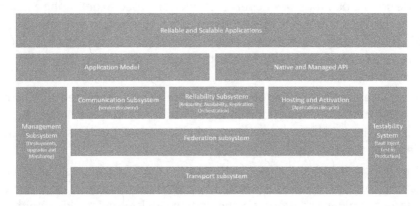

In a distributed system, the capacity to securely interact between nodes in a cluster is significant. At the bottom of the stack is the transport subsystem, which gives reliable communication between nodes. Above image describes transport subsystem lies on the federation subsystem, which groups the different nodes into a single entity called as named clusters, so that Service Fabric can identify failures, do leader voting, and offers consistent routing. The federation subsystem also holds the hosting and activation subsystem, which controls the lifecycle of an application on a single node. The management subsystem maintains the lifecycle of applications and services. The testability subsystem supports application developers test their services in simulated faults before and after deploying applications and services to production environments. Service Fabric gives the ability to determine service locations through its communication subsystem. The application programming models shown in the above picture are layered on top of these subsystems along with the application model to enable tooling.

The reliability subsystem, present on top of the federation subsystem, is accountable for the reliability of Service Fabric services for mechanisms such as replication, resource administration, and failover.

## Transport Subsystem

The transport subsystem executes a point-to-point datagram communication channel. This communication channel is used for interaction within the service fabric clusters and communication between the service fabric cluster. It maintains one-way and request-reply communication patterns, which offers the basic implementation of broadcast and multicast in the Federation layer. The transport subsystem secures the message by using X509 certificates or Windows security. This subsystem is used internally by Service Fabric and is not directly available to developers for programming.

## Federation Subsystem

To know about a set of nodes in any distributed system, we need to have a consistent monitor of the system. The federation subsystem uses the interface primitives offered by the transport subsystem and joins the different nodes into a single cluster. It also provides the distributed systems primitives required by the other subsystems - failure detection, leader option, and consistent routing. The federation subsystem is developed on top of distributed hash tables with a 128-bit token space. For failure detection, the layer uses a leasing mechanism based on heart beating and intervention. The federation subsystem also supports through intricate join and departure protocols that only a single owner of a token exists at any time. This provides leader option and guaranteed consistent routing.

## Reliability Subsystem

The reliability subsystem offers the mechanism to make the state of a Service Fabric service highly available, reliable through the use of the Replicator, Resource Balancer, and Failover Manager.

- The Replicator of Service Fabric makes sure that state changes in the primary service replica will automatically be replicated to secondary replicas, maintaining uniformity between the primary and secondary replicas in a service replica set. Replicator also communicates with the failover component to get the list of functions to replicate, and the reconfiguration agent provides it with the configuration of the replica set. That configuration indicates which replicas the operations need to be replicated. Service Fabric offers a default replicator maned as Fabric Replicator, which is generally used by the programming model API to make the service state highly available.

- The Failover Manager of Service Fabric takes care of load balancing of the nodes, when nodes are created or removed from the cluster, the load is automatically redistributed over the available nodes. If any of the node in the cluster fails, the cluster will automatically reconfigure the service replicas to support availability and reliability.

- The Resource Manager redirects service replicas across the failure domain in the cluster and ensures that all failover units are operational. The Resource Manager also balances service resources across the all the shared pool of cluster nodes to achieve best consistent load distribution.

## Management Subsystem

The management subsystem layer provides end-to-end service and application lifecycle management to provision, deploy, patch, upgrade, and de-provision applications without loss of availability by using PowerShell cmdlets or by using administrative APIS. The management subsystem achieves this by the following services:

- **Cluster Manager:** This is the fundamental service that communicates with the Failover Manager from reliability to place the applications on the nodes based on the service deployment limitations. The Resource Manager in failover subsystem assures that the boundaries are never broken. The cluster manager controls the lifecycle of the applications from provision to re-provision. It integrates with the health manager to ensure that application availability is not fallen from a semantic health perspective through upgrades.

- **Health Manager:** The health manager enables health monitoring of applications, services, and cluster entities. Nodes, service partitions, and replicas send health information, which later consolidated into the centralized health store. This health information provides an overall point-in-time health snapshot of the services and nodes distributed across multiple nodes in the cluster, which can help to take any corrective actions. Health query APIs can be used to query the health events reported to the health subsystem.

- **Image Store:** This service offers storage and distribution of the application binaries (dlls). This service provides a simple distributed file storage where the applications are uploaded to and downloaded from.

## Hosting Subsystem

The cluster manager notifies the hosting subsystem (typically runs on each node), about the services it requires to manage for a particular node. The hosting subsystem then manages the application lifecycle on that node. It communicates with the reliability and health components to guarantee that the replicas are properly placed and remain healthy.

## Communication Subsystem

The Communication subsystem provides reliable messaging within the cluster and service discovery via the naming service. The naming service resolves service names in the cluster and allows the users to manage service names and properties. Using the naming service, clients can securely interact with any node in the cluster to resolve a service name and fetch service metadata.

## Testability Subsystem

It is a set of tools specially designed for testing services built on Service Fabric. The tools let a developer easily find out faults and run test scenarios to exercise and validate the various states and transitions that service will encounter throughout its lifetime, all in a controlled and safe manner. This subsystem also offers a mechanism to run more extended tests that can iterate through various possible failures without losing availability. The testability subsystem comes with a capability of the test-in-production environment.

# Service Fabric Installation and Environment Setup

To develop and run Azure Service Fabric applications on Windows development machine, you need to install the Service Fabric runtime, SDK, and tools. You also require to enable execution of the Windows PowerShell scripts included in the SDK.

## Prerequisites for Windows OS

| OS (Any of the following) | • Windows 7<br>• Windows 8/Windows 8.1<br>• Windows Server 2012 R2<br>• Windows Server 2016<br>• Windows 10 |
|---|---|
| Service Fabric SDK | **Following are the instructions to use Visual Studio 2017:**<br><br>The Service Fabric Tools comes with Azure Development workload in Visual Studio 2017. To use this feature, enable this workload as part of Visual Studio installation.<br><br>In addition to the above, Microsoft Azure Service Fabric SDK and runtime using Web Platform Installer installation is required.<br><br>To install the Microsoft Azure Service Fabric SDK use following link: http://www.microsoft.com/web/handlers/webpi.ashx?command=getinstallerredirect&appid=MicrosoftAzure-ServiceFabric-CoreSDK<br><br>**To use Service Fabric SDK in Visual Studio 2015 (it needs Visual Studio 2015 Update 2 or later) and follow below instructions.**<br><br>For Visual Studio 2015, the Service Fabric tools are installed together with the SDK and runtime using the Web Platform Installer.<br><br>**To Install the Microsoft Azure Service Fabric SDK and Tools access the following link:** |

| |
|---|
| http://www.microsoft.com/web/handlers/webpi.ashx? command=getinstallerredirect&appid=MicrosoftAzure-ServiceFabric-VS2015 **For SDK installation only follow the below instructions** If only SDK installation is required, you can always install the following package: Install the Microsoft Azure Service Fabric SDK through the link: http://www.microsoft.com/web/handlers/webpi.ashx? command=getinstallerredirect&appid=MicrosoftAzure-ServiceFabric-CoreSDK |

## Service Fabric Hosting Model

There are two different types of hosting model supported by Azure Service Fabric.

• Shared Process

• Exclusive Process

Both the models describe how the deployment of application varies on a Service Fabric node and the relationship between replicas of the service and the service-host process.

Let's first understand the basics of application model before proceeding with hosting models.

## The Application Model

An application is a collection of essential services that accomplish certain functions. Service holds a complete or standalone function and can start, run independently of other services. Service is a package of code, configuration, and data. For each service code contains the executable binaries, setup consists of service settings which can be loaded at runtime, and data includes random static data to be consumed by the service. Each component in the following hierarchical application model can be versioned and upgraded autonomously.

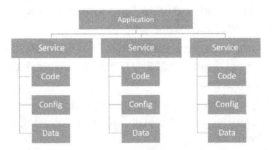

An application type is a classification of an application and contains a package of service types. A service type is a classification of service. The classification can have unlike settings and configurations, but the core functionality remains the same. The instances of service have different service configuration variations of the same service type.

Classes of applications and services are described through manifests (.XML file). The manifests describe applications and services to invoke on which applications can be instantiated from the cluster's image store. The schema description for the ApplicationManifest.xml and ServiceManifest.xml file it comes with the Service Fabric SDK and tools installation, *which is located in the installation folder" C:\ ProgramFiles\MicrosoftSDKs\ServiceFabric\schemas\ServiceFabricServiceModel. xsd".*

To understand the hosting model, let's walk through an example. Let's say we have an *ApplicationType* MyAppType, which has a *ServiceType* MyServiceType. MyServiceType is provided by the *ServicePackage* MyServicePackage, which has a *CodePackage* MyCodePackage. MyCodePackage registers *ServiceType* MyServiceType when it runs.

Let's say we have a three-node cluster, and we create an application **fabric:/App1** of type MyAppType. Inside this application **fabric:/App1**, we create a service **fabric:/App1/ServiceA** of type MyServiceType. This service has two partitions (for example, **P1** and **P2**), and three replicas per partition. The following diagram displays the view of this application as it ends up deployed on a single node:

Service Fabric initiated ServicePackage, which started CodePackage, which is hosting replicas of both the partitions. Nodes in the cluster have an equal view because the number of replicas per partition to be similar to the number of nodes in the cluster. Let's create another service, **fabric:/App1/ServiceB**, in the application **fabric:/App1**. This service has one partition, and three replicas per partition.

## Stateful and Stateless Services

Stateless and stateful applications varies in the way the data related with the application is stored. While some of the stateless applications like a web interface for end users can be really stateless, long-running stateless application might still need to maintain state but this can be done outside the application.

Stateful applications store the data inside. Services built leveraging Reliable Services Framework have access to a large number of APIs that help them query the system, Report health about entities in the cluster, receive notifications about setup and code changes, find and communicate with other dependent services.

| | Stateless | Stateful |
|---|---|---|
| **Data** | • State is stored outside the code | • Resides within code.<br>• Can be maintained expanding Reliable Collections.<br>• Latency is low as code and data are dependent.<br>• State is stored in the compute tier. |
| **Programming Model** | • Guest Executables<br>• Stateless Reliable Services | • Stateful Reliable Services<br>• Stateful Reliable Actor Model |
| **Use case** | • An endpoint<br>• Web interface for end users<br>• API gateway to other services<br>• Proxies<br>• Guest Executable- Existing applications that are migrating to Service Fabric<br>• Guest executables will not be able to expand features of Service Fabric platform e.g. endpoint registration, load reporting | • Gaming, Chating applications, which require low latency reads and writes.<br>• Calculation intensive applications<br>• Data processing on device data received from a wide number of devices<br>• Transactional applications which include workflows<br>• Data Analytics based applications |

*Stateful Vs. Stateless Services layer*

# Monitoring

Service Fabric provides different types of monitoring; It depends on the usage and your requirement, you may choose any of the following monitoring options as per customers need. Monitoring is very essential for any application for better fault recovery, to get insights into user behavior and action, also to keep application healthy and up always.

## Application Monitoring

Application monitoring generally maintains the history of how components of your application are being used. Applications can be monitored to make sure issues that might impact users are caught before. Monitoring your applications can be useful in the following scenarios:

• **Determining application load and user traffic:** Does it require to scale your services to meet user demands or report a potential bottleneck in your application?

- Identifying issues with service communication and remoting across your cluster .

- **Getting insight of user action and behavior:** collecting telemetry in applications can help to understand what user needs to see in your application and can help in extending feature development and better diagnostics for app errors.

- Monitoring can always help to understand what is occurring inside running containers.

Service Fabric supports many options to instrument your application code with the appropriate traces and telemetry. It is recommended to use application insights. Application insights integration with Service Fabric includes tooling experiences for Visual Studio and Azure portal, as well as Service Fabric specific metrics, providing a comprehensive out-of-the-box logging experience.

## Cluster Monitoring

Monitoring your Service Fabric cluster is very essential in ensuring that the platform and workloads are running as planned. Service Fabric aims to keep applications resilient to hardware failures. This goal can be achieved via the platform's system services' ability to detect infrastructure issues and rapidly failover workloads to other available nodes in the cluster. But in some particular case, what if the system services themselves have issues?

To provide the solution to above problem Monitoring the cluster allows staying informed about activity taking place in your cluster, which helps in detecting issues and fixing them effectively.

Service Fabric offers a complete set of events out of the box. These Service Fabric events can be accessed through the EventStore APIs or the operational channel.

- **EventStore:** The EventStore which is available on Windows in versions 6.2 and later, exposes these events via a set of APIs (accessible via REST endpoints or through the client library).

- **Service Fabric event channels:** Service Fabric events are available from a single ETW provider with a set of relevant logLevelKeywordFilters used to pick between Operational and Data & Messaging channels on windows; this is the way in which Service Fabric events can be filtered on as needed by separating outgoing Service Fabric events. Diagnostics are enabled by default at the time of cluster creation, which create an Azure Storage table where the events from these channels are store and can be used in future.

It is recommended to use the EventStore for quick analysis and to get a snapshot idea to measure cluster operation. For collecting the logs and events being generated by your cluster, it is generally recommended to use the Azure Diagnostics extension. This integrates well with Service Fabric Analytics, OMS Log

Analytics' Service Fabric specific solution, which provides a custom dashboard for monitoring Service Fabric clusters and allows you to query your cluster's events and set up alerts.

## Performance Monitoring

Monitoring underlying infrastructure is a primary part of understanding the state of cluster and application resource utilization. Measuring system performance depends on many factors, typically application measured through a **Key Performance Indicators (KPIs)**. Metrics collected from the nodes in a cluster can be mapped with Service Fabric relevant KPIs, as performance counters. These KPIs can help to understand followings:

- **Resource utilization and load:** To scale your cluster, or optimizing your service processes.

- **Predicting any infrastructure issues:** Many issues are preceded by sudden falls in performance; hence KPIs can be used in this case to measure network I/O and CPU utilization to predict and diagnose infrastructural issues.

A list of performance counters that can be collected at the infrastructure level which can be found at performance metrics.

Service Fabric provides a collection of performance counters for both the Reliable Services and Actors programming models. If either of these models being used in your application, these performance counters can provide KPIs that guarantee your actors are running up and down correctly, or that your reliable service requests are being handled quickly enough. Application Insights can be used to collect a set of performance metrics if configured with your application.

## Health Monitoring

The Service Fabric platform includes a health model, which provides extensible health reporting for the status of entities in a cluster. Each node, application, service, partition, replica, or instance, updates continuous health status. The health status can either be **OK, Warning**, or **Error**. The health status is varied through health reports that are issued for each entity. The health status of entities can be checked at any time in Service Fabric Explorer or can be queried via the platforms' Health API. Health reports are customizable and you can modify the health status of an entity by adding your health reports.

Azure Service Fabric introduces a health model that provides rich, flexible, and extensible health evaluation and reporting. The model allows near-real-time monitoring of the state of the cluster and the services running in it. You can easily obtain health information and correct potential issues before they cascade and cause massive outages. In the typical model, services send reports based on their local views, and that information is aggregated to provide an overall cluster-level view.

Service Fabric components use this rich health model to report on their current state. We can use the same mechanism to report the health of our app. If we invest in high-quality health reporting that takes custom conditions, we can detect and fix issues of running application quite easily.

# Cluster Management

## Deploy Application

Now that the application is ready, let's deploy it to a cluster directly from Visual Studio. A Service Fabric cluster is a connected set of virtual or physical machines into which microservices are deployed and managed.

- You can create Service Fabric clusters through the Azure portal by using PowerShell or Azure CLI scripts or from an Azure Resource Manager template.

## Service Fabric Cluster

An Azure Service Fabric cluster is a network-connected set of virtual or physical machines into which your microservices are deployed and managed. A machine or VM that is a segment of a cluster is called a cluster node. Clusters can scale to thousands of nodes. If you integrate new nodes to the cluster, Service Fabric rebalances the service partition replicas and instances across the incremented number of nodes. Overall application performance enhances and contention for access to memory drops. If the nodes in the cluster are being used roughly, you can decrement the number of nodes in the cluster. Service Fabric again rebalances the partition replicas and instances across the decremented number of nodes to make better utilization of the hardware on each node.

Service Fabric permits for the creation of Service Fabric clusters on any VMs or computers running Windows Server or Linux. This promises you can deploy and run Service Fabric applications in an environment where you can opt set of Windows Server or Linux computers that are inter-connected, be it on-premises, Microsoft Azure or with any cloud provider.

Service Fabric allows the creation of Service Fabric clusters on any VMs or computers running Windows Server or Linux, which enables to deploy Service Fabric applications in an environment where you can opt the set of Windows Server or Linux computers that are interconnected, be it on-premises, Microsoft Azure or with any cloud provider.

Service Fabric provides an install package for you to create standalone Service Fabric clusters on-premises or on any cloud provider.

## Any Cloud Deployments Versus On-Premises Deployments

The method for creating a Service Fabric cluster on-premises is similar to the process of creating a cluster on any cloud provider of your choice with a set of VMs. The initial steps to provision the VMs are administered by the cloud provider or on-premises environment that you are using. Once set of VMs with network connectivity are ready to use, then the steps to set up the Service Fabric package, edit the cluster settings, and run the cluster creation and management scripts are identical.

Benefits of creating standalone Service Fabric clusters:

- You are not bound to a particular cloud provider, you can choose any cloud provider of your choice to host cluster.
- Service Fabric applications, once developed, can be run in multiple hosting environments with minimal to no changes.
- Knowledge of building Service Fabric applications transfers from one hosting environment to another.
- Operational experience of managing Service Fabric clusters can be easily transferred from one environment to another.
- Customer reach is unbounded by hosting environment constraints.
- An additional layer of reliability and protection against broad outages exist because the movement of the services from to another deployment environment is easier, if a data center or cloud provider has a blackout.

## Supported Operating Systems for Standalone Clusters

Clusters creation on VMs or computers running these operating systems (Linux is not yet supported):

- Windows Server 2012 R2
- Windows Server 2016

## Advantages of Service Fabric Clusters on Azure Over Standalone

Running Service Fabric clusters on Azure provides advantages over the on-premises option, so if you don't have specific needs for where you run your clusters, then you can opt either to run on Azure or any cloud provider.

- **Azure portal:** Azure portal makes service Fabric clusters easy to create and manage.
- **Azure Resource Manager:** Use of Azure Resource Manager allows easy management of all resources used by the cluster as a unit.
- **Service Fabric Cluster as an Azure Resource:** A Service Fabric cluster is an Azure resource, where you can model it like your need as other resources in Azure.
- **Integration with Azure Infrastructure:** Service Fabric gives advantages to manage the underlying Azure infrastructure for network, OS, and other upgrades to enhance availability and reliability of services.
- **Diagnostics:** On Azure, we provide integration with Azure diagnostics and log analytics.
- **Auto-scaling:** For clusters on Azure, Azure provide built-in auto-scaling functionality due to Virtual Machine scale-sets. In on-premises and other

cloud environments, you have to build your auto-scaling feature or scale manually using the APIs that Service Fabric exposes for scaling clusters.

## Scaling in Service Fabric

Azure Service fabric makes it simple to make scalable applications by managing the services, partitions, and replicas on the nodes of a cluster. Running several workloads on similar hardware allows most resource utilization, however additionally provides flexibility regarding however you decide on to scale your workloads.

Scaling in Service Fabric can be achieved in many different ways:

- Scaling by adding or removing stateless service instances
- Scaling by adding or removing new named services
- Scaling by adding or removing newly named application instances
- Scaling by using partitioned services
- Scaling by creating and removing nodes from the cluster
- Scaling by making Cluster Resource Manager metrics

### Scaling by Adding or Removing Stateless Service Instances

One of the easiest ways to scale within Service Fabric works is to choose stateless services. When stateless service created, there are chances to define an InstanceCount. InstanceCount defines how many running instances of that service's code are created at the starts up.

Let's say, there are 100 nodes in the cluster and assume a service is created with an InstanceCount of 10. During runtime, those 10 running instances of the code could all become too busy or not. One way to scale that workload is to increase or decrease the number of instances based on load. For example, some piece of monitoring or management code can increase the existing number of instances to 50, or decrease it to 5, depending on whether the workload needs to scale in or out based on the load. Take a look at the following code:

```
StatelessServiceUpdateDescription  updateDescription  =  new
StatelessServiceUpdateDescription();
updateDescription.InstanceCount = 50;
await     fabricClient.ServiceManager.UpdateServiceAsync(new
Uri("fabric:/app/service"), updateDescription);
```

### Using Dynamic Instance Count

Service Fabric provides an automatic way to change the instance count for stateless services. It enables the service to scale dynamically with the number of nodes that are available. The way to facilitate automatic scale of services is to set the instance count = -1. InstanceCount = -1 is a direction to Service Fabric that *Run this stateless service on every node*. If the number of nodes changes later, Service Fabric automatically changes the instance count to match with the available valid nodes to guarantee that the service is running on all valid nodes.Take a look at the following code:

```
StatelessServiceDescription serviceDescription = new
StatelessServiceDescription();
serviceDescription.InstanceCount = -1;
await  fc.ServiceManager.CreateServiceAsync(serviceDescripti
on);
```

## Scaling by Creating or Removing New Named Services

A named service instance is a specific instance of a service type within some named application instance in the cluster.

New named service instances can be created, or removed as services become more or less involved. This allows requests to be broadcasted across more service instances, normally allowing load on existing services to decrease. When creating services, the Service Fabric Cluster Resource Manager places the services in the cluster in a distributed manner. The exact decisions are administered by the metrics in the cluster and other installable rules. Services can be created in several different ways, but the most common are either through administrative actions like someone calling New-ServiceFabricService or by code calling CreateServiceAsync. CreateServiceAsync can even called from within other services running in the cluster.

Creating services dynamically is a common practice and can be used in almost all the scenarios. For example, consider a stateful service that represents a specific workflow. Calls designating job are going to show up to this service, and this service is going to perform the steps to that workflow and record progress.

Think of scaling this kind of service. The service could be multi-tenant in some form, and accept calls and starting steps for several copies of the same workflow all at once. Though, that can make the code more complex, since now it has to bother about many various instances of the same workflow, all at different stages and from different customers. Also, remember handling multiple workflows at the same time doesn't solve the scale problem because at some point this service will consume too many resources to fit on a particular machine. These types of issues make the service, not to work as well when the number of simultaneous workflows it is tracking gets larger.

A solution is to form an instance of this service for each completely different instance of the workflow you would like to trace. This is often an excellent pattern and works whether or not the service is stateless or stateful. For this pattern to figure, there is typically another service that acts as a *Workload Manager Service*. The work of this service is to receive requests and to route those requests to alternative services. The manager will dynamically produce an instance of the work service once it receives the message, so expire requests to those services. The manager service may additionally receive callbacks once a given workflow service completes its job. Once the manager receives these callbacks it may delete that instance of the workflow service, or leave it if additional requests are anticipated.

Advanced versions of this kind of manager will even produce pools of the services that it manages. The pool helps make sure that once a replacement request comes in it does not get to look ahead to the service to spin up. Instead, the manager will decide a workflow service that's not presently busy from the pool, or route arbitrarily. Keeping a pool of services out there makes handling new requests quicker since it's less probable that the request must look ahead to a replacement service to be spun up. Making new services is fast, however not free or instant. The pool helps minimize the quantity of your time, the request must wait before being maintained. you may typically see this manager and pool pattern once response times matter the most. Queuing the request and making the service on the background then passing it on is a preferred manager pattern, as is making and deleting services supported some of the following quantity of work that service presently has pending.

## Scaling by Creating or Eemoving Newly Named Application Instances

Creating and deleting whole application instances is similar to the pattern of creating and deleting services. For this pattern, there's a manager service that is making the decision based on the requests that it is seeing and the information it is receiving from the other services inside the cluster.

When should create a new named application instance be used instead of creating a newly named service instance in some already existing application? There are some instances:

- The new application instance is for a client whose code has to run underneath some specific identity or security settings.
  - o Service fabric permits process completely different code packages to run underneath specific identities. To launch identical code package under totally different identities, the activations ought to occur in several application instances. think about a case wherever you have got an existing customer's workloads deployed. These could also be running underneath a selected identity therefore you'll be able to monitor and control their access to alternative resources, corresponding to remote databases or alternative systems. During this case, once a replacement client signs up, you almost certainly don't need to activate their code within the same context (process space). However you may need to manually scale it sometime, this makes harder for your service code to act at intervals the context of a selected identity . You sometimes should have additional security, isolation, and identity management code, rather than using different named service instances within identical

application instance and therefore a similar method area, you'll be able to use completely different named Service fabric Application instances. This makes it easier to outline completely different integrity contexts.

- The new application instance additionally is a method of configuration.
  - o By default, the named service instances of appropriate service type in an application instance will run in the same process on a particular node. Creating more services means more application upgrades to modify the information within the config packages or to deploy new application so that the new services can look up their particular information.
- The new application serves as an upgrade boundary.
  - o Within Service Fabric, differently named application instances serve as boundaries for an upgrade. An upgrade of one named application instance will not affect the code that another named application instance is running. The different applications will end up running various versions of the same code on the same nodes. This can be a circumstance when you need to make a scaling decision because you can opt whether the new code should follow the same upgrades as another service or not. Separate application instances provide greater granularity while doing application upgrades, and also enable A/B testing and Blue/Green deployments.
- The existing application instance is full.
  - o In Service Fabric, application capacity is a concept that you can use to control the number of resources available for particular application instances. However, this application instance is out of capacity for a certain metric. If this particular customer or workload should still be granted more resources, then you could either increase the existing capacity for that application or create a new application.

## Scaling at Partition Level

Service Fabric reinforces partitioning. Partitioning splits a service into several logical and physical sections, each of which operates independently. This is subsidiary with stateful services since none set of replicas has to handle all the calls and manipulate all of the states at once. The partitioning overview provides information on the types of partitioning schemes that are reinforced. The replicas of each partition are spread across the nodes in a cluster, distributing that accommodation's load and ascertaining that neither the accommodation as a whole or any partition has a unique case of failure.

Let's consider a service that works at a range of partitioning scheme with a low key of 0 to 99, and a partition count of 4. In a three-node cluster, the service might be hit with four replicas that share the resources on each node as shown here:

## Availability of Stateless Services

Service Fabric services can be developed either as stateful or stateless. Planning a stateless service needs setting an InstanceCount. The instance count determines the number of instances of the stateless service's application logic that should be running in the cluster. Developing the number of instances is the recommended way of scaling out a stateless service. A stateless service is an application service that does not maintain a local state that requires to be highly available or reliable.

If an instance of a stateless named service crashes, a new instance is automatically created on an available node in the cluster. For example, a stateless service instance fails on Node1 and can recreated on Node3.

## Availability of Service Fabric stateful services

A stateful service has a state connected with it. In Service Fabric, a stateful service is represented as a set of replicas. Each replica is a working instance of the code of the service. The replica also has a reflection of the state for that service. Read and write operations are executed at the Primary. Changes to the state from write operations are replicated to the other replicas in the replica set, called Active Secondaries, and applied. If the Primary replica goes down, Service Fabric makes one of the Active Secondary replicas the new Primary replica.

## Summary

In this chapter we learnt about Service Fabric, and its role in Microservices. Then We learnt about various features, Architecture, Monitoring, Cluster management, and scaling of Azure Service Fabric.

In next chapter we will learn more on Integration point of view of Microservices using various patterns like Circuit breakers, Azure service bus, message queueing and role of API gateways.

# CHAPTER 7

# Integrating Various Components

In the previous chapters, you have been walked through the whats and hows of the microservice architecture, its building blocks, its strengths and features that define it. These are meant to help you effortlessly transition from a microservice novice to a developer. But, unless the various pieces of your microservice solution within your scope is communicating to each composing service, as per need, your solution is incomplete and will be rendered useless.

In this chapter, we will walk you through the Integration steps of components of microservices. We will start with a basic question in the microservices based application, why integration is important? You will see the examples based on a business case. This chapter will highlight the following topics:

- Importance of the integration in microservices based applications
- Synchronous communication
- Asynchronous communication
- Integration patterns
- Azure Service Bus

## Why is Integration Important?

In today's world, data is the source of power, but it has value only if it is used at the right time by the right owner. Else it may act as a dead weight and lead to the problem of useless abundance. In microservices solution, each individual service works independently, without the knowledge or dependency over the other services. But not all services in the business can work like that, and it is important that the services interact with each other for things like, to complete a process, to share details for further processing, to fetch updated values of prices or stocks available, and so on. Thus, on-time delivery of the information between the composing services is vital, to ensure the efficiency, reliability, and performance. Hence, the integration of various components plays one of the most important steps of the microservice solution development.

## What to Avoid During Integration?

The intent of this chapter is to guide you through the integration nuances of microservices. But every time we make a decision for integration, we will have to ensure that we do it in a graceful manner and make the coupling (tight or loose) as per our need. Unless we are making a conscious effort to keep the DO-NOTs out of the solution, chances are that they will creep in. So, what are these common mistakes that we are talking about? The common mistakes that we need to avoid are as follows:

- Overcomplicating the communication design
- Losing sight of timeouts for the asynchronous requests
- Over-compensating the lack of atomic transactions

These are the 3 problems that usually creep into our design when we lose focus of the source of the problem. Then we try to create solutions based on the effects they see rather than getting to the root of a problem. In the upcoming sections, when we discuss, the different types of integration we will also discuss, how we can get things wrong.

## Sample Business Case

To help you walk through the various concepts of integration and testing, let us first look into the sample business case of a *Hotel Aggregator Solution*. A hotel aggregator solution, is one that gives the choice to select a hotel amongst many, that falls within your set criteria, manages your booking and cancellations. The USP of such platforms is basically, the comparison between many hotels that may match your criteria, competitive pricing, and membership benefits.

Such a solution, in the real world, would have a great number of microservices for proper functioning. However, for the sake of simplicity, let us pick up a couple of possible services such as the following:-

- **User Management:** This service will handle users who are either hotel admins or guests . Hotels can add locations, rooms, pictures, facilities, and pricing. Guest registration should only take the basic user details and preferences for sake of offers.

- **Authentication and Authorization:** This service will help a user to log in, log out, manage accounts. For hotel admin, this will also give them access to booking, cancellations, communications that have been made specific to a booking.

- **Booking and Cancellation:** This service helps guest book a room and choose a payment mode and make payment. Guest can also cancel or modify the booking from this service and make a special request. The refunds too will be handled by this service.

- **Search:** This is the most important service for the platform, as this will be the most used service by any visitor. This service is meant to search across thousands of hotels that match the search criteria set by the visitor.

- **Membership:** This service is meant to manage user membership privileges like points, profile, offers, coupons, special packages, and so on.

- **Notification and Alerts:** This is another service that will be widely used. This service is meant to manage all notifications that are sent to guests and hotels for booking and cancellations.

The concepts of integration and testing in this chapter and Chapter 9 will be explained based on the above business case.

## Synchronous (Request-Response) Communication via RESTful HTTP Requests

The basic idea of integration in microservices is that the composing services should talk to each other in a timely manner. But before we get into the technicality of the integration, let us understand the three core concepts of this type of integration. These are as follows:

- Synchronous
- Request-Response
- Restful HTTP

When we call something synchronous, we basically mean something that occurs in exact time or at a regular interval or in the defined order. Thus, synchronous communication would translate to communication that occurs as per the defined order by the business process at a real time.

Request-response communication means every message sent will be acknowledged by the recipient in an agreed form and in a timely manner. Thus, for each message sent, the sender too will receive a message from the recipient which clearly states the success/failure of the event.

Restful HTTP is the architectural style that leverages the power of HTTP verbs and uniform service locaters. Thus, with RESTful HTTP the best of both the architectures are leveraged as follows:

- The statelessness of HTTP ensures, that the server will not remember all the requests made to it.
- The HTTP verbs like GET, PUT, POST, DELETE ensures targeted actions. Thus, specific operational needs could be achieved without doing too much or too less.
- Multiple data exchange format helps to transfer information that is requested by the client, in a format that their system can support.
- Caching is easier to implement with RESTful services. Thus, it helps cut down the number of unique requests that are processed by the server.

Now, with the above keywords being clear, thus the first key concept of integration *Synchronous request-response(communication) via RESTful HTTP requests* seamlessly translates into the *ordered exchange of messages that are guided by the RESTful HTTP architectural styles.*

So, let us first see what such a message flow will look like, taking a scenario from the business case explained above.

A logged in user wants to book a hotel for 2 days. The steps he needs to follow are as follows:

1.  Select the hotel
2.  Select room type
3.  Confirm the dates
4.  Provide the following details:
    a.  Number of guests
    b.  Number of children
    c.  Number of rooms
    d.  Name of the guests
5.  Choose the payment mode
6.  Make the payment on the payment gateway
7.  On successful booking, guest sees the booking details on the screen
8.  On failure of booking, a refund process is initiated for the amount deducted if any in the failed transaction

In the above process, we see a very good scope to use the request - response integration pattern. Let us first see the flow.

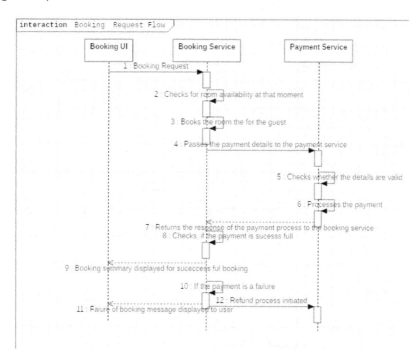

In the above flow, it is required that the booking process waits for the payment process to complete and provide a status (success/failure) as it will show a message based on the outcome. Since it is a transactional process, thus it is necessary for the user to know the outcome of the transaction. Thus, this type of business flow is very apt for request-response communication.

For the RESTful HTTP part, since this would be a transaction-based interaction, it will necessarily be using a secured channel like HTTPS. The use of restful architecture is necessary, as transaction parameters need to be secured and hence a post request if most apt for this. Whether JSON or XML content will be interchanged that completely depends on the integration principles of the payment gateway and the networks they are working with.

## Asynchronous Communication (Event-Driven) via Azure Service Bus

We have discussed synchronous communication above. Now, it is time to understand what asynchronous communication is and why do we need it?

Let us extend our above use case a little bit so that now it looks something like this:

- Select the hotel
- Select room type
- Confirm the dates
- Provide the following details:
    o Number of guests
    o Number of children
    o Number of rooms
    o Name of the guests
- Choose the payment mode
- Make the payment
- On successful booking:
    o a confirmation email is sent to the guest with hotel details and invoice
    o a summary of the booking is sent to the guest via SMS
    o a booking email is sent to the hotel with booking details along with the special request made by the guest
    o 1000 points are added to the customer profile that can be redeemed in the next booking
- On failure of booking:
    o a notification email is sent to the guest with details of the failed transaction
    o a refund process is initiated for the failed transaction

In the above process, we see a very good scope to use the asynchronous pattern. In our above use case, the three main services that would come be amongst each other are as follows:

- Booking Service
- Notification Service

- Membership Service

While Booking Service will be interacting with the Payment Services in a synchronous manner, the interaction with the Notification and Membership Service must be in Asynchronous. So, how do we identify which of these 3 services will be Asynchronous ? Let's break the problem down:

- When a user makes a booking and initiates payment, then request to the payment service must be atomic, it should be secure, and the scope of the program should be back to the user within a very short span of time, as the user will want to know the outcome of the transaction. Based, on the above criteria, the synchronous communication seems apt.

- For the notification (email or SMS) service, the following things need to be considered:

  o The notification is different for the different outcome. So, on success, two emails are supposed to be sent, one to a guest, one to a hotel and an SMS is sent to the guest with the summary.

  o On failure, only a single notification is sent to the guest with the details of the failed transaction.

  o Neither email or SMS will be opened within the application. These will be delivered to the email address and mobile number registered with the solution.

  o Emails and SMS in bulk are normally not sent from a web application, as the protocols used are different, SMTP and the likes of SMPP for email and SMS respectively.

  o The primary services of the solution should not be affected by the performance or the delays of the Notification system.

- The membership service needs to add up points and need not be updated right away. It could be run periodically, and update membership points based on the transactions done during the period.

Thus, we can understand that we:

- Do not want the guest to be waiting for the *booking successful* only after email / SMS is sent.

- We don't want the failure of notification, result in timeout error for the Guest.

- The guest can be alerted of the additional points added after some time.

Based on this we can easily deduce that we can use asynchronous communication. Now, it needs to be seen what type of communication best suits it. As we are using Azure Services in all our previous samples, we find that Azure service bus provides a very seamless solution to the problem we have in hand. Before REST based we understand how Azure Service Bus solves the problem, let us get an overview of what is Azure Service Bus?

Azure supports 2 types of queue mechanism that can support messaging between application and service. These are storage queues and service bus queues. The storage queues are part of storage infrastructure, uses REST-based GET/PUT/PEEK interface and provides a reliable messaging interface. On the other hand, Service Bus queues are part of a broader Azure messaging infrastructure and support queuing as well as publish/subscribe and more advanced integration patterns. (ref- https://docs.microsoft.com/en-us/azure/service-bus-messaging/service-bus -azure-and-service-bus-queues-compared-contrasted)

In our problem, we see the opportunity of using the publish/subscribe model that works well with the event-driven functionality. The following sequence diagram shows the flow of the events:

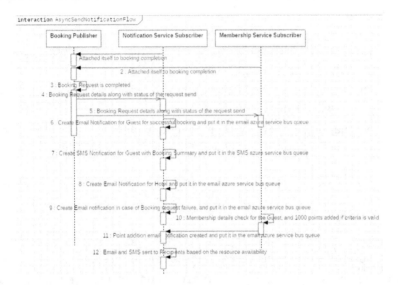

Now the question is *"Why Azure Service Bus?"*, seems relevant here. And the answer to this is as follows:

Microsoft Azure Service Bus is a fully managed enterprise integration message broker. It is commonly used where we need to decouple applications and services from each other. The reliability of the Service Bus as the secure platform for asynchronous data and state transfer is a big clincher where we are looking for high availability without any comprises. Since message exchange is at the core of the Service Bus, data exchange between different applications and services using messages becomes easier, faster and without any comprises. Again, the message in binary format supports JSON, XML, or just text.

When we say that we will use Azure Service Bus Queues, we mean the following:

- Notification Service is attached to Booking Service that has published an event for the booking completion.
- Once a booking is completed, the notification service receives all the data it needs for the email / SMS notification.

- The service in the first part does the following:
  o  Chooses the appropriate email template
  o  Creates the email message
  o  Places the message in the email queue
  o  Chooses the SMS template
  o  Creates the SMS
  o  Places the message in the SMS queue
- The service in the second part does the following:
  o  Checks the email waiting in the queue and sends them out in FIFO order
  o  Checks the SMS waiting in the queue and sends them out in FIFO order
  o  Since the email and SMS queue is independent, it does not matter if one of the processes fails or is not completed
- The Service Bus for the membership can also use a technique called Client Batching, and run only once a day, and send out all membership-based email once at the end of the day.

Azure Service Bus is robust and explaining the entire thing is beyond the scope of this book, however, this could be a great place to start with.

Please follow the given link:

https://docs.microsoft.com/en-us/azure/service-bus-messaging/service-bus-messaging-overview

## Circuit Breaker

In every household, we have a fuse in our main and whenever we are drawing too much of electricity like using geyser, microwave, motors altogether, the fuse tends to trip. In the process, it ensures that our electronics do not get damaged due to sudden power fluctuation and saves us from major accidents. For a solution based on microservices, each component is constantly making remote calls to another component for its processing. For some reason, if one of the components is failing for some reason and other components keep making calls to the failing component, requests that it cannot process will be queued up and will slowly but surely drain it and make it crash. Which may result in other components come crashing down. So, how to stop it? Here is where the Circuit Breaker pattern comes to picture. In other words, the Circuit Breaker Pattern ensures that:

- The service is not naked and has a wrapper.
- The calls to the service are made through the wrapper.
- A threshold limit is set for the failure count for the service.
- The failures are constantly monitored.
- On reaching the threshold limit, all calls to the service is automatically routed to a default error handler.

While there are available frameworks like Polly to implement circuit breaker, it is better to understand what happens in a circuit breaker under the hood. In a circuit breaker, three unique states are identified. These are as follows:

- **Closed:** Under normal conditions, the circuit breaker remains in the closed state. All calls pass through to the services. Now, if the services start failing and the number of failures exceeds a predetermined limit, the breaker trips, and it moves into the Open state.

- **Open:** The circuit breaker returns an error for the calls without executing the function.

- **Half-Open:** After a timeout period that is defined at the initialization, the circuit temporarily switches to a half-open state. This is to check whether the problem still exists. In this state, even if a single call fails, a breaker is once again tripped and again it waits for the timeout period. If it succeeds, the circuit breaker resets back to the normal, closed state and calls are again directed to the services.

The flow between the states looks like this:

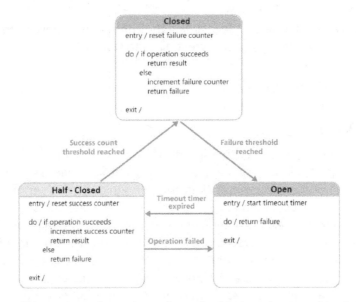

*(ref - https://docs.microsoft.com/en-us/azure/architecture/patterns/circuit-breaker)*

In our problem case, we can assume that the Payment Service will be one of the most critical services and since payment service has a financial impact on the guest, it is judicious to ensure that the failure of this service is monitored, and the circuit break pattern can be easily implemented for this scenario. As mentioned earlier, while we may easily switch to one of the popular frameworks, we can implement a much simpler version like available in the sample.

## Communication Between Services

By now it is well understood that, with microservices, we are trying to separate the features as individual and self-sustaining units of deployment. But while the functions are individually complete and independent, for the sake of business process and solution completeness, these features need to talk to each other. Thus, inter-service communication becomes critical. But as soon as we decide on communication, we need to understand that if done badly, communication can completely bring down the application.

When we are looking for a solution to our communication needs between service, we need to take a scope of the following:

- **Coupling:** whether the communication needs to be loosely or tightly coupled
- **Concise:** how much or how little of the information needs to be exposed
- **Contemporary:** how soon or how late can the messages be sent

Since communication is one of the most important parts of microservices, it is advised that it is better to weigh the options that are available. While trying to pinpoint communications style between services, it should be noted that:

- Understand the criticality of the message between 2 services at a time
- Do not expect a blanket solution
- Target one problem at a time

As discussed earlier, one could choose between synchronous and asynchronous. But these two are at a very high level. Leveraging the power of HTTP and RESTful is critical. It is also advised to leverage the power of the platform one is using. Thus, if you are already using MS Azure, then this itself is a powerful platform that has inbuilt capabilities that can help create reliable and highly available microservices solution.

## Styles of Collaboration

When we want to design collaboration between our services, there are two main ways of doing it. These are as follows:

- Collaboration by request
- Collaboration by event

So, how do they differ? Let us re-look at our Notification Service in terms of these two styles of collaboration.

So, we want to send an email to the guest when the booking is successful and another to the hotel. While on booking failure, we send an email only to the guest.

The above collaboration will look something like the flow shown in the diagram below if we choose to collaborate via request:

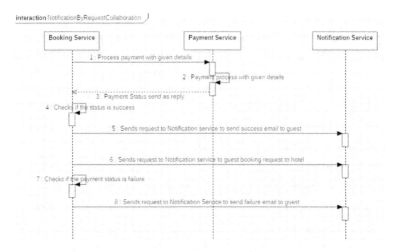

But the same flow will look something different if we choose to use Event Collaboration:

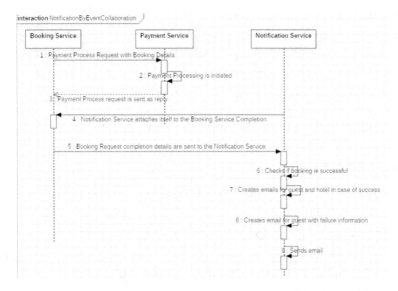

Now, if we compare the two diagrams, we see that the for-request collaboration the responsibility to get the flow going rests on the Booking Service for event collaboration it shifts completely to Notification Service.

So how do we decide whether to use request collaboration or event collaboration? For our given sample, we can choose to ask ourselves questions like:

- Will the workflow of the Request may change at any point in time? If yes, i.e. if additional logic needs to be incorporated to decide the notification type, content or count, then it is better to be done by request collaboration. Then we can make changes to a single service.

- If the number of notification handlers can increase, or notification increases, it is better to use event collaboration. In that case, you will be able to get going just subscribing to additional events published.

Event collaboration comes with the additional segregation of commands and queries. We will explore these a little later in the chapter.

## Integration Patterns

Like any software development problems, integration too comes with a predefined set of challenges and some of them are very common. To solve those recurring problems, a set of integration patterns have been identified. A brief walkthrough of those patterns is given as follows:

- **API Gateway:** The API gateway is an implementation of **Backend for Frontend (BFF)**, a pattern conceived by Sam Newman. The gateway in this pattern acts as a proxy between client applications and services. MS Azure has Azure API management that can be used as the API gateway. The gateway will - accept API calls and then route them to the respective backends, will verify API keys, JWT tokens, and certificates, supports Auth through Azure AD and the OAuth 2.0 access token. It also manages and enforces usage quotas and rate limits thus help in transforming APIs on the fly without code modifications Azure API management also manages the Caching of the backend responses wherever they are set to enhance the application performance and manages the Logging call metadata for analytics and MIS.

- **Event Driven:** In a microservices solution, if you have chosen to implement DB service, then it is important to keep the data in sync across the services else there may be inconsistencies that can be very harmful. Based on our problem case, the room prices are residing in the hotel services DB, while booking is done via Booking Service. So, if the booking service is not aware of the most recent room charges and applicable taxes, then booking may take place with old prices and the guest may have to face issues while check-in. For this, we will need something to notify the Booking Service, whenever the price changes or rooms are added. This concept of publishing your important events so that other services can perform actions accordingly is at the core of the event-driven pattern.

  Thus, if we choose to implement an event-driven pattern to solve our get current room rates for booking problem, we would do the following:

  Implement the Room Management Service in such a way, that it publishes an event whenever a service updates its charges or facilities. And the booking service (dependent service) will subscribe to this event. Now, whenever a booking service receives an event of the change of room rates and it updates its data. This way, our booking services can get and update their room rates repository as and when required.

- **Event Sourcing:** While event-driven pattern ensures that, the dependent services always subscribe to the published events that change the data they need, but how to ensure that the services have published events that one can subscribe to ? That is where the Event Sourcing comes into the picture.

Event Sourcing helps us to ensure that the service will publish an event whenever the state changes and there are services that depend on its change of state. In this pattern, a business entity like Room Charges can have a sequence of state-changing events. The Event Store will persist these events and all these events will be available for subscription or as other services. This pattern helps us simplify our tasks as the need to sync the data model and the business domain. Hence, effectively improving our application performance, scalability, and responsiveness. Event Sourcing Pattern is a guide to an approach on how we can handle the various operations on our data by a sequence of events; the events that are recorded in a store.

- **Eventual Consistency:** When we say Eventual consistency what we mean as an implementation of the data consistency approach. So why is data consistency suggested? Well if we need to scale up our system, we can still ensure that the system still has high availability. In our hotel aggregator problem, the search service is one of the best examples to use the eventual consistency. But first, let us break the problem down.

  o The hotels can register themselves and provide details of the following:
    - Room Types
    - Number of rooms
    - Prices
    - Facilities
    - Location
    - Offers

  o The searchable hotel information is made available to search services

  o Now during the peak season, the number of visitors on the search services can go up considerably

  o To handle the additional visitors the search services may have to scale up

For the above situation, while there is no textbook that will say that this problem needs some type of consistency. But when we need to implement a system that must be highly scalable and highly available, thus consistency can be the perfect strategy for such scenarios. But what type of consistency, Eventual or Strong?

Say now we have made multiple replicas of our search database that is highly indexed and has additional features to create a great search tool. Now due to high load, you decide to replicate the databases. Now, one of the databases is updated and we must replicate the change across all the replicas.

If we choose to go by eventual consistency then, the sync process across all the databases will happen eventually, however, state of data differs amongst the different DB. Thus, we can say that with eventual consistency we get stale data as a trade-off for low latency hence high availability.

Now for data-critical applications, stale data may not be an option. Under such circumstances, strong consistency should drive your sync process. On the other hand, with strong consistency, it means, whenever data changes in a single DB, the write request to all DB replicas are to be made one after another. The access to DB during this period is denied. A ll additional read-write requests that are not part of replication to any of the databases get delayed. Thus, we can say that with the strong consistency we get the latest data as a tradeoff for high latency. Thus, high reliability comes at the price of lower availability.

The choice amongst these two types of consistencies is completely driven by the domain for which the application is being built.

- **Compensating transactions:** In a monolithic application with single DB, we understand the concept of when to implement cascading rollback. But for a microservices application with distributed database similar rollback is not easy to implement and one must strategize the rollback. This is where Compensating transactions comes into the picture. It provides a way to roll back or undo all the tasks that have been performed in a series of steps.

  When one or more services have implemented operations in a series and one or more of them have failed, the logical next step would be to revert all the changes by retracing the path or choose to come to the state from where a different flow of the program could be traversed to. In our problem, when a guest books a room, the **BookingService** marks the room as booked temporarily. Only after the confirmation of the payment process completion and booking completion, **BookingService** calls the **HotelService** to mark the room as booked. And if the payment process fails, then the **HotelService** is called to change the state of the room back to available.

- **Competing Consumers:** Let us understand the problem when an application is running in the cloud. Since it is expected to handle many requests, requests are normally processed asynchronously. This is normally achieved, send the requests through something like a messaging service. With an increase in the number of requests from multiple tenants can lead to an unpredictable workload. This additional workload needs to be balanced across clients/consumers to prevent an instance from becoming/having a bottleneck. The solution to the problem, where the clients are competing for the resources, is message queue. With message queues, we implement a communication channel between the application and the instances of the consumer service. The application pushes the requests in the form of messages to the message queue. The consumer service instances then receive these messages from the queue and process them as per need. This solution helps eliminate instance specific dependency. The pool of consumer service instances can pick and process messages from any instance of the application. Again, with proper implementation, the same message is still available in the queue unless all instances process it. The things that one should keep an eye on, are the message ordering and message reliability.

MS Azure has created a very reliable messaging platform that supports two types of queues. These are as follows:

o   Azure Service Bus

o   Azure Queues

We will explain these in the next section.

## Azure Service Bus

We have already mentioned about publisher-subscriber model. Based on our problem case, we have also explained the need for this event-driven pattern, how and when the services need to publish and subscribe for events. For a small application, we can normally create a something in line with an **EventManager** say **NotificationEventManager**. But let us now try to understand that how the robustness of Azure Service Bus helps us to manage the events and creates a hassle-free microservices platform.

If we want to come up with a very simple definition of Azure Service Bus, we can quote from Gaurav Aroraa's book Building Microservices from .Net Core 2.0 that, *"Azure Service Bus is an information delivery service. It is used to make communication easier between two or more components/services."*

For our Hotel Aggregator Platform, whenever the services like Booking, Hotel Management, Payment, Notification or Membership needs to communicate to one another, they will use Azure Service Bus. Within Azure Service Bus, there are two types of communications supported. These are as follows:

**Brokered Communication or Hired service:** This type of communication is simple; the sender sends the message and the message is delivered in the queue allotted for the recipient. The recipient picks up the message as and when it is available. This completely removes the need for both the sender and the recipient to be online at the same time to send or receive a message. The messaging platform has components like queues, topics and subscription. In our problem, notifications to the guest and the hotel could easily use a brokered communication. For brokered communication, the available components are but the choice of using what depends completely on the problem that we want to resolve. An overview of the components are as follows:

- **Queues:** These are for one-directional communication and act as brokers. The messages are pushed into queues and wait till they are picked by the consumers.

- **Topics:** These too provide one-directional communication where a single topic can have multiple subscriptions. That is, one message may need to go to multiple recipients.

- **Relays:** These provide bi-directional communication flow. They do not store messages (as queues and topics do) but provides a channel to pass messages to the destination application.

**Non-brokered communication:** This is the real-time communication, requires all the participants to be online at the same point of time. The caller calls but it depends on the availability of the receiver whether to receive the call or not. If it receives the call, it will process the call else the caller may attempt a recall. This process may continue a certain number of times based on the criticality. In our problem, the payment process should be implemented via non-brokered communication. This way it can be ensured that the transaction happens successfully else it does not happen.

## Azure Messaging Queue

Azure queues are simply the cloud storage accounts that uses Azure Tables for message or data storage. They provide a way to queue a message between applications. Since it is a simple data structure, it follows the FIFO method, thus the message that goes in first is retrieved first. The messaging concept is simple - a sender sends the message and a client receives it and then processes it. Messages may come with additional attributes attached to them. For example, expiry time is an attribute of the message that is often used. After it is set, the message waiting in the queue will expire at what is set as the expiration time.

Thus, in this chapter, we have taken a sample solution of that of a Hotel Aggregator and introduced to the various concepts of integration and how to identify what fits in a problem and how to identify and map problem introduced due to distributed environment and resolved via integration patterns. We have also identified the things that we need to watch while trying to come up with a solution. Before, we conclude we must remember that no solution can be universal. But common problems have common and tested solutions. Thus, we need to identify the appropriate integration pattern that best suits your needs.

## Summary

In this chapter, you learned to integrate services using a synchronous approach via RESTful APIs using ASP.NET Core and learn asynchronous messaging patterns and techniques using Azure Service Bus. Additionally, they will understand the advantages and limitations of the two approaches and how to make the right choice depending on various scenarios.

API Management is the best bet when it is the case of RESTful services, in the next chapter you will see the complete hands-on integration with API Management.

# CHAPTER 8

# Hands on Integration with API Management

## API Management

The role of API Management in hosting APIs to external, partner, and internal developers to reveal the potential of their data and services. Companies everywhere are looking to extend their operations as a digital platform, creating new channels, finding new customers and driving more in-depth engagement with existing customers. API Management provides the core competencies to assure a successful API program through developer engagement, insights, security, analytics and protection. You can opt for Azure API Management to take any backend system and launch an entire API program based on it.

This chapter offers an overview of common scenarios that involve API Management. It also gives a concise summary of the API Management system's main components. The chapter, then, offers a more comprehensive overview of each module.

## Overview

Administrators create APIs to use API Management. Each API consists of one or more methods, and each API can be attached to one or more services. To use an API, developers need to subscribe to a service that holds that API, and then they can call the API's methods, subject to any usage policies that may be an impact. Common situations include:

- **Securing mobile infrastructure** by gating permission with API keys, preventing DOS attacks by using throttling, or using advanced security policies such as JWT token validation.
- **Allowing ISV partner ecosystems** by giving fast partner onboarding through the developer portal and creating an API facade to decouple from own implementations that are not available for client consumption.
- **Performing an internal API program** by allowing a centralized location for the companies to inform about the availability and latest modifications to APIs, gating access based on organizational accounts, all based on a secured channel within the API gateway and the backend.

The system is created with the following components:

- The API gateway is the endpoint that describes:
  - o  Accepts API requests and routes them to backends

- o    Verifies API keys, certificates, JWT tokens and other credentials
- o    Supports usage quotas and rate limits
- o    Changes your API on the runtime without code modifications
- o    Caches backend responses where set up
- o    Logs metadata requests for analytics objectives
- The Azure portal is an administrative interface where you configure your API program. And use it to:
  - o    Determine or import API schema
  - o    Package APIs into products
  - o    Configure policies like quotas or transformations on the APIs
  - o    Get insights from analytics
  - o    Manage users
- The Developer portal serves as the primary web presence for developers, where they can:
  - o    Read API documentation
  - o    Create an account and subscribe to get API keys
  - o    Access analytics on their usage

# Offloading

Use the gateway to offload functionality from each services to the gateway, particularly cross-cutting concerns. It is recommended to consolidate these functions into one place, rather than to make every service responsible for implementing them. This is particularly true for features that require specialized skills to perform correctly, such as authentication and authorization.

Following are few examples of functionality that could be offloaded to a gateway:

- Authentication
- SSL termination
- IP whitelisting
- Throttling
- Logging and monitoring
- Response caching
- Web application firewall
- GZIP compression
- Servicing static content

Offload is a specialized service functionality to the gateway proxy. This pattern can explain application development by leading shared service functionality, such as the use of SSL certificates, from different parts of the application into the gateway.

## Context and Problem

Some characteristics are commonly used across various services, and these features need configuration, management, and maintenance. A specialized service that is shared with every application deployment develops the administrative overhead and increases the possibility of a deployment error. Any updates to a shared characteristic need to be deployed overall services that share the same feature.

Properly managing security issues e.g. token validation, SSL, encryption certificate management, and other complex tasks can expect team members to have extremely specialized skills. For example, a certificate required by an application should be configured and deployed on all application instances. With every new deployment, the certificate must be managed to guarantee that it does not expire. Any general certificate that is overdue to expire must be updated, verified, and tested on each application deployment.

Other shared services e.g. authentication, authorization, monitoring, logging or throttling can be challenging to implement and run across a large number of deployments. It is better to incorporate this type of functionality, in order to decrease overhead and the risk of errors.

## Solution

Offload few of the features into an API gateway, especially cross-cutting concerns such as certificate management, SSL termination, authentication, protocol translation, monitoring or throttling.

Following diagram presents an API gateway that eliminates inbound SSL connections. It requests data on behalf of the initial requestor from any HTTP server upstream of the API gateway.

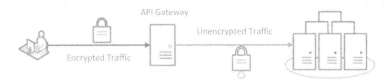

*<<image reference https://docs.microsoft.com/en-us/azure/architecture/patterns/gateway-offloading >>*

Benefits of this pattern include the following:

- Clarify the development of services by removing the requirement to distribute and keep supporting resources, like web server certificates and set up for secure websites. Easier configuration results in simpler management and scalability and offers service upgrades easier.
- Provide dedicated teams to achieve features that require functional

expertise, such as security. This allows your core team to concentrate on the application functionality, leaving these functional but cross-cutting concerns to the appropriate experts.

- Give some agreement for request and response logging and monitoring. Even if a service is not perfectly instrumented, the gateway can be configured to guarantee a minimum level of monitoring and logging.

## Issues and Considerations

- Assure the API gateway is highly available and flexible to failure. Bypass single points of failure by managing many occurrences of your API gateway.
- Assure the gateway is created for the capacity and scaling demands of your application and endpoints. Ensure the gateway does not become a bottleneck for the application and is adequately scalable.
- Only offload characteristics that are used by the whole application, such as security or data transfer.
- Business logic should never be offloaded to the API gateway.
- If you want to trace transactions, think generating correlation IDs for logging purposes.

## When to Use this Pattern

Use this pattern when:

- Deployment has a shared interest such as SSL certificates or encryption.
- A point that is common across application deployments that may have another resource requirement, such as memory resources, network connections or storage capacity.
- You want to move the liability for issues such as network security, throttling, or other network boundary matters to a more specific team.

This pattern may not be suitable if it includes coupling across services.

## Routing

Route requests to different services using a single endpoint. This pattern is helpful when you need to expose many services on a single endpoint and route to the relevant service based on the request call.

## Context and Problem

When a client requires to use multiple services, setting up a separate endpoint for each service and ask the client to manage each endpoint can be difficult. For example, a HotelBooking application provide services such as search, reviews, facilities , booking, and book history. Each service has a separate API that the client must communicate with, and the client must remember each endpoint in order to connect to the services. If an API modifications are done, the client must be updated as well. If later there is a need to refactor a service into two or more separate services, the code must be updated in both the service and the client.

## Solution

Add a gateway in front of a collection of services, applications or deployments. Apply application Layer 7 routing to route the call to the relevant services.

By using this pattern, the client application only requires to know about and interact with a single endpoint. If a service is merged or decayed, the client does not significantly require updating. It can continue making calls to the gateway, and only the routing changes.

A gateway also lets your difficult backend services from the clients, enabling you to keep client calls simple while allowing changes in the backend services, behind the gateway. Client requests can be routed to specific service or services want to handle the anticipated client behavior, enabling you to add, split, and restructure services behind the gateway without breaking the client.

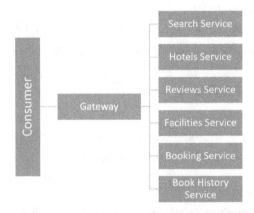

This pattern can further support with deployment, by providing you to control how updates are pushed out to users. Whenever a new version of your service is deployed, it can be implemented in parallel with the existing version. Routing lets you command what version of the service is offered to the clients, giving you the adaptability to use various release plans, whether incremental, parallel, or complete rollouts of updates. Any issues identified after the new service is deployed, can be immediately rollback by making a configuration change at the gateway, without touching clients.

## Issues and Considerations

- The gateway service may propose a single point of failure. Ensure it is appropriately created to meet your availability requirements. Think resiliency and fault tolerance capabilities when implementing.

- The gateway service may add a bottleneck. Assure the gateway has adequate performance to handle load and can quickly scale along with your growth expectations.

- Perform load testing on the gateway to guarantee you don't introduce cascading breakdowns for services.
- Gateway routing is level 7. It can be based on Port, IP, header, or URL.

## When to Use This Pattern

Make use of this pattern when

- Client needs to invoke multiple services that can be accessed behind a gateway.
- You want to clarify client applications by using a single endpoint.
- You need to route incoming calls from externally addressable endpoints to internal endpoints, like exposing ports on a VM to cluster virtual IP addresses.

This pattern may not be appropriate when you have a simple application that have only one or two services.

## Deploy to API Management

In Azure API Management, a product holds one or more APIs also usage quota and the terms of use. Once a product is published to the portal, developers can subscribe to the product and start the use of the product's APIs.

In this section, you will learn how to:

- Create and publish a product
- Add an API to the product

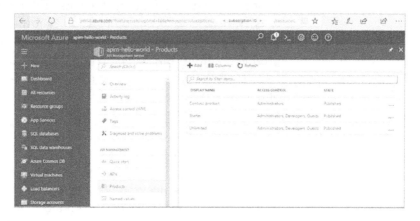

*Prerequisites*

- Complete the following steps: Create an Azure API Management instance.
- Also, complete the following steps: Import and publish your first API.

*Create and Publish a Product*

1. Click on **Products** in the menu on the left to represent the **Products** page.
2. Click on + **Add**.

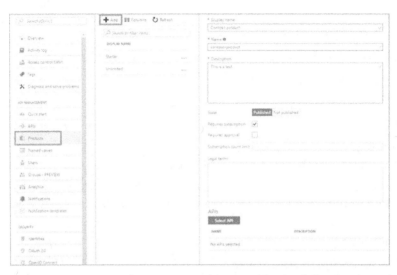

When you create a new product, you need to provide the following knowledge:

| Name | Description |
|---|---|
| Display Name | The name as you wish it to be displayed in the Developer portal. |
| Name | A specific name of the product. |
| Description | The Description field provides you to give detailed information about the product e.g. its purpose, the APIs it gives access to, and other helpful information. |
| State | Click on Published if you desire to publish the product. Before the APIs in a product can be requested, the product must be released. By default new products are not published, and are apparent only to the Administrators. |
| Requires subscription | Select Require subscription if a user is expected to subscribe to adopt the product. |
| Requires approval | Select Require approval if you need an administrator to review and take decision (Accept/Reject) while a user attempts to subscribe to this product. If the box is unchecked, subscription trials are auto-approved. |
| Subscription count limit | To limit the count of various concurrent subscriptions, enter the subscription limit. |
| Legal terms | You can add the terms of use for the product which subscribers must accept in order to use the product. |

## Add APIs to an Existing Product

Products are connections of one or more APIs. You can add various APIs and give them to developers over the developer portal. You can add an existing API through the product creation. You can also add an API to the product later, either from the Products **Settings** or while creating an API.

Developers should first subscribe to a product to gain access to the API. When they subscribe, they take a subscription key that is enough for any API in that product. If you built the APIM instance, you are an administrator then, so you are subscribed to each product by default.

1.   From the **Products** tab, select a product.
2.   Go to the **APIs** tab.
3.   Click on + **Add**.
4.   Choose an API and click on **Select**.

Add/modify subscribers to the product from the **Subscriptions** tab.

You can continue setting the product after saving it by selecting the **Settings** tab.

Define the visibility of a product for subscribers or guest from the **Access control** tab.

## Security and Load Balancing

The availability of the API gateway is primary aspect to ensuring the application availability. API gateway availability needs a load balancer that can offer flexibility to cope with faster changes in microservices, such as versioning and dynamically shifting scale. Furthermore, being exposed to the external network, the API gateway must be able to offer secure transportation and authentication, and different access policies for external clients and internal clients. On addition to this, the API gateway requires protection from DDoS attacks.

Azure API Management service will need to access the internal load-balancer through a VPN connection. This is how we're going to make sure that our backend API hosted on our VMs is never called (as it simply can't be reached externally). Only external connectivity with the backend API will be through the Azure API Management proxy.

To configure Load Balancing, open Azure PowerShell and run the following command:

```
Add-AzureInternalLoadBalancer -ServiceName "[cloud service
name]" -SubnetName "[subnet name]" -InternalLoadBalancerName
"[load-balancer name]" -StaticVNetIPAddress "[IP within
subnet]"
```

## Summary

In this chapter you learned about Azure API management, need of it and other benefits of API management such as offloading, routing, deployment, security, and load balancing.

In coming chapter, we will discuss about Testing strategies of microservices in details and then we will go in details discussion of different types of testing with test driven development.

# CHAPTER 9

# Testing Microservices

In the previous chapters, we have have been introduced to both the development and integration concepts. We started with the whats and hows of the microservice architecture, its building blocks, its strengths and features that define it. We also took up sample use cases and started working on a sample microservice solution. Then we walked through the integration decisions that we need to take. These steps help you to create a complete microservices solution. So do we directly deploy it? *NO*. Of course not. Like any other software, it has to be tested. So does the switch from monolithic or SOA to microservices, change the testing guidelines for us?

In today's chapter, I will walk you through the testing steps of the microservices as a single component and also as an application. I will start with the basics of testing guidelines and then work through the different types of testing that we may have to perform and then finally testing the application as a whole. But let's start with why integration is important? You will see the examples based on a business case. This chapter will highlight the following topics:

- Importance of the testing in microservices based applications
- What are the types of testing that we may need
- TDD
- Test Strategy
- Unit Testing
- Component Testing
- Integration Testing
- End to End Testing
- Performance Testing

## Why is Testing Important?

Testing of any solution is important in order to confirm whether the solution delivers what it promises. As the intent of the application is set, before it is developed, an application is tested to verify the following:

- Are the promised features working as per expectations?
- Is the application flow consistent with the expectations set?
- What happens when an additional load is given to the system?
- How easily does the application recover from the failure?

Depending on the criticality of the process handled and the complexity of the business flow, testing scope and strategy needs to be decided. For microservices, testing is critical. Since microservices are built as small but multiple services that can be deployed as a unit and may give the impression that testing of a monolithic application could be replicated for each of the services. But that would be a big NO. As this will leave out big chunks of untestable code. The challenges that microservices poses are as follows:

- Microservices have multiple services that work together or individually, thus have varying degrees of complexity.
- Microservices are meant to target multiple clients; hence, they have more complex use cases.
- The architectural style of each component/service of the microservice is isolated and independent. Thus, they need to be tested individually and as a system.
- As independent teams working on separate components/services interact with each other. Hence testing thoroughness is dependent on both internal services but also external services.
- Each component/service in a microservice may work independently but may have to access shared resources and each service is responsible for modifying its own database.

## Sample Business Case

To help you walk through the various concepts of testing, we will be using the same sample business case of a *Hotel Aggregator Solution from chapter 7*. The business case of the solution is given as follows:

A hotel aggregator solution, is the one that gives the choice to select a hotel amongst many, that falls within your set criteria, manages your booking and cancellations. The USP of such platforms is basically, the comparison between many hotels that may match your criteria, competitive pricing, and membership benefits.

Such a solution, in the real world, would have a great number of microservices for proper functioning. However, for the sake of simplicity, let us pick up a couple of possible services such as the following:

- **User Management:** This service will handle users who are either hotels or guests. Hotels can add locations, rooms, pictures, facilities, and pricing. Guest registration only should take basic user details and preferences for the sake of personalizing offers.
- **Authentication and Authorization:** This service will help user login, logout, manage accounts. For hotel admin, this will also give them access to booking, cancellations, communications that have been made specific to a booking.
- **Booking and Cancellation:** This service helps guest book a room and choose a payment mode and make payment. Guest can also cancel or modify the

booking from this service and make a special request. The refunds too will be handled by this service.

- **Search:** This is the most important service for the platform, as this will be the most used service by any visitor. This service is meant to search across 1000s of hotels that meets the search criteria set by the visitor.

- **Membership:** This service is meant to manage the user membership privileges like points, profile, offers, coupons, special packages, and so on.

- **Notification and Alerts:** This is another service that will be widely used. This service is meant to manage all notifications that are sent to guests and hotels for booking and cancellations.

Now, let us look at how the given business case that has been developed as a microservice solution, can be tested.

## Types of Testing that We Need

As microservices is a cluster of services that work together to deliver a functionality, thus we need to test the services both individually and as a group. But at the end of the day, microservices is a software and will have the same set of expectation from any other software. The universal guideline for end to end testing of software is represented by V-Model with the side note that not all the steps are mandatory for all types of software. So, what is V-Model? V-Model is a diagrammatic representation, indicating the type of testing is required to test something. Often known as the Verification and Validation model, in its basic form it looks like this:

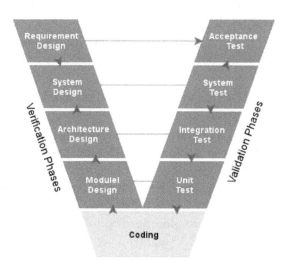

*Figure 1: PC - www.professionalqa.com*

As stated earlier, not all types of testing are important for all solutions, but what type of testing will be conducted, completely depends on the development methodology and the test strategy that has been finalized.

## Test-Driven Development or TDD

As defined by Wikipedia, **Test-driven development (TDD)** is a software development process that relies on the repetition of a very short development cycle: requirements are turned into very specific test cases, then the software is improved to pass the new tests, only."

So, what does that mean? Well, it simply means that, for each specific use case, we would write only the code that helps us pass the tests and no more. To explain it further, let's first check the steps to achieve TDD. TDD development is the repetition of the following steps through the entire development and maintenance cycle. This we will achieve by mapping the steps with respect to our business case.

For the sake of simplicity let us take the simplest use case. A visitor on the aggregator platform can search a hotel by name, place but not together. When the search is to be conducted by name it will be a like search based on the number of characters that have been used for the matching but for search by place, it must match the exact place for the hotel.

Now, let us see how to go about implementing TDD for this use case, so this has basically two functions together. One is a like search by hotel name and another is an exact match for the location. So, the steps are as follows:

- **Step 1: Add a test:** We start with writing a test for the new feature of search. Since there are 2 use cases, we must write two different tests. The tests should define the function of search (or an improvement of the search function, if already existing) function and should be succinct. The developer should clearly understand the feature's specification and requirements. Thus, the developer should understand that:

  o Search by name, should return all hotels that match the characters anywhere in the name across locations. So, it could be one, many or none.

  o Search by location should return all hotels that are listed under that location. So, it could be one, many or none.

  Thorough understanding of the above use cases and user stories along with exception conditions are necessary. Since these are names, thus special characters should not be allowed. However, "&" or "-" and spaces could be part of a name. Thus, these characters should be allowed. The choice of testing framework could be anything that is suitable for the technology stack that is being used for the development. Thus, we see that the key differentiator between TDD tests and writing test cases for unit testing are that the former is written before development while later is after the development of the function. While the difference may seem subtle but is the key differentiator.

- **Step 2: Run all tests and see if the new one fails:** Once the new tests are written, all the tests are run once again, to check what fails and what not. It is excepted that any functionality that is dependent on existing functionality may fail. But, it would be judicious to check if the failing test fails because the new functionality is missing or because the test case itself is incorrect. Thus, we check whether search function breaks the login or the price calculation.

- **Step 3: Write some code:** The next step is to write some code that causes the test to pass. The code we write for the two search functions may not be the most perfect code, but at least it should help pass the test, even if it has been done in the most inelegant way. We will improve on it as per need in Step 5. That is acceptable because it will be improved and corrected in Step 5. At this point, the only purpose of writing the code is to pass the test. One should not write code beyond the need and just enough for the functionality that the test checks.

- **Step 4: Run tests:** The tests are re-run and checked if anything is failing. If a test fails, then they need to be corrected till the point that none of them fails.

- **Step 5: Refactor code:** Once the base version of the code is achieved that passes the test criteria, then all the

- **Repeat:** Run the steps again until the functionality is perfected.

The flow in TDD is shown in the diagram given as follows:

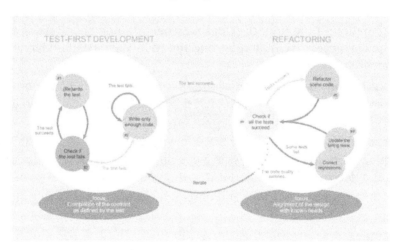

*Figure 2: PC - https://en.wikipedia.org/wiki/Test-driven_development*

## Test Strategy

A test strategy defines the approach for software testing that is required for the application. It is derived from the business requirement and takes into the scope of the domain of the application, compliances and industry-specific benchmarks, if any. Test strategy is created at the beginning of the project and mostly remains unchanged throughout the lifetime of the project. A standard test strategy will document the following:

- **Scope and objective:** The objective of the business and how much falls within the scope of testing.
- **Business Issues:** Budget of the project, the time required for testing, number of resources, infrastructure, and licensing needs falls under business issues and needs to be considered before the actual testing starts.
- **Testing approach:** What are the different types of testing that is needed (performance, load, stress, functional etc.) and whether the testing is only manual or automation or both are some of the crucial points which define the testing approach.
- **Test deliverables:** What are the different documents required from the testing team, how they would keep the record of the testing cycles etc. will be included here.
- **Defect tracking approach:** Tools that will be used for tracking the defects and guidelines the communication between the testing team and the development team and how the lifecycle of the defect is also determined at this stage.
- **Training:** If there is some complex or new tool is introduced in the business then it is helpful if the team members are given proper training. What type of training and the responsible person to conduct such training is defined here.
- **Automation:** If the project or business needs automation testing then the script language, tool used, reporting and code maintained is planned in test strategy.
- **Risks:** Nobody can anticipate all the risks beforehand, but obvious risks can be anticipated and can be avoided if planned properly. Also, solutions to those risks could be documented for future references.
- **Responsibility Matrix:** In any SDLC, everybody owns a responsibility. Test Strategy also clearly defines, who owns what and who is the authority to sign off at different levels.

The test strategy should include the description and guidelines to conduct the following:

- Unit tests
- Component tests
- Integration tests
- Contract tests
- End to end tests
- Performance tests

We will walk through each of these steps one by one in later sections.

## Unit Testing – Testing Each Unit of Development

The intent of Unit Testing is - *Unit tests exercise the small pieces of software such* as a function in the application to determine whether they produce the desired output given a set of known inputs.

It is worth noting that unit testing alone doesn't provide guarantees about the behavior of the system. But unit testing process ensures that the validation of the intent of each of functions written for the use cases. The basic guidelines for unit testing are to create simple test stubs for a simple feature. Test both the negative and the positive scenarios. Ensure all the paths of the program flow is tested. So, if a function has an if and else condition, create enough test stubs to test both the sections.

## Component Testing – Testing a Component as a Whole

Once the unit testing has been done thoroughly, then it is required to test the microservice in isolation. So, for an Identity Service, once the unit testing is completed. Then all the service needs to be tested in entirety. So, the following functions within the scope of identity service need to be tested one after another like the following:

- Logging in of the user
- Forgot password
- Password Reset
- Access to authorized modules
- Change password
- Logout

## Integration Testing – Testing the Multiple Components With Each Other

Once the component testing of the individual service is completed, as the next step it is required that the communication between two services needs to be verified. It is mandatory to check whether the two services are working together. Within this scope, we need to check the following:

- Whether the requests from one service is responded in a timely manner
- Is, there any accessibility issues?
- Does the environment need additional access?
- Is there any need to validate the source of the requests?

An integration test thus verifies the communication paths and interactions between components and helps identify interface defects. The calls to the service must be made with integration to external services, which should include error and success cases. This way the integration testing validates that the system is working together seamlessly and that the dependencies between the services are present as per expectation.

## Contract Testing – Testing What is Exposed Externally

Contract testing helps with verifying of the interactions at the boundary of an external service thus helps assert that the service meets the expectations of the contract expected by a consuming service. A service should be treated as a black box during contract testing. This type of testing should treat each service as a black box and all the services must be called independently and their responses must be verified.

A *contract* defines how a service call (where a specific result or output is expected for certain inputs) is referred to by the consumer contract testing. The idea is, if two consumers are consuming the same service and is developed as per the contract then response received from the service should be easily accepted by the calling service.

## End to End Testing – Testing the Application as a Whole

The role of end-to-end tests is to ensure everything ties together and there are no high-level inconsistencies between the microservices. End-to-end tests also help verify that a solution meets all the external requirements and achieves its goals, thus helps in testing the entire system, from end to end.

The tests also verify that the entire process, all the use cases and workflows correctly , inclusive of all the services and along with DB integration. Thorough testing of operations that affect multiple services ensures that the system works together as a whole and satisfies all the requirements.

## Performance Testing

The intent of the performance testing is to check whether the application performs as per expectation and delivers the capability under an expected workload. The outcome of the performance test is not that of getting errors as they have already been tested. The purpose is to identify the following:

- Threshold limits
- Speed
- Scalability
- Stability

For any solution, the idea is to have all the above parameters based on the industry benchmarks. If the application is not able to achieve it then there are different ways of boosting the performance like:

- Ramping up the infrastructure
- Moving resource or request intensive services to the individual or multiple servers
- Using load balancers
- Identifying queries that may result into bottlenecks and tweaking it
- Using cache and improving caching policies

Following are the different types of testing which fall within the scope of performance testing:

- **Load testing:** In this type of testing, we test the behavior of the system under various circumstances of a specific load. It also covers critical transactions, database load, application servers, and so on. With load testing, we can validate that an application with a given configuration of the server can efficiently handle the given load.

- **Stress testing:** In this approach, the system is put under regress testing to find the upper limit capacity of the system. The standard practice is that load benchmark achieved in load testing is used as a multiple increased till the application crashes.

  Let us help you understand with an example. Say from load testing we understand that the application can handle up to 1000 TPS (transaction per sec). So, for stress testing, first, the TPS is going to be increased to 2000, if it works fine then increased to 3000 and thus kept on increasing till it crashes at 6000 TPS. So, now we know that the application cannot handle a load of 6000 TPS but is able to handle a load of 5000 TPS. So, the maximum value lies between 5000 to 6000. Now, we can go ahead and put a load of 5500 TPS. If it succeeds, then the maximum TPS lies between 5500 to 6000. And, with the similar process you come to number, say 5625 TPS. But it is always advisable to keep around 15% of buffer and not stress the application in production with the value received from stress testing.

  It also determines how a system behaves in this critical situation when the current load goes above the expected maximum load.

- **Soak testing:** Also known as endurance testing, the purpose of this test is to monitor memory utilization, memory leaks, or various factors that affect the system performance.

- **Spike testing:** In this approach, we make sure that the system can sustain the urgent workload spikes. One of the best ways to determine performance is by suddenly increasing the user load all at once.

## Sociable Versus Isolated Unit Tests

Sociable unit tests contain concrete collaborators and cross boundaries. On the other hand, solitary tests are those that ensure the methods of a class are tested. Martin Fowler has explained very well at (https://martinfowler.com/bliki/UnitTest.html) regarding:

- **Sociable tests:** This is a test which confirms that the application is working as per our expectation. In this environment, other applications behave correctly, run smoothly, and produce the expected results. It also helps to test the functioning of new functions/methods, including other software for the same environment. Sociable tests may resemble system testing as these tests behave like system tests.

- **Isolated unit tests:** As the name suggests, you can use these tests to perform unit testing in an isolated way by performing stubbing and mocking. We can perform unit testing with a concrete class using stubs.

Let us take an example, our Search Service uses **HotelInfo** classes. Now, let's assume you want to test the **GetHotelDetails** method of the **HotelInfo** class. The **GetHotelDetails** method needs to invoke some functions on the **HotelDetail** and **AvailbaleForBooking** classes. If you intend to have unit tests that are solitary, you don't want to use the real **HotelDetail** or **AvailbaleForBooking** classes here, because a fault in either, would cause the **HotelInfo** class's tests to fail. Instead, we need to use **TestDoubles** for the collaborators. This practice is called isolated unit test. Again, had we chosen to use the actual of the **HotelDetail** and **AvailbaleForBooking** classes then it would be known as Sociable unit tests. Sociable unit tests are good when it is easy for you to segregate the exceptions of the tested from the exceptions of the testable class.

## Stubs and Mocks – When to Use What?

If you have done a quick search for the two words Stub and Mock you would have come across a definition like – *Stubs are returned, canned responses to calls made during the test; mocks are meant to set expectations.* What does it really mean? Well, here it is.

**Stubs:** Stubs are meant to return a stub object that is a valid response within the application scope. Thus, whatever be input to the stub, it will always return the same output. So, for our application, we may write a stub that will always return three hotels from Delhi. The stub definition could look something like the following code:

```
public class HotelInfo
    {
        public int HotelID { get; set; }
        public string HotelName { get; set; }
    }
    public interface IHotelManager
    {
        List<HotelInfo> GetHotelListForLocation(string
        location);
    }
    public class HotelManager : IHotelManager
    {
        public List<HotelInfo> GetHotelListForLocation
        (string location)
        {
            //Some complex business logic might goes here.
            May be DB operation
            return new List<HotelInfo>();
        }
    }
```

```
//Stub implementation to bypass actual Extension manager
class.
public class StubExtensionManager : IHotelManager
{
    public List<HotelInfo> GetHotelListForLocation
    (string location)
    {
        return new List<HotelInfo>() {
            new HotelInfo(){ HotelID = 100, HotelName =
            "Ma Sharda Business Suites"},
            new HotelInfo(){ HotelID = 101, HotelName =
            "Royal Getaway"}
        };
    }
}
```

**Mocks:** A mock object is nothing but a fake object in the system that helps us decide whether the unit test has passed or failed. It does so, by checking whether the object under test interacted as expected with the fake object. Usually, we do not write more than one mock per test. If it seems confusing, let us look at an example to check it.

```
public interface IServiceProvider
    {
        void searchService(String location);
    }
    //Mock extenison service provider
    public class MockSearchService : IServiceProvider
    {
        public string ErrorMessage = null;
        public void searchService(string location)
        {
            if (location.Contains("!") || location.
            Contains("@") ||
            location.Contains("#")
            || location.Contains("$") || location.
            Contains("%") |
            location.Contains("^")
            || location.Contains("*") || location.
            Contains("(") ||
            location.Contains(")"))
            {
                ErrorMessage = "Incorrect Location";
            }
        }
    }
    //Actual incomplete ExtensionManager functionality
```

```
public class SearchManager : IServiceProvider
{
    public void searchService(string location)
    {
        throw new NotImplementedException();
    }
}
public class SearchAnalyzer
{
    public IServiceProvider provider = null;
    public SearchAnalyzer(IServiceProvider tmpProvider)
    {
        provider = tmpProvider;
    }

    public void SearchCheck(string location)
    {
        provider.searchService(location);
    }
}
[TestClass]
public class MockTest
{
    [TestMethod]
    public void TestIncorrectLocationName()
    {
        //Act
        MockSearchService mockobject =
        new MockSearchService();
        //Inject mock object now
        SearchAnalyzer analyzer = new
        SearchAnalyzer(mockobject);
        //Action
        analyzer.SearchCheck("De$%");

        //Assert
        Assert.AreEqual(mockobject.ErrorMessage,
        "Incorrect Location");
    }
}
```

## Using Pact-Net-Core

In a consumer-driven test, our goal is to ensure that we test all the services, internal components, and services that depend on or communicate with other/ external services. Pact-net-core helps us achieve this. It is written in a way to guarantee that contracts would be met by all interfacing services.

Let us see how it helps us achieve our goal:

- The execution is very fast
- It helps identify failure causes
- It does not require a separate environment to manage automation test integration

To achieve your goals while working with Pact, there are two steps to it. These are as follows:

- **Defining expectations:** In the very first step, the consumer team needs to define the contract. Pact helps to record the consumer contract, which will be next verified when replayed.
- **Verifying expectations:** In the second step, the contract is shared with the provider team and then the provider service is implemented to fulfill the same. The replaying of a contract on the provider side to help fulfill the defined contract:

Consumer-driven contracts help mitigate the challenges of microservice architectures with the help of an open source tool called Pact-net.

## Managing All Tests – Tips No One Tells You

In this section, we will not be discussing the usual walk through of the test projects, but we will walk you through the steps to ensure that you have written tests for all the types of testing that have been identified in the test strategy.

So, here are the steps that need to be followed:

- **Setting up the environment:** In line with our development environment we can choose our testing environment and below is what we can use:
  - Visual Studio 2017 Update 3 or later
  - .NET Core 2.0
  - C# 7.0
  - ASP.NET Core 2.0
  - xUnit and MS tests
  - Moq framework
- **Project Structuring:** It is advised that since it is a microservice solution, thus each service has been created as a separated deployable unit i.e. as a separate project. Thus, the unit test cases for each service should also be separated from that of the other services and hence moved to an individual project. The advantages of such segregation are as follows:
  - The unit test project will only refer to one service and only include the references of this service and its dependencies, nothing else.
  - The naming conventions of the service project could be reused.
  - As the development team which worked on the service project, will be working on this, they will be easily able to identify the functionalities which are breaking due to certain changes.

o    Based on the complexity of the service, the guidelines to the test a service can completely be changed.

The project structure should look something like the following:

```
✓🗀 Solution 'Chapter9' (10 projects)
  ▷ +🗂 Booking.ComponentTests
  ▷ +🗂 Booking.Payment.IntegrationTests
  ▷ +🗂 Booking.PerformanceTests
  ▷ 🌐 Booking.Service
  ▷ +🗂 Booking.Service.UnitTests
  ▷ 🌐 Booking.UI
  ▷ +🗂 Booking.UI.UnitTests
  ▷ +🗂 Payment.PaymentGateway.ContractTest
  ▷ 🌐 Payment.Service
```

- **Stubs and Mocks:** The stubs could be created that could be reused as per Solution Architecture or Test Strategy. However, mocks will be more targeted and should be used to test out a certain functionality.
- Tips and Tricks on each type of testing:
  o    **Unit Testing:** When writing unit test cases, ensure that all the input parameters are tested along with all the possible paths that a program could take. A unit test case should also handle all the negative scenarios that are expected. For negative scenario testing, it is also to be checked whether the exceptions are gracefully handled, and a user gets some meaningful response and is not left dangling clueless. For unit testing of functions that are expecting data from external entities, at first, isolated unit testing should be performed with the help of stubs and later sociable unit testing should be performed.
  o    **Component Testing:** Within the unit testing project, component testing project can be included. However, they should run only after the unit tests have successfully passed. The aim of component testing is to cover and test all the business process workflows that are covered by the service.
  o    **Integration Testing:** For integration testing, again ensure that you create separate projects for each interaction flow. There are two ways to structure your integration test projects:
    ▪    **Group all the test cases for two or more services in one:** This means if we need to test the integration between our **IdentityService** and **MembershipService**, we write all the associated test cases in one project.

- **Group all test cases for a single flow in one:** This means that if we need to test the search functionality, then we group all the test cases in one project that may refer to multiple services.

  Whatever structuring guideline you may employ, ensure that any change in the main function, should be tested across with all the types of testing.

  o **Contract Testing:** For this type of testing, it is best to test a business flow and thus refer to all external services. The external services may share a sandbox URL that you may need to test with. The idea of the sandbox is that it exposes different types of interactions (request and response) in known contracts. Thus, you can check whether your application contracts are working with external APIs or not. In case of any issues, you may have to check the integration policies of the contracts exposed by the third party and take their help to resolve the issue, assuming no bugs have been identified within your program logic.

  o **End to End testing:** The end to end testing will ensure that all the layers of application and any external sources that alter the state of your data or system is thoroughly tested. In today's world, it is hard to test an application with a single tool. So, one may have to choose tools that effectively test each layer.

  o **Performance Testing:** This is best tested with automation testing. However, a single iteration of performance testing will not be of any help and you may have run multiple iterations and create numerous stubs. While performance testing of monolithic architecture results to change server configuration abruptly. But for microservices, it is advised to perform performance testing on individual services and plan their deployment accordingly. This way server could be selectively upgraded for more resource intensive application.

- **Continuous Integration:** Since microservices development mostly happens in a distributed team, it is always great to use a continuous integration tool like VSTS, Bamboo, CC.Net and to tweak the configuration to run all the tests before anyone can check in. This is a good way to confirm that changes do not cause a breaking build. If you are not using a tool per se , then creating a MSBuild file and run it with MSTest.exe with the set configurations is a good way to achieve it.

- **Iterations:** While testers work with the preset strategy, it is often hard for developers to come up with the exact iterations they need to test a piece of code. There is no hard and fast rule. If you have tested all traversal path of the program, it is fine. Again, the measure of complexity is another indicator. So, run the inbuilt complexity analysis tool and if the ratio of code to complexity is too high, it is good a have more than one iteration for that piece of code.

## Summary

In this chapter, we have tried to understand the importance of testing an application, different types of testing. We have also walk through the types of testing and what fits for microservices and how to plan the testing for your application. The aim of the application is to help you understand the importance of testing, its types, its nuances, and its do's and don'ts so that you can maximize your benefits from your testing efforts.

# CHAPTER 10

# Extending Application with Logging

In the previous chapters, we have been introduced to both the development, integration followed by the concepts of testing. We walked through microservice architecture, its building blocks, its strengths and features that define it. We also took up sample use cases and started working on a sample microservice solution. Then we walked through the integration decisions that we need to take. These steps help you create a complete microservices solution. Next we understood the importance of testing, how a test strategy helps, different types of testing that we may need to perform and tips about writing test cases. Thus, we are now ready with a solution that can be assumed to be ready for the deployment. But are we missing something. It is a big YES. While a code may be ready feature wise, but we also have to do couple of things that helps us monitor and manage the application when it goes live.

In this chapter, I will walk you through the different types of logging, tools and of course some tips and tricks to do things better. I will start with the basics of logging guidelines and then work through the different types of logging that we may have to perform and then finally logging through various tools that are available for microservices inlcuding one by Azure. But let's start with why logging is important? You will see the examples based on a business case. This chapter will highlight the following topics:

- Importance of logging/monitoring
- Instrumentation and telemetry
- Azure diagnostics
- Azure storage
- Logging techniques and implementations (Elmah, NLog, Log4Net)
- Circuit breaker
- Possible topics: Azure API Management
- A brief overview of the ELK stack

## Why is Logging Important?

Let us assume that it is almost 1 month to the peak of the holiday season. And based on the last year booking details, people are bound to start planning and booking the holidays. To beat the prices of a competition, the company has decided to give 20% off on all the bookings for the next 3 days. So, the expected thing happens. A record number of visitors start booking on the application. But the application starts crashing after first 3 hours.

- How do the system adiministrator find out that the application is crashing?
- How will the maintenance team understand what is the root of the problems?
- How will the developers identify the exact piece of code that may be causing the issue?

Now, you may think that some of the customers may inform the team, but since the site is already crashing, there is no point in visiting the site and of course customer care on the phone will not have the right option for you to log this issue. So, what could be done?

Well, the answer to this is *Logging*. To help you walk through the various concepts of logging, we will be using the same sample business case of a *Hotel Aggregator Solution* from Chapter 7 and 9.

## Types of Logging

Logging is a way in software development, to maintain a track of the events that are happening in an application. One can use the logging throughout the flow of the application and ensure that details of the exception are logged in detail, so that they can later be used to trace back to the root cause of the exception. But logging is not one flat action that covers everything. The purpose of you plan to you the log is very important and will influence your decision on:

- How you maintain logs?
- How much details will you write into logs?
- Till how many days will you store the logs?
- How are you going to read the logs?
- Who will be able to read the logs?

The different types of logging that are known in application development are:

- **Audit Trail:** This type of logging is done at the highest level. This log is maintained for each event in application every single time and may log as little or as much information required based on whether the Log is Informational, Warning or an Error. Sometimes for critical functions or for a secured application, all the actions that are performed by single user after login is also tracked through this type of login. During audit trail, the amount of log generated cannot be estimated also one log entry has no relation to next log entry. Thus, the convention of maintaining audit trails are mostly in files.

- **History:** This type of log is mostly maintained when we need to track all changes that is made to critical data. The change of data is made in the database. The data within the database is mostly relational in nature, hence the most practical thing is maintaining data history in database itself. However, to ensure that the database performance is not hit by such historical data, thus it should be done along with strong archival policies that are strictly followed.

- **Error Logging:** In case of error logging, the idea is to capture as much data as possible of the exception that occurred. But another thing is to ensure that the occurrence of the error is notified too. Thus, error logging must be done in three steps given as follows:
  - o  **Step 1:** Log exception details in the log file.
  - o  **Step 2:** Put a mechanism in place to send email notifications to the system administrator regarding the error.
  - o  **Step 3:** Ensure code returns friendly error codes, to pin point exact piece of code that threw the exception. This would help developers to recreate the error and find the resolution faster.

## Instrumentation and Telemetry

Instrumentation and Telemetry are two things that form a very integral part of logging. So, let us try to understand them individually at first and then with the concept of logging.

Instrumentation is often defined as follows - *"Most applications will include diagnostic features that generate custom monitoring and debugging information, especially when an error occurs. This is referred to as instrumentation and is usually implemented by adding event and error handling code to the application."* - MSDN

Thus, in more simpler words we may say, Instrumentation is a way where we develop diagnostic capabilities within an application.

The logged data from informational events may not always be useful and may seem like burden in terms of storage cost. But when there is an issue with the application, the data from informational events are as valuable as that from error or warning messages. Thus, the application developed with capabilities, that amount of log data captured can be changed simply by updating the application configuration so that the diagnostic and instrumentation systems can collect event data from all three types that is information, warning and error and thus resolve the issue at the earliest. It is also practical to continue to run the application in the extended reporting mode for some time just to be alert that the error does not recur intermittently.

Telemetry, on the other hand, in its most basic form, is the process of gathering information that is generated by instrumentation and logging systems. It is mostly performed using asynchronous mechanisms that supports massive scaling and the wide distribution of application services. It can be defined as follows: *The process of gathering remote information that is collected by instrumentation is usually referred to as telemetry.* -MSDN

In large and complex applications, information is usually captured in a data pipeline and stored in the form that makes it easier store, faster to analyze and create informational data at various levels of granularity. The purpose of such information is to understand the trends, gain insight into usage and performance patterns, and detect and isolate faults, thus make decisions to help improve application and business generated from it.

Though, Azure has no built-in system that directly provides a telemetry and reporting system of this type, a combination of the features exposed by all the Azure services, Azure diagnostics, and application insights can help you create telemetry mechanisms that may span the range of simple monitoring mechanisms to comprehensive dashboards.

The complexity of the telemetry mechanism is not fixed and is often influenced by the following:

- Size of the application i.e. basically a measure of the number of roles or virtual machine instances, the number of ancillary services it uses, the distribution of the application across different data centers, and other related factors.

- Different stake holders who may want to see and analyze the data.

- How the data will be used like to improve SLA, plan new support products like BOTs that help resolve the issues etc.

For critical applications, like banking and health care systems, Instrumentation, and telemetry helps to create power monitoring systems that helps improve the application performances via different types of monitoring, like the following:

- **Health monitoring:** We monitor the health of a system along with its various components at a given frequency. This way we can ensure that the system and its components are performing as expected and in case of any issue, the problem could be identified at the earliest. An exhaustive health monitoring system can help keep tabs on the overall system health like CPU usage, memory utilization, processes, and so on. How the monitoring is achieved, and this differs from being in the form of pings or extensive health monitoring endpoints, which emit the health status of services along with some useful metadata at that point in time.

- **Availability monitoring:** Availability monitoring is like health status monitoring with a subtle difference. The difference is, focus is on the availability of systems rather than a summary of the health at that moment. The factors that may influence the availability of systems are dependent on various factors, such as:
  o Overall nature and domain of the application,
  o The number of services, and service dependencies
  o Infrastructure or environment.

  With availability monitoring systems, low-level data points are captured that are related to the factors mentioned above and represents them to make a business-level feature available. Many times, availability monitoring parameters are used to track business metrics and service level agreements (SLA) between the solution provider and the client.

- **Performance monitoring:** Key Performance Indicators (KPI) helps us ascertain how is the application performing at any point of time. While the overall KPIs of one application may differ from the other, however, some of the common KPI of a large web-based system are as follows:

o    Requests served per hour

o    Concurrent users served per hour

o    Average processing time / users to perform business transactions, for example, completing a booking request

Additionally, performance is also measured by some common system-level parameters that are also used during health monitoring like:

o    CPU utilization

o    Memory utilization

o    I/O rates

o    Number of queued messages

If any of these KPIs are not met by the system as per the agreement, an alert is raised. During the process of analyzing performance issues, historical data from previous benchmarks captured by the monitoring system is used for troubleshooting. This also helps in creating a FAQ document for the support staff, so that they can quickly close an issue that keeps recurring.

- **Security monitoring:** In these days we are driving towards creation of intelligent systems. These systems thus need smarter monitoring systems. Something that can detect the following unusual parameters:

o    Data pattern requests

o    Unusual resource consumption patterns

o    Detect attacks on the system

Specifically, in the case of DoS, attacks or injection attacks can be identified proactively prevented and risks could be mitigated, and teams can be alerted on time.

Part of security monitoring is to maintain audit trails of authenticated users and maintain history who have the accessed the physical system. Since, specific domain may have specific security needs, often the security monitoring system are put in place to ensure that the compliance requirements are duly satisfied. Security is a cross-cutting concern of distributed systems, including microservices. There are multiple ways of getting the right data from the system. The good thing about security monitoring is, one can get data from various tools that are not part of the system but may be a part of the infrastructure or environment in which the system is hosted. Again, once may choose to bring in the data collected from external sources within the scope of the system and maintain them in logs or DB. Thus, different types of logs and database entries.

## Diagnostics Tools within Azure

Azure diagnostics logs help us to collect diagnostic data for a deployed microservice. We can also use a diagnostic extension to collect data from various sources. *Azure Diagnostics* is supported by web and worker roles, Azure virtual machines, and all *Azure App* services. Other Azure services have their own separate diagnostics.

If your Azure cloud service is responding slowly or is not working as per your performance expectation, the first thing that you would like to know, if there's a CPU or memory bottlenecks. Or again, if it fails unexpectedly or doesn't restart, it is good to see the system logs too. With Azure SDK 2.8, *Azure Diagnostics* telemetry is within the Application Insights. How does this help? How about seeing your *Azure Cloud Services* projects and Azure Windows VMs. Perf counters, Windows event logs, and app traces will all be displayed alongside the response times inside your app by the *Application Insights*.

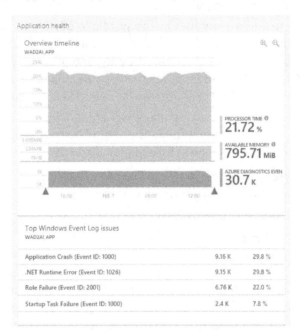

*Figure 1: PC - https://azure.microsoft.com/en-us/blog/azure-diagnostics-integration-with-application-insights/*

The steps to achieve it is simple and given as follows:

- If you haven't published your *Cloud Service* project yet:
  - o In Solution Explorer, open the properties of each web or worker role (the role, not the project).
  - o Check send diagnostics data to Application Insights.
  - o Select the Application Insights resource for your app.
  - o Next, Publish the service.

- If your Cloud Service or Virtual Machine is already running:
  - o In Server Explorer or Cloud Explorer, right-click the Cloud Service or Virtual Machine and select Enable/Update Diagnostics.
  - o Check send diagnostics data to application Insights.
  - o Select the application insights resource for your app.
  - o Apply the updates.

Once these steps are done successfully, next is how you view the diagnostics in the Application Insights? The diagnostics will automatically show up in the telemetry portal. And to view the KPIs you need to do the following –

The diagnostic telemetry will show up in the Application Insights portal.

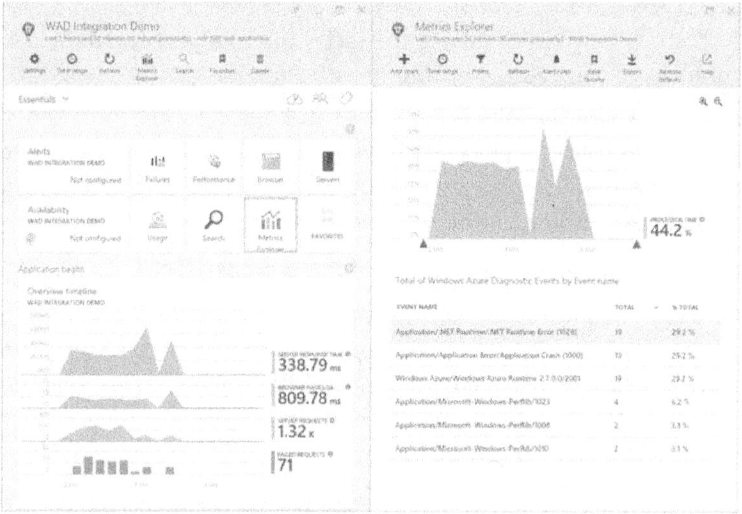

*Figure 2: PC - https://azure.microsoft.com/en-us/blog/azure-diagnostics-integration-with-application-insights/*

- For Windows event log
  - o To investigate individual events, use Search.
  - o You can use Metrics Explorer to see counts of different types of event. You can create various diagnostic charts and view event-based data at various levels of granularity.
- **Application traces and ETW traces:** Use Search to find and inspect log traces and analyze the details of the issue.
- **Performance counters:** Open the Servers tile from the overview blade or else create your own custom charts of them using tools within Metrics Explorer or Application Insights Analytics. The Available Memory and % Processor Time performance counters can be found under the Performance Counters category, while others can be found under Custom Metrics. This way one can view all the KPI critical to the application.

Once you have setup your application insights portal, it is time to use the combined diagnostics. Azure Diagnostics and Application Insights SDK provide complementary views of your live application. Thus, you can get views from the system perspective, performance counters, role lifecycle data and other Windows events. And you can add on to the collected data as the SDK sends data from inside your app, about requests, exceptions, dependencies, and any custom telemetry you may choose to add. It is seen that each one is switched on by a single option, and one can send the data streams to the same resource in the Azure portal, thus it is easy to set up, and provides great diagnostic value as the combination of the two streams. The scenarios in which it may add more value are as follows:

- **Poor performance:** You'll see system events and performance data to help diagnose the issue.
- Role crashes, recycles or failure to start – the role lifecycle data is invaluable for identifying this type of problem.

Seeing all the data in one place, one does not need to log in to the VM or go looking at multiple places looking for the event logs – it's all there, where you can correlate app and system telemetry. Thus, Azure Diagnostics creates a powerful tool by bringing everything on the same window in simple and easy steps.

## Persisting Diagnostic Data with Azure Storage

While Azure Diagnostics brings all the diagnostic information at one place, for analysis purposes, it is important that we decide to persist it in some form. Azure Storage fulfills our need to persist diagnostic data. Since Azure diagnostics logs are not permanently stored as they are rollover logs, that is, they are overwritten by newer ones. Azure diagnostics logs can be either stored in a file system or transferred via FTP; better still, it can be stored in an Azure storage container. There are different ways to specify an Azure storage container for diagnostics data for the specified Azure resource (in our case, microservices hosted on the Azure app service). These are as follows:

- CLI tools
- PowerShell
- Azure Resource Manager
- Visual Studio 2017 with Azure SDK 2.9 or later
- Azure portal

The steps to using the Azure Storage are as follows:

- Specifying a storage account:
  - o The storage account for storing application-specific diagnostic data is specified in the **ServiceConfiguration.cscfg** file of the storage account. The simple configuration driven storage account helps maintain separate accounts for development and production. Or in case the application is configured with CI and CD, it can be mentioned as dynamic deployment variable.

o    The account information is defined as a connection string in a configuration setting and looks something like the following:

```
<ConfigurationSettings>
    <Setting name="Microsoft.WindowsAzure.Plugins.
    Diagnostics.DevConnectionString" value="
    UseDevelopmentStorage=true" />
</ConfigurationSettings>
```

o    One can change this connection string to provide account information for an Azure storage account.

- Azure Storage Schema: The structure of Azure table storage for storing diagnostic data is as follows:
   o    If the storage is in the form of tables, we will find the following tables schema:
      - **WadLogsTable:** The table is meant to store the log statements written during code execution, using the trace listener.
      - **WADDiagnosticInfrastructureLogsTable:** This table specifies the diagnostic monitor and configuration changes.
      - **WADDirectoriesTable:** This includes the directories that the diagnostic monitor is monitoring. This includes IIS logs, IIS-failed request logs, and custom directories. The location of the blob log file is specified in the container field and the name of the blob is in the RelativePath field. The AbsolutePath field indicates the location and the name of the file as it existed on the Azure virtual machine.
      - **WADPerformanceCountersTable:** This table contains data related to the configured performance counters.
      - **WADWindowsEventLogsTable:** This table contains Windows' event tracing log entries.
   o    For a blob storage container, the diagnostic storage schema is as follows:
      - **wad-control-container:** This is only for SDK 2.4 and previous versions. This contains the XML configuration files that control Azure diagnostics.
      - **wad-iis-failedreqlogfiles:** This contains information from the IIS-failed request logs.
      - **wad-iis-logfiles:** This contains information about IIS logs. custom: This is a custom container based on the configuring directories that are monitored by the diagnostic monitor. The name of this blob container will be specified in WADDirectoriesTable.

Thus, depending on the application needs, you may choose to use tables or blob storage container to store your diagnostics data.

## Logging Techniques and Implementation of ELMAH, nLog and Log4net

With increasing complexity of the application and to provide better user experience the demands from logging has vastly increased. Logs are expected to be used multifold and are often based on key application decisions. Thus, simple logging techniques will not suffice the needs. Because of which many logging frameworks are used in the industry to provide logging robustness along with developer friendly integration steps and user-friendly experience. The common thing about these frameworks are as follows:

- **Configuration driven:** Most of the logging frameworks are configuration driven. That means, you just need to add a configuration within your application configuration file and your logger starts referring to the work.

- **Multi-level logging support:** The frameworks help you configure logs to target each level of Information, Warning, and Error. Thus, one may choose to log as little or as much information wherever necessary.

- **Different Types of loggers:** Each framework may expose additional types of loggers but the most common loggers are as follows:

  o **Event Log:** The logs for this type are written in the system event log.

  o **File Log:** The logs are written into a file at a given location with a given name. However, you may choose the following:

    ▪ **Standard:** There is a single file by that name and you keep writing to that file.

    ▪ **Rolling File:** File is overwritten based on size or day.

  o **Console:** The logs are written on the console window.

  o **DB:** The logs are written into specific table. The configuration contains a DB connection string for the database that has the table along with the insert command. One also need to set parameter for the number of queued up requests before the insertion happens.

- **Extensibility:** All the frameworks expose APIs. Thus, if required, based on domain and application needs, one may extend the logger with additional features or integrate it with other tools.

Based on the above techniques, the three very well know tools are given as follows:

- **ELMAH:** The name is the acronym for Error Logging Modules and Handlers and is .Net Open Source Project. A highly powerful tool, it is sad that it has not received the attention it deserved. If you need event-driven development, then ELMAH should be your go-to tool for logging. Once you have integrated ELMAH into your application and configured appropriately, this is what you get without changing anything within your ASP.Net code:

  o Logging of nearly all unhandled exceptions.

o    A web page to remotely view the entire log of recoded exceptions.

o    A web page to remotely view the full details of any one logged exception.

o    In many cases, you can review the original yellow screen of death that ASP.NET generated for a given exception, even with customErrors mode in your ASP.Net config file being turned off.

o    The e-mail notification of each error at the time it occurs.

o    RSS feed of the last 15 errors from the log.

o    Several backing storage implementations for the log, including in-memory, Microsoft SQL Server and several contributed by the community.

A step by step ELMAH setup tutorial can be found here: https://docs.microsoft.com/en-us/aspnet/web-forms/overview/older-versions-getting-started/deploying-web-site-projects/logging-error-details-with-elmah-cs

It can be easily said that the power of ELMAH is highly unused in ASP.Net space and it is good to explore it, find its untapped power that makes your application logging robust.

- **NLog:** This is another powerful tool that is used widely as it could be used within different types of application. You can easily download and integrate Nlog within your application with couple of simple configurations. NLog has all the common features of the framework listed above:

  o    Enable Internal logging: A simple configuration like one given below, helps identify the root cause of the issues:

```
<nlog internalLogFile="c:\logDetail.txt"
internalLogLevel="Trace">
    <targets>
        <!-- target configuration here -->
    </targets>
    <rules>
        <!-- log routing rules -->
    </rules>
</nlog>
```

  o    Multi-level logging helps store targeted information based on levels on the production. Thus, reducing the load of storing unnecessary information and analyzing the same.

  o    **Filters to suppress statements:** We can configure filter to suppress certain type of information with a simple configuration given as follows:

```
<logger name="*" writeTo="file">
    <filters>
        <when condition="lengthundefined'${message}')
        >100" action="Ignore" />
    </filters>
</logger>
```

o     Custom targets can be created for additional features to logging for example we can create a custom target to write to Azure Storage.

o     Customizing the message layouts are easy and can be done simply by writing a configuration like this:

```
${longdate}|${level:uppercase=true}|${logger}|
${message}.
```

You can check the customizable field here: https://github.com/NLog/NLog/wiki/Layout-Renderers

o     You can use the Diagnostic Contexts to Log Additional Fields. If you need to create, you can create a dictionary of data that can be used as properties within your logging, this becomes useful. Say something like setting guest's name on the context and then include that in every logging statement. Since the guest's name would be different per transaction, you would not want to set it at a global scope. To achieve this, you would use the **Mapped Diagnostics Context (MDC)**. For global variables, you can use the **Global Diagnostics Context (GDC)**. Properties stored in GDC is shared across all threads in your application and is also available to be included in your logs.

o     **Log4Net:** This is another logging framework, like that of nLog. But the thing about log4net is that it is highly configuration driven and exposes many variables which makes logging at any level with minimum effort. The logging types are exposed as appenders and APIs for appenders are easily available thus making it easy to extend.

So, it would not be incorrect to say that by using any of the above 3 tools, ELMAH, nLog, and Log4Net, you can easily achieve logging what not and create a robust application in entirety.

- **Workload spikes:** One of the best ways to determine performance is by suddenly increasing the user load all at once.

## Summary

In this chapter, we have tried to understand the importance of logging and how through logging application can be maintained in production . We have also understood the need and the power of instrumentation and telemetry and what are there in Azure for Diagnostics and Storage. We have also understood the various logging techniques and what to look for, in a logging framework and discussed about some of the best in market logging tools. The expectation after this chapter is, you will be able to create a microservice application starting from design, development, integration, , testing and logging.

# CHAPTER 11

# What is Next?

In the previous chapters, we have completed our application with the implementation of logging. Where we have tried to understand the importance of logging and how through logging, an application can be maintained in production. We have also understood the need and the power of instrumentation and telemetry and what are there in Azure for Diagnostics and Storage. We have also understood the various logging techniques and what to look for in a logging framework and discussed about some of the best in market logging tools. The application till previous chapter is discussed in such a manner so that after the previous chapter, you will be able to create a microservice application starting from design, development, integration, testing, and logging.

In this chapter we will revisit all the chapters and discuss important points that should be remembered while one writing application based on microservices architecture by explaining:

- What and why
- Why we took a use case and what we discussed
- Testing, Integration, and deployment
- Security and logging
- Who is using microservices in the industry

## What and Why

The journey of this book has started with the definition, with explanation of the microservices in *Chapter 01*. Where we have discussed many important things to thoroughly understand the subject.

## What are Microservices

Let us understand what microservices mean; Microservices is an architecture pattern, offer a better way to build to decouple components within an application boundary. Microservice architecture is a style of designing software systems which divide significant software applications into many small services that can run independently. Each of the microservices has its own team working on it, so they are entirely separated from each other. This allows every service to run its own unique process and communicate autonomously without having to rely on other services or the application as a whole. The main crux of microservices architecture can be defined with its two fundamental advantages as defined below:

## Microservices are Modular and Independent

When we say, Microservices are loosely coupled; it means each service is small and designed to solve specific business function. Microservices are broken down into multiple service components by design, which can be developed by a small development team so that each of the services can be developed and deployed independently without compromising the integrity of the application. In a microservice architecture-based approach, each microservice owns its process and data so that it will be independent of a development and deployment point of view. Typically, a tiered approach is taken with a back-end store, middle-tier business logic, and a front-end *user interface (UI)*. Microservice has evolved over the past couple of years to build distributed applications that are for the cloud. Any programming language can write it and use any framework.

## Microservices are Decentralized and Cross-functional

The ideal organization for microservices has small, engaged team where each team is in charge of a business function made out of various microservices which can be independently deployed. Teams handle all parts of development for their microservices, from development to deployment, and hence all level of team members required to deliver Microservices from developers, quality engineers, DevOps team, and Product architects. This organization design is consistent with Conway's law, which says that the interface structure of a software system will reflect the social fabric of the organization that produced it. The code is organized around business capabilities.

## Why Microservices?

In previous section we have gone through the What part of the microservices, where we understand about the microservices by discussing its definition and advantages. Now, the bigger question is why microservices, when we have plenty of other architectural solutions in place. We have discussed the monolithic application and SOA to answer this question.

## Discussing Monolithic

In monolithic software, we mainly built as a single unit. The monolithic software is designed to be self-contained; components of the program are interconnected and interdependent rather than loosely coupled as is the case with modular software programs. In a tightly-coupled architecture, each component and its associated components must be present in order for the code to be executed or compiled.

The monolithic architectural style is a traditional architecture type and has been widely used in the IT business. The term monolithic is not new and has come from the UNIX world. In UNIX, most of the commands exist as a standalone program whose functionality is not dependent on any other program.

Enterprise applications are built in 3 layers: A data access layer, Business layer /

Service layer and UI/Presentation layer. It is a single layered software application in which the presentation layer and data access layer are consolidated into a single program on a single platform.

- **Presentation layer:** Presentation (UI) layer in which user interacts with an application, all client-side logic, client-side validation related logics taken acre by this layer.

- **Business Logic layer:** Business Logic layer contains all the logic related to business context, which is a middle layer communicating between Presentation and data access layer.

- **Data access layer:** Data Access layer contains all the logic related to backend or Database.

In a traditional web application, the client (a browser) posts a request. The business tier executes the business logic, the database collects/stores application-specific persistence data, and the UI shows the data to the user.

A monolithic app which is designed without modularity, each layer is tightly coupled. If the changes are required in one business function, the entire application needs to be rebuilt and deployed. The major problem with this design is, it's not designed for scalability and fault tolerance. If an exception occurs in one module, then the entire system will fail to function. Technical debt from a monolithic code base is a measurable reality in traditional DevOps. With monolithic code, even isolated components receive the same memory, as well as sharing access to the program itself. While that may present it a little easier to code interfaces and execute applications, it ultimately takes away the adaptability that should be a part of the agile development process.

Deploying such a monolithic application will become another hurdle. During deployment, you will have to make sure that each and every component is deployed accurately; otherwise, you may end up facing a lot of problems in your production environments.

## Discussing SOA

In the previous section, we discussed the monolithic architecture and its limitations. We also addressed why it does not meet our enterprise application requirements. To defeat these issues, we should take a modular method where we can separate the components.

**Service-Oriented Architecture (SOA)** is basically the group of services. Service-Oriented Architecture describes a set of principles and patterns for designing and developing software in the form of interoperable services. It is an architecture pattern where services are the logical representation of a repeatable business activity that has a specific business outcome. These services interact with each other. These services are generally business functionalities that are built as software components. The communication can comprise either simple data passing, or it could connect two or more services regulating some activity.

SOA architecture presents a connection between the implementations and the consuming applications, creating a logical view of sets of services which are ready for the use, invoked by a standard interface and management architecture.

## Understanding Service in Service-oriented Architecture

To make SOA more effective, we need a clear understanding of the term Service.

Service, in this case, is an essential conception of SOA. It can be a part of the code, program, or software that gives functionality to the other systems. This piece of code can communicate directly with the database or indirectly through different service. Moreover, it can be used by clients directly, where the client may be a website, a windows app, mobile app, or any other device app.

Services are what you connect together using Web Services. Service is the endpoint of a connection. Also, service has some type of underlying computer system that supports the connection offered. This section provides information on the specification of services. Typically, services interact with other systems via some communication channel, generally the HTTP protocol.

Service is a logical design of a repeatable business activity that has a specified outcome (e.g., Booking Service, Provide Hotel information, reports). A service is self-contained and may be composed of other services. It has three components: an interface, a contract, and implementation. The interface defines how a service provider will fulfill requests from a service consumer, the contract outlines how the service provider and the service consumer should communicate, and the implementation is the actual service code itself. Because the interface of service is separate from its implementation, a service provider can execute a request without the service consumer knowing how it does so; the service consumer only worries about consuming services.

## SOA - Architectural Principles

As a Service Oriented Architecture, it adheres to few principles, in this section; we will discuss SOA Architectural Principles.

- **Standardized service contract:** Services adhere to a standard communications agreement, as outlined collectively by one or more service-description documents in a given set of services.
- **Service longevity:** Services should be designed to be long-lived. Where possible, services should avoid driving consumers to change if they do not need extra features, if you invoke a service today you should be capable of calling the same service forever.
- **Service abstraction:** The services act as black boxes, that is, their inner logic is hidden from the consumers.
- **Loose coupling:** Services maintain a relationship that minimizes dependencies and only maintain an awareness of each other. Implementations are environment-specific – they are constrained or enabled by context and must be described within that context.

- **Service contract:** Services adhere to a communications agreement as defined collectively by one or more service description documents. Services are self-contained.

- **Service abstraction:** What is specified in the service (contract, service), it hides logic from the outside world. Above what is specified in the service contract, services hide logic from the outside world.

- **Service reusability:** Logic is divided into services with the intention of promoting reuse.

- **Service discovery:** Ability to optimize performance, functionality, and cost. More natural introduction of system upgrades.

## Why We Took a Use Case and What We Discussed

After discussion and understanding the theoretical part of the Microservices, one should require creating a real-world application. To fulfill the needs, we have taken lot of real-world scenarios with their use cases. The considering a use-case is a way to depict a whole project.

In our use case, we have discussed:

Online hotel booking application is taken as an example to make you understand Microservices architecture in this book. Using the same application, we will learn the challenges of the Monolithic application, then how SOA made it better and Microservices made it most accessible.

This is an online hotel booking system where a user can search a hotel in a given city with the different category of rooms, check the hotel availability, Price, facilities and Book it.

Our actual project having following folder structure:

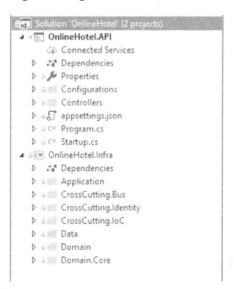

*11 1 – Folder hierarchy of online hotel project*

The above image is showing the folder structure of our online hotel booking project, through-out the book, we have taken the above app and worked on it with the discussion of various components of microservices.

## Testing, Integration and Deployment

Testing is a very crucial thing for any application, main part of success for an application depends upon good testing. Integration is the part how our application is integrated with different modules, components, external or internal apis and deployment is the final stage where we deploy our app to various environment like development, QA, Staging or production etc.

### Why is Testing Important?

Testing of any solution is important in order to confirm whether the solution delivers what it promises. As the intent of the application is set before it is developed, an application is tested to verify the following:

- Are the promised features working as per expectations?
- Is the application flow consistent with the expectations set?
- what happens when additional load is given to the system?
- how easily does the application recover from the failure?

Depending on the criticality of the process handled and the complexity of the business flow, testing scope and strategy needs to be decided. For microservices, testing is critical. Since microservices are built as small but multiple services that can be deployed as a unit and may give the impression that testing of a monolithic application could be replicated for each of the services. But that would be a big NO. As this will leave out big chunks of untestable code. The challenges that microservices poses are as follows:

- Microservices have multiple services that work together or individually, thus have varying degrees of complexity.
- Microservices are meant to target multiple clients; hence, they have more complex use cases.
- The architectural style of each component/service of the microservice is isolated and independent. Thus, they need to be tested individually and as a system.
- As independent teams working on separate components/services interact with each other. Hence testing thoroughness is dependent on both internal services but also external services.
- Each component/service in a microservice may work independently, but may have to access shared resources and each service is responsible for modifying its own database.

### Why is Integration Important?

In today's world, data is the source of power, but it has value only if it is used at the right time by the right owner. Else it may act as a dead weight and lead to the problem of useless abundance. In microservices solution, each individual service works independently, without the knowledge or dependency over the other services. But not all services in the business can work like that, and it is important that the services interact with each other for things like, to complete a process, to share details for further processing, to fetch updated values of prices or stocks available, and so on. Thus, on- time delivery of the information between the composing services is vital, to ensure the efficiency, reliability, and performance. Thus Hence, the integration of various components plays one of the most important steps of the microservice solution development.

## *Integration Testing – Testing the Multiple Components with Each Other*

Once the component testing of the individual service is completed, as the next step it is required that the communication between two services needs to be verified. It is mandatory to check whether the two services are working together. Within this scope, we need to check the following:

- Whether the requests from one service is responded in a timely manner
- Is, there any accessibility issues?
- Does the environment need additional access?
- Is there any need to validate the source of the requests?

An integration test thus verifies the communication paths and interactions between components and helps identify interface defects. The calls to the service must be made with integration to external services, which should include error and success cases. This way the integration testing validates that the system is working together seamlessly and that the dependencies between the services are present as per expectation.

## Docker in the Project and CI/CD

In our book, we used docker as a container. Docker is a container management service. The tagline of Docker is developed, ship, and run anywhere. Docker is an instrument intended to make it less demanding to make, send, and run applications by utilizing compartments. Containers enable developers to bundle up an application with the greater part of the parts it needs, for example, libraries and other dependencies and ship everything out as one bundle which can then be deployed anywhere.

Apart from above, we have also discussed about CI/CD:

*Visual Studio Team Services (VSTS) offers a highly customizable **continuous integration (CI)** and **continuous deployment (CD)** pipeline which automatically deploy ASP.NET Core web app to a Windows **virtual machine (VM)** in Azure.*

Continuous integration is a method that encourages developers to integrate their code into a main branch of a shared repository early and often. Instead of developing features in isolation and integrating them at the end of a development cycle, code is combined with the shared repository by each developer multiple times during the day.

## Security and Logging

Security is very important for any application. Secured applications are one of the best to use in the chapter.

### Why is Logging Important?

Let us assume that it is almost 1 month to the peak of the holiday season. And based on the last year booking details, people are bound to start planning and booking the holidays. To beat the prices of a competition, the company has decided to give 20% off on all bookings for the next 3 days. So, the expected thing happens. A record number of visitors start booking on the application. But the application starts crashing after first three hours.

* How do the system adiministrator find out that the application is crashing?
* How will the maintenance team understand what is the root of the problems?
* How will the developers identify the exact piece of code that may be causing the issue?

Now you may think that some of the customers may inform the team, but since the site is already crashing, there is no point in visiting the site and of course customer care on the phone will not have the right option for you to log this issue. So, what could be done?

Well, the answer to this is Logging. To help you walk through the various concepts of logging, we will be using the same sample business case of a *Hotel Aggregator Solution* from Chapter 7 and 9.

The different types of logging that are known in application development are as follows:

* **Audit Trail:** This type of logging is done at the highest level. This log is maintained for each event in application every single time and may log as little or as much information required based on whether the Log is Informational, Warning or an Error. Sometimes for critical functions or for a secured application, all the actions that are performed by single user after login is also tracked through this type of login. During audit trail, the amount of log generated cannot be estimated also one log entry has no relation to next log entry. Thus, the convention of maintaining audit trails are mostly in files.

* **History:** This type of log is mostly maintained when we need to track all changes that is made to critical data. The change of data is made in the database. The data within the database is mostly relational in nature, hence the most practical thing is maintaining data history in database itself. However, to ensure that the database performance is not hit by such

historical data, thus it should be done along with strong archival policies that are strictly followed.

- **Error Logging:** In case of error logging, the idea is to capture as much data as possible of the exception that occurred. But another thing is to ensure that the occurrence of the error is notified too. Thus, error logging must be done in three steps given as follows:

  o   Step 1 – Log exception details in the log file.

  o   Step 2 – Put a mechanism in place to send email notifications to the system administrator regarding the error.

  o   Step 3 – Ensure code returns friendly error codes, to pin point exact piece of code that threw the exception. This would help developers to recreate the error and find the resolution faster.

Till now, if you have read this book and did not skip any chapter, you can create your own application based on microservices architecture.

## Who is Using Microservices in the Industry

Let's discuss a bit about, who are using microservices, in the industry.

- **Uber:** Uber erstwhile UberCab is based out of Sans Francisco, USA, founded in year 2009. They are mainly into transport business share basis cab facilities. They have moved from classical monolithic to SOA and then microservices, you can read out more interesting stories from the official page of their engineering team: https://eng.uber.com

- **Netflix:** Netflix is American media service provider founded in 1997, they have shifted to microservices to provide better service to their users. You can read details from here: https://medium.com/netflix-techblog

- **iSafe mobile app:** iSafe is an initiative for the organizations, universities and group to make sure everyone is safe. iSafe is an Indian company and they have capability to report a tip for any unusual activities happening around us. They are using microservices for better service. You can read more from their official pages: http://isafe.net.in and you can try them from: https://play.google.com/store/apps/details?id=com.iSafe.net

- **Amazon:** Amazon erstwhile Cadabara Inc. is an American ecommerce and cloud computing company. They are using microservices for their electronic ecommerce platform. You can read more about them: http://highscalability.com/amazon-architecture

Apart from above, there are more big organizations those are using microservices viz. Ebay, Sound Cloud, Gilt, Hailo, Lending club etc.

www.ingramcontent.com/pod-product-compliance
Lightning Source LLC
La Vergne TN
LVHW022308060326
832902LV00020B/3334